Offensive Speech, Religion, a
the Limits of the Law

Offensive Speech, Religion, and the Limits of the Law

NICHOLAS HATZIS

OXFORD
UNIVERSITY PRESS

OXFORD
UNIVERSITY PRESS

Great Clarendon Street, Oxford, OX2 6DP,
United Kingdom

Oxford University Press is a department of the University of Oxford.
It furthers the University's objective of excellence in research, scholarship,
and education by publishing worldwide. Oxford is a registered trade mark of
Oxford University Press in the UK and in certain other countries

First Edition published in 2021

Impression: 1

Published in the United States of America by Oxford University Press
198 Madison Avenue, New York, NY 10016, United States of America

British Library Cataloguing in Publication Data

Data available

Library of Congress Control Number: 2020948243

ISBN 978-0-19-875844-0

DOI: 10.1093/oso/9780198758440.001.0001

Printed and bound in the UK by
TJ Books Limited

Acknowledgements

I received invaluable advice from colleagues and friends who discussed with me the issues explored here or commented on draft chapters. I am indebted to Eric Barendt, Lior Barshack, Vincent Blasi, Sionaidh Douglas-Scott, Leslie Green, Kent Greenawalt, George Letsas, Ian Loveland, Virginia Mantouvalou, Yoram Shachar, the late Stavros Tsakyrakis, and the anonymous reviewers for Oxford University Press. For discussions on religion in constitutional law, and for unfailing support over many years, I am grateful to Nicos Alivizatos. My greatest debt in writing this book is to Gerald Neuman, who encouraged my initial interest in the relation between speech and religion and gave detailed comments on the manuscript.

I presented some of the ideas developed in the book in a series of lectures on free speech at the Radzyner Law School, The Interdisciplinary Center Herzliya in Israel. I thank Dean Amnon Lehavi, Lior Barshack, and the members of the faculty for the invitation and hospitality, and my students at the IDC for their lively interest and their questions and contributions in the lectures.

At the Press, Alex Flach and Jamie Berezin were generous with their help during the time it took to complete the work, and Brianne Bellio was instrumental in turning the manuscript into a book.

Chapter 6 incorporates some material first published in my article 'Lying, Speech and Impersonal Harm' (2019) 38 Law and Philosophy 517, and I thank the publisher and editors for permission to republish here.

Contents

Table of Cases

CANADA

ISRAEL

UNITED KINGDOM

UNITED STATES

EUROPEAN COURT OF HUMAN RIGHTS

EUROPEAN COMMISSION ON HUMAN RIGHTS

Table of Legislation

List of Abbreviations

ACHR	American Convention on Human Rights
ECHR	European Convention on Human Rights
ECtHR	European Court of Human Rights
ICCPR	International Covenant on Civil and Political Rights

Introduction

> I learn belatedly, thanks to the seaside indolence of August on a Dalmatian island that piles up stacks of outdated newspapers and weeklies, that in Denmark they have purged—I imagine from the schools—a tale by Hans Christian Andersen with a Christian ending, or Christian elements in any case, so as not to offend the faithful of other churches. In its respectful stupidity, this is a decisive step in the universal history of censorship. In this case, it is a well-intentioned censorship, moved by a concern not to upset cultural or religious minorities. But censorship, after all, is always well-intentioned: it seeks to protect morality, one's country, the family, institutions, order, society, progress, the people, the children, health.

This is the beginning of a short essay by Claudio Magris on censorship.[1] In a few sentences, he captures some of the main aspects of the problem of offensive speech: that offence has become a major preoccupation in Western, liberal democracies; that religion is very often at its root; that sometimes the mere expression of a different viewpoint is thought of as offensive; that offence to beliefs is linked to issues about respect for the person holding the beliefs; that purging from public space what is considered offensive aims at protecting people's feelings; and that those who argue for restrictions are motivated by a particular view of the role of speech in society.

In this book, I explore how these themes matter for the way we think about free speech and the legal right to freedom of expression. While most of what I will say applies to offensive speech more generally, the focus is on speech which offends religious beliefs and sensibilities. Religion has been at the heart of global controversies about free expression, sparked by, among others, the Danish cartoons and the *Charlie Hebdo* publications. On several occasions, the

[1] Claudio Magris, 'A New Writer: The Censor' in *Snapshots* (translated by Anne Milano Appel) (Yale University Press 2019) 69.

Offensive Speech, Religion, and the Limits of the Law. Nicholas Hatzis, Oxford University Press. © Nicholas Hatzis 2021.
DOI: 10.1093/oso/9780198758440.003.0001

result was violence and death. But even discussions about offence to religion are often very intense and agitated, conducted with a passion which is unusual when talking about other matters of public interest. Coping with what we experience as profoundly upsetting is always complicated, but it appears that we find it easier to put up with insults to our beliefs about, say, politics or society; offence to religious beliefs activates a different kind of visceral reaction on the part of the offended. This particular difficulty with religious insults is reflected in judicial practice, the prime example being the European Court of Human Rights. As we will see in Chapters 3 and 4, the Court consistently shies away from any meaningful scrutiny of measures which restrict religiously offensive speech, showing wholesale deference to the views of national authorities. By contrast, it scrutinizes restrictions on political speech much more strictly, even when the speaker's message is profoundly offensive, and has ruled that the offensiveness of a political view is not sufficient reason for banning its public expression.

The question underlying this book is when, if ever, is the government justified in silencing those who offend the religious beliefs of their listeners? Starting from the fact that speech is usually considered a privileged activity compared with other forms of human conduct, I explore the normative reasons which may support or negate offensive speech bans. In order to show how those reasons operate in constitutional practice I use cases from various jurisdictions but it is not the purpose of the book to offer a complete description of the law under any particular system.

Often, I draw on US case law and First Amendment theory. A common objection raised in debates on freedom of expression is that the American model, with its very strong protection of speech, is so exceptional that it is of limited value when we consider speech regulation in other liberal democracies. I think this concern is exaggerated. The First Amendment model developed, to a considerable degree, as a response to the reality that American society was increasingly plural—in politics, religion, and ways of life; enhanced protection for the public expression of diverse views was seen as a way of negotiating the inevitable tensions brought about by the experience of difference. Nowadays, most Western societies are similarly plural and diverse and face the same dilemmas which have led to some of the landmark judgments of the US Supreme Court. I am not suggesting that American law should be transplanted in other legal systems but it seems to me impossible to discuss freedom of expression without looking closely at the theory and practice of the First Amendment, which, with subtlety and sophistication developed over the course of more than a century, offers valuable insights regardless of jurisdiction. Besides, all liberal systems, while casting the interests involved in free speech disputes in different ways, accord speech a privileged position in the sense that they acknowledge that there is something particularly important in being able to speak our minds.

Further, I am not aiming at constructing a theory of offensive speech, the sort of system of principles or comprehensive methodology which can be applied whenever a communication causes offence. I doubt that this is either desirable or possible. Rather, I will attempt to flesh out the moral content of the claims for offensive speech prohibitions and explore how the values justifying free expression affect how we understand the conflict between speech and the protection of religious sensibilities, taking into account the institutional arrangements which guarantee, and impose limits, on speech. While my suggestion is that the arguments for proscribing offensive expression are unpersuasive (with some very limited exceptions), I hope that the discussion will be interesting for readers with diverse views on the role of speech for the political life in our plural societies.

* * *

The first two chapters set the scene. In Chapter 1, I explore the nature of offence as a constellation of unpleasant feelings stirred up when our expectations to be treated in a particular way are disappointed. In the offended state of mind, psychic pain is caused by the clash between internal reality and the external world. Legal systems usually proscribe several types of offensive conduct but offence caused by speech poses particular challenges because of the importance of free expression for individuals and society. I propose that for the purpose of assessing a political community's response through its institutions to communications which offend some of its citizens, the category of offensive speech should be construed narrowly and distinguished from speech which promotes hatred. The two are morally different, and it is a mistake to borrow arguments from the hate speech debate to support the restrictions on expression which offends.

Then, in Chapter 2, I consider the structure of the claim that the government ought to proscribe religiously offensive speech, and the sort of reasons that can be invoked to support it. The claim, a form of practical reasoning, implies that respect for religious beliefs is a value and that by banning religious insults the government realizes that value. However, coercive restrictions on liberty ought to be based on reasons which all reasonable citizens can be expected to find acceptable, regardless of their personal views on what constitutes an ethical life. This is usually described as a public reason requirement. My suggestion is that even public reason theories that allow for reliance on religious grounds on some occasions, cannot accommodate the use of coercion against speakers who offend religious sensibilities. The fact that an act or opinion is sinful or otherwise wrong from a religious perspective is not a proper ground for its prohibition.

Is there a non-religious basis for regulating sacrilege and profanity? A common strategy is to say that protection from offence to religious beliefs is part of the more general right to freedom of religion. When the government proscribes offensive speech is giving effect to that right, and this is a reason which can justify the exercise of its coercive force over speakers and be accepted by everyone as legitimate, independently of their views about God and the sacred, because we all have an interest in living under a regime which protects religious freedom. This is the issue addressed in Chapter 3. I argue that although freedom of religion is an important right, believers have no right-based claim to be protected from unpleasant feelings caused by religious insults. It is, therefore, erroneous to interpret, as the European Court of Human Rights does, the legal right to religious freedom as including a right not to suffer offence to one's religious beliefs. In turn, this means that cases on religious offence do not involve a conflict between two fundamental rights, namely speech and religion.

The position that religious offence is a proper target for state coercion also entails a broader view about the nature and functions of public discourse and the place of religious speech in it. That view considers public discourse as a highly regulated space for orderly discussion, with the role of the regulator reserved for the state, which can set the terms for what can be said publicly. One of its central themes is the distinction between content and style: the government cannot generally proscribe unpopular, anti-religious speech which is moderate and respectful but can legitimately intervene when the speaker has exceeded the limits imposed by norms of civility. Chapter 4 offers an argument against this approach. It suggests that it is better to think of public discourse as the locus of an open deliberative process where all citizens have an equal claim to speak even if what they say is abusive or offensive. This way it performs a legitimizing function for the exercise of democratic authority by the state and allows individuals to discern, even in decisions with which they disagree, a trace of their moral agency. Such conditions make possible for society a process of self-reflection, which is necessary for change and progress.

Two important limitations on governmental power to regulate speech follow from this understanding of public discourse. On the one hand, freedom of speech covers both the substance and the manner of expression. Speakers can address the important and difficult issues around the role of the sacred in human life in a civil and moderate manner but it should also be possible to use humour, satire, mockery, sarcasm, and abuse. On the other hand, the agenda and rules of public discussion are not value-neutral issues situated outside public discourse to be determined by the government. They are part of it—substantive norms subject to constant debate and reinterpretation.

The themes of religious speech in public debate and the civility norms relied on to restrict religious offence are pursued further in relation to blasphemy, and its most recent reincarnation as defamation of religion, in Chapter 5. Blasphemy laws have been the usual response to the problem of speech which offends religion and remain rather common even in liberal, democratic legal systems. The first part of the chapter traces the transformation of blasphemy from an offence aimed at the protection of Christianity to a much broader, inclusive norm which protects all religions (and, in some cases, non-religious conscientious beliefs) from vilification and insult. I argue that the even this modernized version should be rejected both because it raises serious concerns about vagueness and unequal enforcement and because it is incompatible with free expression values.

Subsequently, I address the question whether modern blasphemy laws can be justified as a means for safeguarding public order. The argument in their favour rests on the idea that those whose beliefs are offended may become indignant and resort to violence, so the government ought to prohibit expression which has this effect. This position starts from the correct premise that the government has a legitimate interest in maintaining peace and order but concludes, wrongly, that this should be achieved by silencing non-violent speakers. Instead, the morally sound course of action is to arrest those who cannot control their rage and threaten to become violent when their beliefs are insulted.

In Chapter 6 I discuss, and reject, two further arguments for restricting offensive speech which targets the beliefs of religious minorities. The first is that it insidiously reinforces negative stereotypes about them, eventually leading to discrimination against their members. I explore what exactly is meant by the claim that speech leads to discriminatory acts and what causal link between expression and discrimination ought to be required for the government to suppress religious insults. The second argument is that offending religious beliefs is a form of intolerance towards those who hold them, so when the government is restricting communications which offend, it gives effect to the value of toleration. My discussion focuses on the kind of moral obligations which flow from toleration. I defend the view that a commitment to toleration should always leave some room for the expression of a negative attitude towards that which is being tolerated and that, in principle, speech is the appropriate means for conveying such an attitude.

***

Finally, some clarifications. First, the arguments in this book do not depend on any particular view about the appropriate relation between religion and the state. Secularists who support a strict separation between the two will probably also think that it is impermissible for the government to silence speakers who offend the religious sensibilities of listeners. But it is entirely possible to think that religious viewpoints have their place in our common life as a political community and that it is appropriate for the state publicly to acknowledge the importance religion has in the lives of many of its citizens and still disagree with prohibitions of religiously offensive speech. Put differently, there is no necessary link between support for strict secularism and the rejection of censorship of religious insults.

Secondly, the book does not discuss all the cases where offence is morally relevant reason for determining an actor's conduct. My concern is exclusively with whether the state can coerce speakers into silence when listeners find their messages offensive. Clearly, there can be other circumstances where the fact that someone will be offended can count as reason against speaking in a particular manner. If I find my friend's religious beliefs entirely absurd or misguided but know that by ridiculing them I will make him feel deeply insulted, I may decide to temper my language, and this may be what is required of me as a friend. The fact that one has a right to speak does not necessarily mean that speaking is the right thing to do. The fact of offence, then, is reason guiding my conduct.

Thirdly, the discussion in this book proceeds on the assumption that religion is on the receiving end of the insults. The offence-giver is the speaker who attacks religious beliefs and the offence-taker is the devout person whose beliefs are insulted. The position I argue for is that the speaker has a right to express his or her views in a manner which can be respectful or insulting, and that the believer has no claim to be protected from the unpleasant feelings caused by the insults. But the same holds true if the beliefs insulted are secular, with the offensive speech stemming from religious speakers. There are many instances where religious views, and the way they are expressed, can be experienced by non-religious listeners as very offensive. The arguments against prohibitions of speech apply to such cases with equal force. If the law denies its protection to believers whose religious sensibilities are insulted, it ought to do the same when the devout attack the sensibilities of the secular causing them offence.

1
The Nature of Offence

Feeling offended is a universal experience. Even the most thick-skinned of us, those who can routinely brush off whatever others say or do and move on with their lives, have, at times, felt offended. The emotional experience of having suffered offence varies from mere irritation and annoyance to profound and intensely felt shock; the more serious the offence, the deeper and more long-lasting the wound inflicted by it will be. *The Iliad* begins with an offended Achilles sulking in his tent—Agamemnon, the leader of the Greeks, has taken away his slave girl, Briseis—and refusing to fight, thus bringing the campaign to conquer Troy to a standstill. Achilles's insult is not caused merely by the loss of a possession but by the symbolism entailed in Agamemnon's action. When the two of them quarrelled in the presence of the other kings, Agamemnon boasted: 'I will then lead off the fair-cheeked daughter of Briseus, going myself to your cabin—your own prize—so that you know well how much greater than you I am'.[1] The effect of these words, Homer tells us, was that 'in Peleus' son pain grew; in his shaggy breast was the spirit divided and two ways pondered the matter, whether to draw from the sheath of his thigh his keen-whetted sword blade, make the assembly disperse, then cut down Atreus' scion, or to desist from his anger and put a strong curb on his spirit'.[2] For both the offence-giver and the offence-taker, it is the symbolic significance of the offensive conduct which determines their experience of it.

Insults strike at the view we have of ourselves and our expectations to be treated by others in a certain way—with respect, consideration, deference. They imply that the offence-giver occupies a superior position, looking down on the victim of the insult, who is made to feel belittled. 'Insult is about humiliation and the assertion of superiority, the assertion or assumption of dominance'.[3] This explains why offence causes psychic pain. Our understanding of who we are and our sense of self-worth are inevitably influenced by how others see and treat us. When we receive insults instead of respect this

[1] Homer, *The Iliad* (translated by Rodney Merrill) (The University of Michigan Press 2009) Book 1, 185–86.

[2] ibid 188–92.

[3] Jerome Neu, *Sticks and Stones: The Philosophy of Insults* (Oxford University Press 2008) 4.

Offensive Speech, Religion, and the Limits of the Law. Nicholas Hatzis, Oxford University Press. © Nicholas Hatzis 2021.
DOI: 10.1093/oso/9780198758440.003.0002

understanding is shaken and, depending on the nature of the offence and our emotional capacity for working through it, we may be shattered altogether. This can make us feel that we are under attack, inferior, worthless. As Homer knew, in the offended state of mind insults eat us from the inside, arousing murderous rage.

In the example from *The Iliad*, offence was intentional and directed to a specific person. It is also possible to cause offence to others without referring to them directly, or even unintentionally. A derogatory comment made in the media about a group with a certain characteristic, such as religion, race, ethnic origin, or sexuality, can make someone who has that characteristic feel insulted, even though the comment was not addressed to her as an individual. But offence can also be caused without the offence-giver intending to insult.[4] This can happen because he was careless, ignorant, or inconsiderate. He may have entirely failed to notice the risk of giving offence when he was reasonably expected to have known about it, or he was aware of the risk but he accepted it and did or said something which could be interpreted as an insult. Such conduct resembles the legal concept of negligence: the offence-giver has failed to exercise reasonable care not to insult others. In ethics and in law we usually think of injuries caused with intent as more blameworthy than inadvertent injuries. The latter may benefit from an excuse, as, for example, when it was not reasonably possible for the offence-giver to have known that his conduct could offend. Yet, even unintentional insults leave the victim with a bitter taste in the mouth.

It is not necessary for offence to be caused by acts of a specific individual, as it is possible for a person to experience unpleasantness by merely thinking of a state of affairs which he finds generally offensive. One may be offended at the thought of world poverty, or climate change, or the level of illiteracy in some countries. These are cases where offence is caused by a social phenomenon which the offended party thinks is incompatible with her values while being, at the same time, too complicated and widespread to be attributable to individual people. It may be argued that such offensive states of affairs, the impersonal forces of history or the economy notwithstanding, could not have come about unless a number of specific individuals had behaved in a reprehensible manner. For instance, it may be said that the 'very rich' are largely responsible for the unequal distribution of wealth and, therefore, world poverty or that the 'environmentally indifferent citizens' are largely responsible for

[4] For more on unintentional insults see Neu (n 3) 18–24.

climate change. While there may be some truth in those statements, the pool of the people whose conduct is under scrutiny is too large and undifferentiated, and their relationship to the actual offended mental state is too remote to allow us to attribute in a meaningful way offence to conduct. Therefore, it is better to think of offence taken at such states of affairs as a type of impersonal offence whose cause cannot be traced to a specific person.

Finally, there are cases where, although it is possible to relate offence to an individual, it would be unreasonable to ascribe to him any kind of responsibility for the unpleasant mental state he has caused to others. The sight of a seriously wounded person covered in blood after a car accident may be experienced by a witness as an offence to the senses, but it would be absurd to say that he is in any way morally culpable for the observer's discontent.[5] In such cases, the issue of blameworthiness does not even arise.

The range of words and actions which can offend is limitless. Given that what counts as an insult is determined by several factors—social conventions, history, personal expectations, susceptibility to offence—different societies, and different people within the same society, will develop their own understanding of offensiveness. Faced with the ubiquitous nature of offence, a legal system needs to determine whether it is ever justified to use the coercive force of the state to prevent and punish it, and, if so, under what circumstances this should be done. In this chapter I look, first, at some general considerations about the law's response to offence and then turn to the more specific issue of offence caused by speech.[6]

[5] The example is from Joel Feinberg, *The Moral Limits of the Criminal Law, vol 2: Offense to Others* (Oxford University Press 1985) 2. Feinberg classifies it as an offended state of mind in the broad sense to distinguish it from what he calls offence in the 'strict and narrow sense' which, in addition to suffering a disliked mental state, includes attributing that state to the wrongful conduct of another and resenting the other for causing the offence.

[6] I am using offence and insult interchangeably to describe a mental state. In *Brutus v Cozens* [1973] AC 854 Lord Reid attempted to distinguish, for the purpose of statutory interpretation, 'insulting' conduct from other conduct which people may find upsetting. The case concerned a member of the audience at Wimbledon who interrupted the match of a South African player to protest against apartheid. The spectators became angry and he was later prosecuted for violating s 5 of the Public Order Act 1936, which provided that 'any person who in any public place or at any public meeting uses threatening, abusive or insulting words or behavior with intent to provoke a breach of the peace or whereby a breach of the peace is likely to be occasioned, shall be guilty of an offence'. The magistrates held that his conduct was not insulting to the spectators but the Divisional Court set aside the judgment, stating that conduct which affronts others and shows disrespect or contempt for their rights counts as insulting for the purposes of the Act. In the House of Lords, Lord Reid held that the meaning of 'insulting' in the statute was the ordinary meaning of the word and its determination was a matter of fact, not law. The term 'affront' used by the Divisional Court was too vague and contempt for the rights of the person as opposed to contempt for the person himself was not as such insulting. He noted that 'there are many grounds other than insult for feeling resentment or protesting' (at 862) and that spectators may have been angry but they were not insulted within the meaning of the 1936 Act.

Legal Constraint of Offence

The most comprehensive and influential exploration of how the law should respond to offence can be found in the work of Joel Feinberg, who develops what he describes as an 'offence principle': 'it is always good reason in support of a proposed criminal prohibition that it would probably be an effective way of preventing serious offense (as opposed to injury or harm) to persons other that the actor, and that it is probably a necessary means to that end'.[7] The offence principle supplements the 'harm principle'[8] and extends the reach of the state's power, which can be exercised to prevent both harm and offence to others. Feinberg's theory differs in this fundamental respect from the classic formulation of liberalism developed by John Stuart Mill, who insisted that the prevention of harm to others is the only aim for which state coercion may be used legitimately. Taken together, the harm and offence principles 'duly clarified and qualified, between them exhaust the class of morally relevant reasons for criminal prohibitions'.[9]

Offence, Not Harm

The term offence could be used to describe a very broad range of unpleasant mental states, such as irritation, discomfort, anger, rage, disgust, aversion, shame, humiliation, disappointment, and so on; one way or another, they can all be described as offensive for the person experiencing them. Those states become normatively significant when 'caused by the wrongful (right-violating) conduct of others'.[10] It is with offence in this normative sense that the offence principle deals, seeking to determine when the government is justified in restricting individual liberty to prevent it.

An offence principle is necessary only if offence is morally different from harm. It is possible to think that the relationship between the two is that offence is a minor or less serious form of harm, with both of them occupying different places in the same scale of bad things that can happen to the victim.[11]

[7] Feinberg, *Offense to Others* (n 5) 1.

[8] Joel Feinberg, *The Moral Limits of the Criminal Law, vol 1: Harm to Others* (Oxford University Press 1984).

[9] ibid 14.

[10] Feinberg, *Offense to Others* (n 5) 1–2.

[11] See eg Donald Vandeveer, 'Coercive Restraint of Offensive Actions' (1979) 8 Philosophy and Public Affairs 175, 178, who takes the view that offence constitutes harm, their difference being one of degree ('When people are offended, they are harmed-typically in a mild way, but not always. "Harm" tends to range over cases where individuals are made seriously to mildly worse off; "offence" tends to range over cases where individuals are made less seriously to mildly worse off').

Understood in this manner, offence does not require a separate set of rules but can be dealt with under the harm principle, the only question being how the requirements of the harm principle may need to be adapted to accommodate injury caused by offence. Feinberg argues persuasively that while offence is, indeed, a less bad thing than harm, it constitutes a distinct category, and the two should not be placed on the same scale. Offence can perhaps reach on occasion a level of seriousness which causes harm to the victim, so the harm principle will become applicable. But those cases are the exception, not the norm. Usually, the effect of offence on the victim is an unpleasant emotional experience and 'the offended mental state in itself is not a condition of harm.'[12]

Another way of explaining the distinct nature of offence is that, unlike harm, it does not affect negatively the victim's opportunities for pursuing her interests and goals.[13] When one suffers physical injury or one's property is damaged, one's resources are diminished, making it more difficult or impossible to engage in activities and projects which give meaning to one's life. Harm 'is prospective rather than backward-looking: it involves a diminution of one's opportunities to enjoy or pursue a good life.'[14] Offence, by contrast, is about a specific experience, in the sense that it produces a disliked mental state without depriving us of future opportunities. The unpleasant feelings will usually disappear when the offensive conduct stops but even if they linger on they do not, as such, cause a 'prospective loss of resources.'[15]

Conditions Legitimising Coercion

Feinberg divides offensive conduct in two broad categories. He uses the term 'offensive nuisances' to describe the unpleasant or annoyed mental states which are usually the result of an unavoidable attack on the observer's senses; loud noises and foul smells are typical examples of such types of offence.[16] As the term itself suggests, this category is modelled on the common law tort of nuisance, which protects an individual's interests in her land. The aspect of the tort which is particularly relevant for the analogy with offensive conduct is that which protects against activities which do not cause physical damage to land but interfere with the landowner's peaceful enjoyment of it. In the common

[12] Feinberg, *Offense to Others* (n 5) 3.
[13] A P Simester and Andreas von Hirsch, *Crimes, Harms, and Wrongs* (Hart Publishing 2014) 109.
[14] ibid.
[15] ibid.
[16] Feinberg, *Offense to Others* (n 5) ch 7.

law, noise, smoke, smells, and vibration are typical instances of this type of nuisance, which cause 'personal inconvenience' and affect 'the senses or the nerves'.[17]

However, offensive conduct may strike at one's sensibilities, moral, religious or other. Then the experience of offence is not aroused by an attack on the senses but tends to take a more deeply felt character, and usually persists even after the act which initially caused it has ceased. For example, one may be insulted by the burning of the national flag, the desecration of a religious symbol, or certain forms of sexual activity. Often, the offence is caused by the mere thought that those things have taken place, without the offended party having witnessed them. It is the fact that one's idea of patriotism or religious devotion, or sense of sexual propriety, have been disturbed that arouses the feeling of insult, and consequent injury. Those are instances of 'profound offence', in which the offence derives mainly not from the perceptual experience of the offending act but from its cognitively mediated content, which is what is really considered by the observer to be an affront to her sensibilities.[18] Offensive speech belongs to this category.

Feinberg notes that for the offended person both types of offence are 'objectionable for roughly the same kind of reason ... they are annoying distractions, unwelcome demands on one's attention, a bother that must be coped with however inconvenient it may be at the time to do so'.[19] While he is right about the similarity of the reasons which make them objectionable, the explanation seems to leave something out. I think that the similarity lies in the fact that both types of offence are underpinned by an encroachment on boundaries.[20] Offensive nuisances breach a boundary around one's person, which is perceived with one's senses and defines a space where one expects to be undisturbed by unwanted physical stimuli. Offence to sensibilities violates an internal boundary, intruding into one's mental space which is shaped by conscious and unconscious processes. Here, offensive conduct disturbs one's peace of mind, stirring up thoughts and emotions which one would have liked to avoid.

There are three ways in which the law may respond to offensive behaviour: leave it completely unregulated; regulate, and usually prohibit, certain, but not all, offensive acts; or prohibit all types of offensive behaviour. The third way is not an option for a liberal political system as it leaves very little room

[17] *St Helen's Smelting Co v Tipping* (1865) 11 HL Cas 642, 650.
[18] Feinberg, *Offense to Others* (n 5) 14, 51.
[19] ibid 9.
[20] On the significance of boundaries see Neu, *Sticks and Stones* (n 3) ch 1.

for individual liberty, while the first is not usually followed because even liberal systems do not subscribe to John Stuart Mill's principle that only harm to other people can justify punishment. Had that view been adopted, the infliction of mere offence would never be punishable. The second model is the most common, with the law prohibiting some offensive activities on the basis of a set of criteria which vary from case to case but often include the seriousness of the offence, the number of people affected, and the specific issue to which offence relates.

Most instances of regulation of offensive nuisances will be uncontroversial and take place through private law or administrative regulations. The prevention and punishment of offence to sensibilities presents more complicated issues. An obvious objection is that it is a form of moralism since it allows the state to punish people not for harming others but for making them upset or distressed.[21] Of course, all legal systems enforce morality regularly but we do not object to it because usually the immoral act also causes harm to others. Murder is morally wrong and harms the victim, so its punishment falls within the harm principle. When, however, the alleged immorality does not involve harm to another person the law's intervention aims at the enforcement of morality as such. Put differently, if we allow offence to count as a legitimizing reason for state coercion we have abandoned the liberal premise that harmless activities should not be prohibited because some people consider them (rightly or wrongly) as immoral. Feinberg has responded to the objection by clarifying and qualifying the offence principle through two 'mediating' criteria: the seriousness of the offence and the reasonableness of the offending behaviour. I will not discuss his theory in detail here, but I will give a brief description, which, although it does not do justice to its subtlety, will help to clarify what is usually meant by the thesis that the prevention of profound offence to one's sensibilities legitimizes the use of state coercion.

The seriousness of the offence, Feinberg says, is to be determined by four factors: its magnitude, whether it can be reasonably avoided, whether the offence (or the risk of being offended) was voluntarily taken, and whether the offended state is the result of one's abnormal susceptibility to offence.[22] The magnitude of the offence depends, in turn, on its intensity, duration, and extent: the more intense, extensive, and long-lasting the offence, the more serious it is considered to be. All aspects of the criterion of seriousness relate to the

[21] Feinberg discusses legal moralism in detail in *Harmless Wrongdoing* (Oxford University Press 1990).

[22] Feinberg, *Offense to Others* (n 5) 35.

person being offended and the way she has experienced the offence; some of them, such as the intensity and the possible abnormal susceptibility to offence are predominantly subjective in nature, while others such as the duration and reasonable avoidability of the offence are of a more objective character.

Once the seriousness of the offence has been assessed, the focus shifts to the offensive conduct and the person engaging in it in order to determine its reasonableness. Again, Feinberg gives a list of factors against which reasonableness is to be measured: the importance of the offensive conduct to the actor himself, its social utility, the existence of non-offensive alternative opportunities to engage in the conduct, the actor's motives, and the nature of the locality where the conduct takes place. Those general factors are supplemented by a subject-specific one—freedom of expression—because of the great social value and the importance which speech has for individuals and society.[23]

What follows, then, is an exercise where the legislator or the judge is expected to place the seriousness of the offence and its reasonableness on the scales and 'read the balance'.[24] In some cases, the application of one of the criteria will be enough to tilt the scales one way or the other. The typical example is consent. If the offended person has accepted the offensive conduct or the risk of being offended, he cannot claim the protection of the law regardless of the relative weight the other factors possess: 'the *Volenti* standard preempts all the rest when it clearly applies'.[25] In cases where consent does not apply, the other criteria must be considered. Freedom of speech also has increased weight, albeit not of the same preemptive force as consent. The presumption in favour of speech covers its content fully, in the sense that, no matter how offensive an opinion is for some people, the state is not morally justified in using its coercive force to protect the offended party. The manner of expression, however, does not share this privileged status, and can be properly balanced against the other criteria.[26] Thus, there is an internal moral hierarchy of the various

[23] Feinberg does not include a reasonableness requirement in his test for the determination of the seriousness of the offence.

[24] Feinberg, *Offense to Others* (n 5) 44.

[25] ibid 45.

[26] ibid 44. The distinction between the content of the speech and the manner in which it is expressed is a familiar one from First Amendment law, and I will return to it in later chapters. Restrictions based on the content of speech are subject to strict scrutiny while content-neutral restrictions are subject to intermediate scrutiny, which leaves more room for state regulation of speech. Classic examples of content-neutral measures include time, place, and manner restrictions. See eg *Clark v Community for Creative Non-Violence* 468 US 288, 293 (1984): 'Expression, whether oral or written or symbolized by conduct is subject to reasonable time, place and manner restrictions ... restrictions of this kind are valid provided that they are justified without reference to the content of the regulated speech, that they are narrowly tailored to serve a significant governmental interest, and that they leave open ample alternative channels for communication of the information.'

considerations which the decision-maker must weigh: consent has absolute preemptive force and where it applies trumps the other criteria and offers unqualified protection to the offensive conduct; free speech ranks below consent but above the other criteria as the content of the expression is privileged regardless of its offensiveness but the manner of the expression is not; finally, the remaining considerations carry relative weight depending on the circumstances of each case.

The use of the terms 'balancing' and 'balance', and the metaphor of the scales, are both familiar to lawyers, as the judicial process is often described as a balancing exercise where the judge has to weigh competing interests. In constitutional adjudication balancing has been used to explain how constitutional courts resolve claims involving conflicts between rights (for example speech vs. privacy) or rights and legitimate public interests (such as public order or the confidentiality of judicial proceedings).[27] Balancing does not imply that there is an automatic mathematical way of coming to a clearly correct answer; what the model does is to identify all the morally relevant considerations and the way they should be applied, and place them before the decision-maker, who needs to exercise her judgment when dealing with specific cases. It is always possible that she may strike the balance erroneously, in which case we can say that her decision is morally wrong but not illegitimate in the sense of taking into account impermissible factors.[28]

Feinberg's theory starts from a liberal point of view and his aim is to establish appropriate limits to the desire of governments to regulate offensive conduct. One may doubt whether the project—constructing an offence principle which legitimizes coercion against some offensive conduct without collapsing into moralism—can succeed. It may not be possible to remain true to the type of the liberal view of the law Feinberg defends while maintaining at the same time that the law should protect one's moral sensibilities from offence.[29] Thus, A P Simester and Andreas von Hirsch have recently criticized his offence principle

[27] For discussions of balancing in constitutional and human rights law see generally Francisco Urbina, *A Critique of Proportionality and Balancing* (Cambridge University Press 2017); Jacco Bomhoff, *Balancing Constitutional Rights: The Origins and Meaning of Postwar Legal Discourse* (Cambridge University Press 2013); Stephen Gardbaum, 'A Democratic Defence of Constitutional Balancing' (2010) 4 Law and Ethics of Human Rights 79; Stavros Tsakyrakis, 'Balancing: An Assault on Human Rights' (2009) 7 International Journal of Constitutional Law 468; Robert Alexy, 'Balancing, Constitutional Review, and Representation' (2005) 4 International Journal of Constitutional Law 572; T Alexander Aleinikoff, 'Constitutional Law in the Age of Balancing' (1987) 96 Yale Law Journal 942; and Louis Henkin, 'Infallibility under Law: Constitutional Balancing' (1978) 78 Columbia Law Review 1024.

[28] Feinberg, *Offense to Others* (n 5) 45–46.

[29] See Larry Alexander, 'Harm, Offence and Morality' (1994) 7 Canadian Journal of Law & Jurisprudence 199; Anthony Ellis, 'Offense and the Liberal Conception of the Law' (1984) 13 Philosophy and Public Affairs 3.

as being too broad and relying excessively on the consequences of offending acts.[30] They suggest that an offence principle can legitimize coercion through the criminal law only if two additional requirements are met: the offending conduct constitutes a wrong[31] and involves, ultimately, some type of harm. The latter condition relates to situations where offensive conduct which is not harmful per se might cause indirect harms to others.[32] This leads to an overlap of the offence and harm principles.

The fact that Simester and von Hirsch find it necessary to invoke harm within the offence principle shows how difficult it is to justify the prohibition of offensive conduct which insults a person's sensibilities. In the case of offence caused by speech, the difficulty is greater because of the special position speech occupies in the range of human activities.

Offence Caused by Speech

My concern in this book is with offensive speech and, specifically, speech which offends religious sensibilities. I use the term 'speech' in a broad sense, encompassing not only spoken or written words but also expressive conduct in the form of acts undertaken, wholly or primarily, for their symbolic content. Many of the things we do in everyday life carry some sort of symbolism but they would not necessarily qualify as speech in this sense because the expressive element is not the dominant factor. The US Supreme Court has provided a useful test for expressive conduct: whether 'an intent to convey a particularized message was present, and [whether] the likelihood was great that the message would be understood by those who viewed it'.[33] A range of offensive behaviour with symbolic significance would not satisfy the test. For example, some people may be offended by the thought that others have extramarital or premarital or homosexual sex. Those sexual acts are not a form of speech because, although they have a symbolic meaning concerning sexual mores, they are not undertaken by the actors with the main aim of conveying a message. But sometimes

[30] Simester and von Hirsch, *Crimes, Harms, and Wrongs* (n 13) pt III.

[31] As we saw earlier in this chapter, Feinberg also takes wrong to be a necessary element of the actions covered by his offence principle, referring to offence 'caused by the wrongful (right-violating) conduct of others'. Simester and von Hirsch criticize him for indirectly abandoning this requirement when he states that 'there will always be a wrong whenever an offended state ... is produced in another without justification and excuse'. See Feinberg, *Offense to Others* (n 5) 2. They suggest that 'this supposes a general, prima facie duty not to generate offended mental states in others: consequently, the general requirement for a wrong disappears': Simester and von Hirsch, *Crimes, Harms, and Wrongs* (n 13) 96.

[32] Simester and von Hirsch, *Crimes, Harms and Wrongs* (n 13) 112–17.

[33] *Spence v Washington* 418 US 405, 410–411 (1974).

the symbolic element may be the principal consideration in what is otherwise a non-speech activity. An interracial couple walking hand in hand down a busy street in a big city does not usually amount to any kind of statement; doing the same in a small conservative town with a history of racial discrimination is very different. In the latter case, what is (usually) a non-symbolic act acquires a dominant symbolic meaning because of the circumstances in which it is performed.[34]

In moral and political philosophy, and in law, speech is usually considered an activity which is unlike other forms of conduct. Constitutions and human rights documents single out speech as a fundamental right and offer it a higher level of protection compared to non-speech activity. This reflects an understanding that there is something especially valuable in free and unrestricted communication which sets it apart form a general liberty claim to be allowed to conduct our lives in the way we want. We can think of this privileged position of speech as the free speech principle.[35]

That principle does not mean that communicative activities can never be restricted; it means, though, that we require the government to provide particularly cogent reasons for interfering with freedom of expression. In constitutional adjudication, this often translates into strict judicial review tests (stricter than those applied when the conduct interfered with is not speech), which the government must satisfy for its measures to pass muster. Silencing a speaker to prevent offence to the listeners is difficult to reconcile with this privileged position of expression. Eric Barendt considers it a paradigmatic example of negating the free speech principle: 'It would be inconsistent with any free speech principle, worthy of the name, if a publication could be stopped on the ground merely that it is offensive to some people'.[36] Similarly, the former judge of the English Court of Appeal, Stephen Sedley, suggests that 'wherever a democracy draws the boundary of free speech, it surely cannot be at a point which protects individuals or groups from offence or insult on account of their ideas: freedom to speak only within such limits is a form of bondage'.[37] Feinberg also acknowledges the difficulties offensive speech raises for his theory by giving freedom of expression increased weight in the balancing of competing interests. Thus,

[34] The example is given by Feinberg, *Offense to Others* (n 5) 27.

[35] See generally Alon Harel, 'Freedom of Speech' in Andrei Marmor (ed), *The Routledge Companion to Philosophy of Law* (Routledge 2012) 599, 600–601; Eric Barendt, *Freedom of Speech* (Oxford University Press 2005) 6–7; Frederick Schauer, *Free Speech: A Philosophical Enquiry* (Cambridge University Press 1982) 7–9.

[36] Barendt, *Freedom of Speech* (n 35) 7.

[37] Stephen Sedley, 'The Four Wise Monkeys Visit the Marketplace of Ideas' in Stephen Sedley, *Ashes and Sparks: Essays on Law and Justice* (Cambridge University Press 2011) 401.

the starting point for the discussion about how the law should treat offensive speech must be that the offence principle and the free speech principle are in stark tension.

The Offended State of Mind

Insults are a narcissistic injury to our view of ourselves. The way we react when our expectations clash with the offensive conduct of others will be determined by the organization of our personality and the emotional resources we can draw upon for negotiating infringements by external reality on internal mental states. The experience of offence is subjective and calls for an understanding from the point of view of the offence-taker. Yet, it is not uncommon to think that in some cases feeling offended, notwithstanding the victim's sincerity, appears to be unjustified or excessive. There are two important considerations in this regard: hypersensitivity and irrationality.[38]

The person who is ready to feel deeply insulted at the slightest disappointment or provocation is probably excessively sensitive to offence. Living with others requires some degree of resilience and if the law were to interfere whenever someone cried 'I am offended!', much of social interaction would be impossible. The law of nuisance incorporates this standard by making the sensitivity of the claimant a factor in assessing whether the interference with land complained of was reasonable.[39] Similarly, in offensive speech cases we might think that a hypersensitive offence-taker was not *justifiably* offended. However, we would still need to make allowances for personal history and social context. If A calls B a 'lunatic' and B takes this to be a grave insult instead of a mere annoyance, he is probably overreacting. Regardless of whether the statement is true, we know, after all, that there is nothing morally wrong with having mental health problems.[40] But if, say, B's family was shunned in the past because a relative was mentally unwell or B lives in a small community where the stigma attached to mental illness persists, what at first sight appears to be abnormal sensitivity to words might be a justified reaction to an offensive statement.

[38] Neu, *Sticks and Stones* (n 3) 6–7.

[39] *Robinson v Kilvert* (1889) 41 Ch D 88 (no actionable nuisance when the defendant interferes with claimant's 'exceptionally delicate' activity).

[40] I am leaving aside the case where B's distress is not caused by the statement itself but by the fact that A may have revealed, if a third person was present while talking to B, sensitive information about him without his consent. Here, the wrongness of A's statement lies in the breach of confidentiality which compromises B's interest in controlling what personal information about him is disclosed to others.

Moreover, the unpleasant mental states associated with offence may be caused by irrational beliefs. If A, while quarrelling with B, shouts at him 'drop dead', B might understandably feel annoyed or angry but if he becomes extremely anxious because he believes that he will soon die then he is being irrational. As words have no magic power to kill, the mental state produced in B by A's speech is caused by an irrational belief.[41]

Those who disagree with governmental bans on religiously offensive speech might be tempted to dismiss altogether the offence felt by some listeners as a product of abnormal sensitivity or irrationality. While in some cases this might be true, we have no reason to think that it is always true. A believer who belongs to a minority religion which is ridiculed publicly and consistently by the majority need not be hypersensitive to feel offended. Nor should those who reject religion treat religious offence as being caused by irrational beliefs. Within a religious outlook, the belief in the sanctity of a particular figure or the respect accorded to a religious symbol are reasonable beliefs for the person holding them.

The way we understand offended mental states bears on the issue of how the law should treat offensive communications. If we prioritize, as we should, the subjective element there is a danger that the category of 'offensive speech' becomes too broad and, as a result, the amount of speech that falls within the offence principle and needs to be subjected to the balancing test is vast. Any message or opinion can feel offensive to some person, depending on circumstances and context. John Stuart Mill warned against the tendency to feel insulted by whatever we dislike:

> There are many who consider as an injury to themselves any conduct which they have a distaste for, and resent it as an outrage to their feelings; as a religious bigot, when charged with disregarding the religious feelings of others, has been known to retort that they disregard his feelings, by persisting in their abominable worship or creed.[42]

If we are like Mill's bigot, any criticism or disagreement, or even the assertion of views different from our own, will be an insult. But then no discussion on politics, society, religion, or any other topic could take place safely and remain beyond the reach of governmental coercion.

[41] On irrationality and mental distress see Judith Jarvis Thomson, *The Realm of Rights* (Harvard University Press 1990) 253–54.

[42] John Stuart Mill, *On Liberty and the Subjection of Women* (Alan Ryan (ed)) (Penguin 2006 [1859]) 95.

If everything one disagrees with or finds upsetting is offensive, then the concept of offensiveness cannot do much work; so, in a liberal political system 'offensive speech' needs to be more circumscribed when used in the context of legal discourse.[43] I think that the notion of profound offence can be usefully supplemented by Jerome Neu's idea of offence as an attack on moral identity: 'In insult, the self—one's moral identity, the core conditions of both self-respect and self-esteem—is under assault, even if the siege is the result of the indifference and negligence of others rather than their active and malicious intentions.'[44] In the context of discussing how a political community should respond through its institutions to communications which insult some citizens, speech can be properly described as offensive when it causes profound offence which is reasonably felt by the victim as an attack on his moral identity. I am not suggesting that this be treated as a test to be applied by courts to all legal disputes about speech which causes offence; nor is it meant as a general definition. Rather, it is meant as a way of thinking about offensive speech which, hopefully, will make sense to people with a range of different views on the ethical life. Its basis is still on the emotional experience of feeling offended, an experience which is complex, often inconsistent, and not amenable to precise definition because it engages the fundamental conditions of one's self-understanding. As is always the case with our psychic life, external events, like the encounter with some forms of conduct or speech, acquire an internal meaning determined by the structure of our personality and our unconscious wishes, motives, and phantasies.

Thus, this approach is open to the criticism that it remains too subjective. The criticism is valid but there are two answers. First, the suggestion is that we use our best critical account of what speech should be considered offensive. This will not fully allay fears about subjectivity but, I think, it is better than trying to construct a supposedly objective test with some kind of common metric of offensiveness. Secondly, even when some speech qualifies as properly offensive, it does not follow that the government is justified in banning it, only that it becomes legitimate to perform the weighing up exercise and ask whether there are persuasive reasons supporting its prohibition.

[43] An alternative view would be to have a low threshold for offensiveness which would allow most complaints about offensive speech to pass to the second stage where they are balanced against competing considerations, including freedom of expression. In this model, almost all the moral work is done at the second, balancing stage. I think that a more limited notion of offensive speech is preferable because subjecting the exercise of a right to a balancing test as a candidate for prohibition and punishment itself involves moral cost, even if, in the end, the conduct at stake is not banned.

[44] Neu, *Sticks and Stones* (n 3) 31.

Unwitnessed Insults

In what circumstances, if any, might unpleasant mental states caused without the complainant having witnessed the offensive conduct count as properly offensive, and is it ever legitimate to put them on the scales against the competing considerations which favour the offender's action? Consider the example earlier in this chapter of the person who disapproves of and is scandalized by the sexual lives of his neighbours. His moral sensibilities may be offended by the 'bare knowledge' that others are engaging in those sexual acts or even the 'very bare knowledge' that, since such acts are legal, others might be engaging in them anywhere, at any time.[45] In either case, the distress he suffers relates to his own thoughts and fantasies about what he considers to be immoral. The issue of unwitnessed insults is important for a world where communication happens mostly online—described by Timothy Garton Ash as a cosmopolis[46]—making it possible for information to travel instantly everywhere.

A variety of offensive speech instances will raise bare knowledge issues. The easiest example is that of symbolic acts which take place in private. The fanatical atheist who expresses his hatred of religion by regularly burning copies of the Bible in his fireplace, with closed windows and without telling others about it, need not bother us because his act, although offensive for many believers had they witnessed or known about it, does not communicate anything to others. The fact that the pious Christians who live next door know of his anti-religious zeal and imagine with horror all the sacrilegious acts he might be performing in secret cannot mean that they have suffered offence in the sense described above.

However, the same individual may be more open about his compulsive Bible burning. He still does it in the privacy of his home, away from the prying eyes of others, but does not make a secret of it. Then the offence suffered by his Christian neighbours is much more specific and derives from their actual knowledge of the offensive, but unwitnessed, act. Still, this is not an instance of religiously offensive speech which is a proper candidate for the balancing exercise that may lead to its prohibition. The unpleasant feelings they experience—shock, anger, indignation—are caused by the affront to their religious sensibilities. They believe that Bible burning is wrong, possibly a sin, and what they object to, and are indignant about, is the wrongness of the act.

[45] The terms are suggested by Feinberg, *Offense to Others* (n 5) 61.

[46] Timothy Garton Ash, *Free Speech: Ten Principles for a Connected World* (Atlantic Books 2016) 19: 'Cosmopolis exists in the interconnected physical and virtual worlds and is therefore, to borrow a phrase from James Joyce's *Finnegan's Wake*, "urban and orbal" '.

But they cannot claim that they have been themselves wronged, as individuals, by the commission of the unwitnessed, and allegedly immoral, act.[47] Their offence is taken 'on behalf of [their] moral principles or [their] moral regard for precious symbols'.[48] The claim to prohibit their neighbours' conduct may be supported by legal moralism (punishment for harmless conduct because it is immoral) but not by the offence principle.

A third variation is when the Bible burning takes place publicly. There are different degrees of publicity our atheist may seek: he may do his burning more or less discreetly in his garden, where he can only be observed by the neighbours next door; or he may build a large ceremonial pyre visible to passers-by; or he may film the entire event and post the video online for the world to see. Can someone who lives down the road and has not witnessed the event with his own eyes but was informed by others in the neighbourhood claim that he has been offended in a sense which might justify punishing the Bible burner? How about the insulted complainant who lives in another city or country and has heard that there is a video depicting Bible burning? A number of cases of religiously offensive speech are variations of this example. In *Otto-Preminger-Institut v Austria*,[49] a case to which I will return in Chapter 3, the European Court of Human Rights upheld the seizure by the police of a blasphemous film. The film was scheduled for a very limited run of six showings in an art cinema and there had been moderate publicity about it. Before the first showing, the local Catholic diocese filed a criminal complaint, and the cinema director was prosecuted and the film seized, so neither its supporters nor its detractors had a chance actually to see it. The latter were offended at the mere thought that something which was inconsistent with the creed of their religion and insulted their religious sensibilities was advertised and would be publicly available at a cinema. This is an example of offence caused by the mere knowledge of the offending communication, which is outside the scope of any reasonable offence principle.

By contrast, the Danish cartoons, which so angered Muslims around the world, were widely publicized and seen by very many people, although not by everyone who felt insulted: a large number of those who expressed their rage in demonstrations in several countries had probably not seen the actual

[47] Feinberg, *Offense to Others* (n 5) 67–69. Another way of describing this state of affairs would be to say that they have been offended but not insulted. This nomenclature reserves the term 'insult' for what Feinberg has described as offence caused by the wrongful conduct of others (and thus potentially subject to punishment) and the term 'offence' for other types of offensive conduct.

[48] ibid 68.

[49] (1995) 19 EHRR 34.

cartoons, perhaps making a conscious effort to stay away from what they knew would cause them great distress. Yet, they could not avoid hearing about them, reading about them on the internet, and discussing them with their friends. The topic was so conspicuous that inevitably it entered their thoughts, arousing feelings of profound insult. While the offended feelings were not necessarily a case of hypersensitivity, or the product of irrationality, it is difficult to see how the believers were wronged as individuals by the publication. The publicity and furore surrounding the cartoons do not alter the fact that their emotional distress was caused by the bare knowledge of the offending communication.

Although unseen and unheard insulting messages would not normally be considered an attack on an individual's personality, there is a case where they qualify as candidates for prohibition: if public space is so saturated with them that the offended person can only avoid them at great cost, or not avoid them at all.[50] If, say, the cartoons were reprinted as large posters and placed in every street in the city centre, and shown on billboards in the main square, it would be very difficult for believers to move around without always being exposed to them. The unpleasant mental states they would have to endure would no longer be caused solely by their relentless, all-consuming thinking of the blasphemous images; the external world would be a constant reminder of the insult, adding another layer of injury. Their profound offence, initially the result of knowing that the cartoons exist, would be so aggravated by the need constantly to try to avert their eyes that they could reasonably claim that the posters affected them personally in a way which undermined aspects of their personality. Even then speech may prove to have greater weight but considering the possibility of prohibition and performing the balancing exercise is compatible with a strong commitment to freedom of expression.

Speech can qualify as properly offensive, and thus come within the scope of governmental coercion, when it causes profound offence which can be reasonably considered an attack on the victim's moral identity. Unwitnessed insults can be profound in character but will usually lack the additional, personal, element. Thus, offensive words, images, and symbolic acts of which the victim has no direct experience would not usually pass the threshold of the necessary offensiveness. The exceptions are cases where the insulting communication is thrust upon the victim, making it unreasonably costly, or impossible, to avoid it.

[50] See the discussion in Feinberg, *Offense to Others* (n 5) 162.

Types of Religious Speech

The Venice Commission of the Council of Europe[51] has proposed a tripartite categorization of religious speech which is the target of legal sanctions: blasphemy, religious insult, and incitement to religious hatred.[52] The subject matter—religion—is common but there are differences of focus, content, and manner of expression. Yet, as the Commission acknowledged, it might not always be easy to pin down such differences. For example, blasphemy traditionally referred to showing disrespect or contempt for God or another revered figure, while religious insult and hatred are about the effect of speech on people. But, as we will see in Chapter 5, blasphemy gradually changed its emphasis from the protection of God and the idea of the sacred to the protection of the believers themselves, and of public order. It became lawful to deny God's existence and criticize religious faith but speech had to be civil and moderate so as not to offend believers and cause strife in the community. This is, broadly, the rationale for modern blasphemy provisions in the Western world.

Further, the Commission distinguished between insult and hatred but did not explain what the difference consists of. It pointed out that in the relation to the former 'the relevant European provisions appear to cover the different concepts' (often at the same time) of 'insult based on belonging to a particular religion' and 'insult to religious feelings'.[53] It then noted that there is no generally acceptable definition of hate speech and cited the working definition from Recommendation (97)20 of the Committee of Ministers of the Council of Europe:

> the term 'hate speech' shall be understood as covering all forms of expression which spread, incite, promote or justify racial hatred, xenophobia, anti-Semitism or other forms of hatred based on intolerance, including: intolerance expressed by aggressive nationalism and ethnocentrism, discrimination and hostility against minorities, migrants and people of immigrant origin.[54]

[51] The European Commission for Democracy through Law, usually referred to as the Venice Commission because it meets in Venice, is a body of the Council of Europe providing advice on matters of constitutional law and policy.

[52] European Commission for Democracy through Law (Venice Commission), 'Report on the Relationship between Freedom of Expression and Freedom of Religion: The Issue of Regulation and Prosecution of Blasphemy, Religious Insult and Incitement to Religious Hatred' CDL(AD)(2008)026 (2008).

[53] ibid para 28.

[54] ibid n 15. The definition of hate speech by the European Court of Human Rights is equally unhelpful, making intolerance a necessary element of hate speech: 'all forms of expression which spread,

Even in those descriptive efforts to explain what are essentially evaluative concepts, the difficulty in drawing a line between religious offence and religious hatred is evident. Both types of speech express a negative reaction, like antipathy and rejection, towards people with a certain religious viewpoint, and the implication is that the difference is a matter of degree, with hatred being an extreme form of negativity. The author of Recommendation (97)20 tried to ease the definitional strain by creating a hate speech patchwork where every form of strong dislike has its place. Is xenophobic and nationalist discourse always a form of hate speech? Is the expression of intolerant feelings (all intolerant feelings or only some of them?) hate speech? When does verbal hostility towards migrants and immigrants, distasteful and repugnant but lawful in most jurisdictions, become a punishable crime?

This conceptual confusion carries over to public debate about religious offence. Critics of the Danish cartoons, which were undoubtedly offensive for believers, described them as so abusive as to be hate speech against Muslims, and legal claims were brought against the newspapers which published them in Denmark and France, which were subsequently rejected by courts. Those arguments borrow the terminology and conceptual apparatus of the hate speech discourse for application in cases of religious insult, thus conflating the two. And while the view of the Venice Commission that offence and hatred should not be treated in the same way as a matter of law is correct, we need to know more about the normative characteristics of the two types of speech which require this differential treatment. There are two related questions: first, how can religious offence be distinguished from religious hatred in a manner which is morally sound and consistent with free speech doctrine; secondly, if there are persuasive arguments for banning hate speech, can they also support a prohibition of religious offence?[55]

incite, promote or justify hatred based on intolerance (including religious intolerance)'. See *Gunduz v Turkey* (2005) 41 EHRR 5 para 40.

[55] Here I am discussing religious hatred insofar as it helps to elucidate the concept of offence. A discussion of the rights and wrongs of hate speech laws generally, or religious hatred offences in particular, is beyond the scope of this book. From the very extensive literature on hate speech see eg Nadine Strossen, *Hate: Why We Should Resist it with Free Speech, Not Censorship* (Oxford University Press 2018); Eric Heinze, *Hate Speech and Democratic Citizenship* (Oxford University Press 2016); Alexander Brown, *Hate Speech Law: A Philosophical Examination* (Routledge 2015); Jeremy Waldron, *The Harm in Hate Speech* (Harvard University Press 2012); Michael Herz and Peter Molnar (eds), *The Content and Context of Hate Speech: Rethinking Regulation and Responses* (Cambridge University Press 2012); Ishani Maitra and Mary Kate McGowan (eds), *Speech and Harm: Controversies Over Free Speech* (Oxford University Press 2012); Ivan Hare and James Weinstein (eds), *Extreme Speech and Democracy* (Oxford University Press 2009) particularly pts II and III; Steven J Heyman, *Free Speech and Human Dignity* (Yale University Press 2008) ch 10; Anthony Lewis, *Freedom for the Thought That We Hate: A Biography of the First Amendment* (Basic Books 2007); Mari J Matsuda, Charles R Lawrence III, Richard Delgado, and Kimberlé Williams Crenshaw, *Words That Wound: Critical Race Theory, Assaultive Speech and the First*

The Relevance of Hatred

Definitions of hate speech often display an element of circularity.[56] This is inevitable if one is trying to define a thing or a form of conduct by reference to one of its constitutive elements. It thus appears easier to delineate hate speech as a legal concept when the criterion is something other than the emotion of hatred itself. Some hate speech provisions prohibit communications which are an incitement to further wrongful conduct, such as discrimination or violence. The International Covenant on Civil and Political Rights requires the proscription of 'any advocacy of national, racial or religious hatred that constitutes incitement to discrimination, hostility or violence' (Article 20.2) and the American Convention on Human Rights refers to 'any advocacy of national, racial, or religious hatred that constitutes incitement to lawless violence' (Article 13.5). Further, section 130 of the German Criminal Code punishes incitement to hatred 'against a national, racial or religious group or a group defined by their ethnic origin' which is done in a manner 'suitable for causing a disturbance of public peace'.[57] In those examples the consequences of speech on people or public order are the factor which distinguishes hatred from other forms of aggressive speech, like insults. Even if the content is the same, the communications which count as hateful and fall within the scope of the prohibition are only those which are likely to have further effects, which are the evil the law aims at suppressing.

This model reflects a well-known distinction in the theory and practice of free speech, that between speech and conduct. John Stuart Mill, while passionately defending the right to speak, noted that:

> no one pretends that actions should be free as opinions. On the contrary, even opinions lose immunity, when the circumstances in which they are expressed are such as to constitute their expression a positive instigation to some mischievious act. An opinion that corn-dealers are starvers of the poor, or that private property is robbery, ought to be unmolested when simply

Amendment (Westview Press 1993). Specifically on religious hate speech see Richard Moon, *Putting Faith in Hate: When Religion is the Source or Target of Hate Speech* (Oxford University Press 2018) and Jeroen Temperman, *Religious Hatred and International Law* (Cambridge University Press 2015).

[56] See Heinze, *Hate Speech and Democratic Citizenship* (n 55) 23, who gives the example of the definition in Ivan Hare and James Weinstein 'General Introduction' in Ivan Hare and James Weinstein (eds), *Extreme Speech and Democracy* (Oxford University Press 2009) 4: 'In its purest form, hate speech is simply expression which articulates hatred for another individual or group, usually based on a characteristic (such as race) which is perceived to be shared by members of the target group.'

[57] See https://www.gesetze-im-internet.de/englisch_stgb/englisch_stgb.html.

> circulated through the press, but may justly incur punishment when delivered orally to an excited mob assembled before the house of a corn-dealer, or when handed about among the same mob in the form of a placard.[58]

Defining hateful communications by reference to the pernicious conduct they trigger (violence or discrimination against believers, breach of public peace) has the advantage of creating a boundary around the religious hatred offence, which acknowledges the moral significance of the difference between speech and action. Evidently, it is not without its problems, the most important of which is the issue of causation. If the causal link between speech and harm required for speech to count as hateful is too lax, the law will also catch communications which have the tendency to cause harmful effects, usually in the long term, rather than immediately incite violence or discrimination. Often, the determination will depend on the manner of expression and tone of language.[59] Moderate and serious criticism, even if harsh, will not be considered as a cause for further harm, and therefore, a form of hate speech. But it is easier to argue that abusive attacks, ridicule, and profanity tend to cause further harms and should be proscribed as hate speech. Where this happens, the dividing line between religious offence and religious hatred becomes obliterated.

It is even more difficult to distinguish between the two where the religious hatred offence proscribes hateful messages as such, without requiring evidence of any further harm. This is the approach of Canadian and English law. Section 319(2) of the Canadian Criminal Code punishes a speaker who 'wilfully promotes hatred against any identifiable group', a provision which was found to be compatible with the right to freedom of expression in the seminal case of *R v Keegstra* concerning anti-Semitic slurs. The aspect of the judgment which is relevant for the discussion here is the Canadian Supreme Court's explanation of what properly counts as hate speech. Chief Justice Dickson held that 'the term "hatred" connotes emotion of an intense and extreme nature that is clearly associated with vilification and detestation'.[60] Thus, the term 'as used in s.319(2) does not denote a wide range of diverse emotions, but is circumscribed so as to cover only the most intense form of dislike'.[61]

This construction was probably an effort to read section 319(2) in a speech-friendly way but, if this was the aim, it is doubtful whether it was achieved.

[58] Mill, *On Liberty* (n 42) 64.
[59] Robert Post, 'Hate Speech' in Ivan Hare and James Weinstein (eds), *Extreme Speech and Democracy* (Oxford University Press 2009) 124, 134–36.
[60] *R v Keegstra* [1990] 3 SCR 697, 777.
[61] ibid 778.

When is the expression of dislike so intense as to count as hatred instead of strong antipathy and disapproval, emotions which also cause their targets serious distress and perhaps psychological injury but whose expression is not prohibited? The Supreme Court directs judges to look at the content and manner of expression and assess which messages are beyond the limits of acceptable dislike. But in so doing, they will inevitably end up applying the norms of respect which prevail in society at a particular time so the law becomes a way to silence speech which falls foul of those norms.[62]

This issue comes into focus when we consider the Court's understanding of the nature of hate speech. Dickson CJ approved of the view that promoting hatred 'is properly understood as a practice of inequality'.[63] Stated this way, the position is wrong. The hateful bigot ranting against those he despises is not practising inequality. It is possible to argue that repeated instances of vilification and abuse of a group will gradually poison societal attitudes and affect the way its members are viewed, so over time it becomes acceptable to deny them benefits, housing, education, or employment to which they would otherwise be entitled. That would certainly be a case of discrimination. However, unless the specific speaker has also done something along those lines, the expression of his hatred is not an instance of inequality. Dickson CJ's view blurs the difference between speech and conduct.[64] When this distinction is removed from our understanding of hate speech, the only distinguishing characteristic of hatred becomes the lack of conformity with societal norms of respect. In fact, this concern was raised before the Court. It was argued that section 319(2) required an inference from the communication at stake whether the speaker intended to promote hatred, which created the danger that judges would see hatred in every message they disliked or found offensive. The Court quickly dismissed it with the dubious assurance that it was enough to direct themselves (or the jury) that not everything distasteful is a form of hate speech.

The UK Parliament made the expression of religious hatred an offence with the Racial and Religious Hatred Act 2006, which in section 1 creates 'offences involving stirring up hatred against persons on religious grounds'. The 2006 Act amended the Public Order Act 1986, which now provides that 'a person who uses threatening words or behaviour, or displays any written material which is threatening, is guilty of an offence if he intends thereby to stir up religious hatred' (s 29B(1)); religious hatred is defined as 'hatred against a group of persons

[62] Post, 'Hate Speech' (n 59) 135.
[63] *R v Keegstra* (n 60) 756.
[64] Barendt, *Freedom of Speech* (n 35) 174.

defined by reference to religious belief or lack of religious belief' (s 29A).[65] The government's initial intention was to criminalize speech that was also 'abusive' and 'insulting', in analogy with section 18 of the 1986 Act, which punishes incitement to racial hatred by 'threatening, abusive or insulting words or behaviour'. The plan was met with strong criticism from MPs, peers, and civil society organizations for its effect on freedom of expression and eventually only 'threatening' communications were banned. Moreover, only intentional incitement of religious hatred satisfies the *mens rea* of the new offence. And further to assuage fears about excessive restrictions on speech, the following clause was added to the Act:

> Nothing in this Part shall be read or given effect in a way which prohibits or restricts discussion, criticism or expressions of antipathy, dislike, ridicule, insult or abuse of particular religions or the beliefs or practices of their adherents, or of any other belief system or the beliefs or practices of its adherents, or proselytising or urging adherents of a different religion or belief system to cease practising their religion or belief system' (s. 29J).

Like its Canadian counterpart, on the one hand, section 29B(1) does not require incitement to unlawful conduct; the intentional utterance of a hateful message is enough to trigger its application. On the other hand, thanks to the section 29J clause, there is recognition that religious hatred and religious offence are legally different and that protection for speech about religion does not stop at the moderate and the inoffensive. The scope of the offence is thus considerably more limited, particularly because antipathy, dislike, ridicule, insult, and abuse are expressly mentioned as protected instances of the exercise of free speech rights.[66]

When Parliament was debating the new offence, the then Home Secretary stated that the Bill was 'about protecting people, not faiths'.[67] This statement, which appears to combine support for freedom of expression with the correct intuition that individuals should not be abused or attacked on account of their religious affiliation, can be linked to broader arguments about respect. It

[65] For more on the 2006 Act, including its legislative history, see Kay Goodall, 'Incitement to Religious Hatred: All Talk and No Substance?' (2007) 70 Modern Law Review 89; Anthony Jeremy, 'Practical Implications of the Enactment of the Racial and Religious Hatred Act 2006' (2007) 9 Ecclesiastical Law Journal 187; Peter Cumper, 'Outlawing Incitement to Religious Hatred: A British Perspective' (2006) Religion and Human Rights 249; Ivan Hare, 'Crosses, Crescents and Sacred Cows: Criminalising Incitement to Religious Hatred' (2006) Public Law 521.

[66] Attacks on people and disturbances of public peace were anyway covered under s 5 of the Public Order Act 1986 which punishes persons causing harassment, alarm or distress by words or actions.

[67] Cited in Eric Barendt, 'Religious Hatred Laws: Protecting Groups or Belief' (2011) 17 Res Publica 41, 43.

is often said that when arguing publicly about religion one ought to approach other people's beliefs with seriousness and moderation and express one's disagreement in a respectful manner. Intemperate and insulting speech shows disrespect for both the belief and those who adopt it as part of their view of what life is worth living, because the belief is part of the believer's identity. An alternative approach would be to try to disentangle respect for believers from respect for their beliefs.[68] This argument may be based on a now well-known distinction developed by Stephen Darwall between recognition respect and appraisal respect.[69] Recognition respect is owed to all persons by virtue of their humanity and does not depend on an assessment of their qualities or achievements; the mere fact that I see in them another human being is reason enough for me to respect them. Appraisal respect is owed only when it is merited, and involves a positive judgment about this person's character or achievement in a specific pursuit. Applied to the debate about religious speech, this understanding of respect supports a claim that individual believers should be accorded recognition respect and that we should refrain from doing anything which fails 'to give proper weight to the fact that they are persons'.[70] By contrast, the fact that they believe X is not reason to respect X, or respect them for believing X. This is a form of appraisal respect which is due only if we are persuaded that there is something positive in X. If not, we should be free to question, criticize, and ridicule X—in short, be disrespectful towards the religious belief or practice—without risking the accusation that we failed to respect the believer. The belief and the believer are not identical, so attacking a religious belief or practice is not the same as attacking the person who holds the belief or engages in the practice. The Home Secretary's statement about the aim of the 2006 Act (protecting people, not faiths) could be read to mean that the religious hate speech offence was meant to safeguard the kind of recognition respect everyone is owed as an attribute of one's humanity but not coercively enforce appraisal respect for any sort of religious belief.

But this justification for hate speech prohibitions may be undermined by the difficulty in assessing what the target of the attack actually is. We have seen that English law considers religious hatred as the 'hatred against a group of persons defined by reference to religious belief or lack of religious belief'. Since the members of the group, and thus beneficiaries of the protection, are

[68] As suggested by Timothy Garton Ash, *Free Speech* (n 46) 261–67.
[69] Stephen L Darwall, 'Two Kinds of Respect' (1977) 88 Ethics 36.
[70] Darwall states that 'to have recognition respect for persons is to give proper weight to the fact that they are persons'. See ibid 39.

defined through their beliefs, how can we differentiate between the belief and the person of the believer? As Eric Barendt has noted:

> the group is constituted or characterized by their common or shared beliefs. It is impossible to distinguish, say, a vituperative attack on the wearing of the niqab or burqa from an attack on Muslims generally, or between a vicious satire on the Catholic Church as an institution and its bishops from hate speech against Catholics.[71]

The question with which we started was how to distinguish religious offence from religious hatred in a way which adequately reflects their moral difference. That the two are different is not in doubt, and even legislators setting out to punish hate speech, and judges upholding the constitutionality of hate speech offences, accept that a line must be drawn between them, yet we still lack a satisfactory way of drawing it. We can usually identify and understand hatred experientially: we feel that it exists in interpersonal relationships and the social worlds in which we live; we may have detected it in other people's feelings towards us; and, if we have a reasonable degree of self-understanding and honesty, we can admit that we have experienced it towards others. But defining a legal category—hate speech—by reference to an emotion—hatred—is probably a mission destined to fail, largely perhaps because it is hard to distinguish from offence.

'Dignity' and 'Basic Standing'

It is better to follow Jeremy Waldron's suggestion and avoid getting 'bogg[ed] down in a futile attempt to define "hatred" '.[72] Waldron has provided a powerful defence of hate speech prohibitions premised on the effects of hate speech on vulnerable persons. What hate speech is calculated to do, he argues, is 'compromise the dignity of those at whom it is targeted, both in their own eyes and in the eyes of other members of society'.[73] This dignity is not a metaphysical attribute but the 'basic social standing'[74] everyone is entitled to as an equal member of our community going about his or her business. The expression of hatred 'aims to besmirch the basics of [the] reputation'[75] of its targets and

[71] Barendt, 'Religious Hatred Laws' (n 67) 49.
[72] Waldron, *The Harm in Hate Speech* (n 55) 36.
[73] ibid 5.
[74] ibid.
[75] ibid.

deprive them of the assurance that they will not need 'to face hostility, violence, discrimination, or exclusion by others'.[76] In so doing, it also injures the public good of inclusiveness, 'reawakening living nightmares of what this society was like—or what other societies have been like—in the past'.[77]

Thus, instead of first defining hate speech and then asking whether particular communications fit the definition, Waldron develops a normative account of the wrongness of hate speech and advocates the application of hate speech prohibitions where that wrongness is manifest. This is the most promising way of distinguishing between offence and hatred. If we need to know, like the Canadian Supreme Court, whether a specific expression of dislike is so extreme so as properly to count as the promotion of hatred we can ask whether its effect is to undermine the basic social standing of those it targets; anything short of that effect, no matter how distasteful, insulting, or abusive the message is, should fall outside the scope of a hate speech prohibition. This assessment will not always be obvious; nor does Waldron so claim. In fact, he concedes that religious speech will pose a special challenge for his view.[78] Indeed, on occasion, it will be difficult to differentiate between the insecurity the members of a minority may feel from the harm hate speech inflicts on their dignity or on inclusiveness as a public good.[79] The answer may depend on the conditions prevailing in a particular society and the way they have come about through a succession of historical events. This is an advantage of Waldron's account: it eschews strong claims of universal applicability, remaining sensitive to history and the political reality in diverse communities.

Moreover, it is possible to be sympathetic to his analysis of the wrongness of hate speech without agreeing with his conclusion in favour of its regulation. For example, it can be doubted whether the sort of dignitarian harm he has in mind can justify the proscription of hateful messages; whether there is adequate evidence that hate speech actually subordinates vulnerable individuals; whether hate speech laws are effective in protecting vulnerable individuals; and it is also argued that hate speech bans undermine the legitimacy of the enforcement of anti-discrimination laws because they deprive those with extreme opposition

[76] ibid. 4. There are points in the book which suggest that the justification for regulating hate speech is not that it has negative consequences for the status of vulnerable people but that it constitutes harm per se, irrespective of its further effects. For example, he says that hate speech 'can become a world-defining activity' (at 74) because it is 'largely performative' (at 166), and a 'speech act' (at 167). But overall the best understanding of his argument is that hate speech can be proscribed as an injury inflicted on the members of groups targeted by it. This aspect of Waldron's account is discussed in Eric Barendt, 'What Is the Harm of Hate Speech?' (2019) 22 Ethical Theory and Moral Practice 539, 543–546.

[77] Waldron, *The Harm in Hate Speech* (n 55) 4.

[78] ibid 118–21.

[79] Barendt, What is the Harm of Hate Speech? (n 76) 541.

to equality of their say in political discourse.[80] But none of those criticisms is necessarily incompatible with the view that some forms of speech can have seriously injurious effects for members of vulnerable groups. Besides, those who oppose hate speech laws do not claim that the expression of hatred is harmless but that the harms are not such so as to justify silencing the speakers or are outweighed by competing reasons for allowing haters to speak.

The focus on the wrongness of hate speech also shows that it is mistaken to borrow arguments from the hate speech debate to support the prohibition of offensive speech (the second question mentioned earlier in this chapter). We have seen that offence is a multi-layered mental state which involves one's self-esteem and the esteem one is accorded by others. Hate speech legislation does not aim to protect listeners from the unpleasant feelings stirred up when they receive insults and ridicule instead of deference and respect. Its main object is to sustain everyone's equal moral position as an ordinary member of society, and any protection of feelings resulting from this affirmation of equal status is incidental. Waldron himself emphasizes this difference and stresses that legislators enacting hate speech laws should be vigilant not to end up protecting people from the effect unpleasant speech has on their feelings.[81] The warning certainly applies with equal vigour to administrators and judges who interpret such laws in individual cases. In the context of religious speech, he argues further, this distinction between offence and hatred, and between the justifications for regulating each one, is both necessary and feasible, despite the inevitable grey areas.[82] He summarizes his position as follows: 'offence, however deeply felt, is not a proper object of legislative concern'.[83]

A similar dignitarian explanation of the wrongness of hate speech is part of a general theory of the First Amendment developed by Steven Heyman. His account, which he describes as a rights-based view of free speech, is based on the idea that expression is wrongful when it infringes other rights people have and exercise as individuals and members of the community. With the exception of cases where the value of speech is so important so as to outweigh the injury, such as the enhanced protection of political speech against defamation suits, communications which violate other rights can legitimately be restricted

[80] Those points are developed respectively in Heinze, *Hate Speech and Democratic Citizenship* (n 55) 153–58; Robert Mark Simpson, 'Dignity, Harm and Hate Speech' (2013) 32 Law and Philosophy 701; Strossen, *Hate* (n 55) ch 7; and James Weinstein, 'Hate Speech Bans, Democracy, and Political Legitimacy' (2017) 32 Constitutional Commentary 527 and Ronald Dworkin, 'Foreword' in Ivan Hare and James Weinstein (eds), *Extreme Speech and Democracy* (Oxford University Press 2009) v.

[81] Waldron, *The Harm in Hate Speech* (n 55) 114.

[82] ibid at 120: 'But the basic distinction between an attack on a body of beliefs and an attack on the basic social standing and reputation of a group of people is clear'.

[83] ibid 105.

in principle. Which way the scales will come down will depend on context and the particular characteristics of each case. Applied to hate speech, the theory suggests that 'speech of this sort violates the target's right to personal security, the community's right to public peace, or both'.[84] However, insulting speech like the Danish cartoons falls outside the scope of the rule because it does not attack Muslims as human beings or advocate violence or discrimination against them.[85]

Both Waldron and Heyman understand the dignitarian harm inflicted by hate speech as being capable of objective determination. It is a 'social reality'[86] constituted by attacks 'on the status [of others] as human beings and members of the community'.[87] This argument works on a different plane from that where offence arises, because whether one's basic standing as a citizen is assaulted cannot depend on the subjective feelings which form the constellation of the offended mental state. Damage to basic standing is a social fact. Therefore, vicious criticism of, say, Anglicans in England, will probably feel to many of them upsetting and painful but cannot jeopardize their dignity and status as equal citizens; it is offensive, but not hate speech. Or, as Waldron puts it, 'a person's dignity or reputation has to do with how things are with respect to them in society, not with how things feel to them'.[88] Bans on offensive speech are about how things feel to us, targeting psychic injury caused when the view we have of ourselves, and of what is our due, is frustrated by external reality.

To recapitulate: the best case for regulating hate speech rests on the idea that it assaults a vulnerable individual's basic standing as an equal member of society. Speech can properly count as promotion of hatred only where this pernicious effect is present. Harsh criticism, antipathy, ridicule, or abusive language, which may have an adverse psychological impact on their targets, are not hate speech, but cases of offensive speech. At the root of offence is an unpleasant emotional experience, which is unlike the injury inflicted on the victim of hate speech which happens at the level of the external world. Justifying the regulation of offensive speech requires different arguments from the ones used in the hate speech debate. The rest of the book explores whether such persuasive arguments exist.

[84] Heyman, *Free Speech and Human Dignity* (n 55) 165. Heyman refers to a 'right' to peace held by the community but it is probably better to think of this as a public interest or public good rather than a right in the strict sense.
[85] ibid 182.
[86] Waldron, *The Harm in Hate Speech* (n 55) 108.
[87] Heyman, *Free Speech and Human Dignity* (n 55) 182.
[88] Waldron (n 55) 106.

2

Reasons for State Action

Following the riots after the publication of the Danish cartoons, the UN Special Rapporteur on Contemporary Forms of Racism, Racial Discrimination, Xenophobia and Related Intolerance, Doudou Diène, took the view that the cartoons should be seen 'as a debate on the balancing of two rights, freedom of expression and freedom of religion',[1] and was later quoted by the press as stating that 'the cartoons are absolutely insulting', that 'this publication explicitly shows a lack of understanding and emotion for believers', and that 'beliefs should not be humiliated under the veil of freedom of expression'.[2]

Those statements are typical of the way public discussion of offensive speech is often conducted. One way of thinking about them is that they are claims about what is the morally appropriate practical attitude of citizens in public space, and which values it should give effect to. They include questions such as how we should address one another, what topics are properly topics of public interest, and what words and tone of language we should adopt when speaking publicly so as to make life with others possible in pluralist societies. We can also think of them as more specific claims about how the law should treat offensive communications and what is the best interpretation of the constitutional and statutory provisions which are relevant for the determination of that question once it has become the object of legal contestation.

Those two aspects of the debate are linked but not identical: we often make claims about what is the right thing to do without expecting the intervention of the law for the enforcement of moral duties. For example, kindness, generosity, and empathy are all important virtues, and a society whose members practised them to some degree would be an easier and happier place in which to live, but we do not think that it is the government's business to punish the callous and the unkind. In the arguments about offensive speech, disentangling the issue of the morally appropriate attitude when one speaks publicly from that of the coercive regulation of speech through the law has been particularly difficult.

[1] Cited in Robert Post, 'Religion and Freedom of Speech: Portraits of Muhammad' (2007) 14 Constellations 72, 79.

[2] ibid 79 and n 47.

Offensive Speech, Religion, and the Limits of the Law. Nicholas Hatzis, Oxford University Press. © Nicholas Hatzis 2021.
DOI: 10.1093/oso/9780198758440.003.0003

From the assertion that sacrilege and profanity are an insult to the feelings of the religious believer, the move to saying that religiously offensive speech should be banned is quickly made. This chapter looks at the assumptions on which this move rests by exploring the structure of the claims for silencing offensive speakers through state coercion. First, I discuss what it means for the state to have a reason to act; then I explore what sorts of reasons can be validly invoked to justify state action and how they bear on the issue of prohibiting religiously offensive speech.

Offence as Reason for Action

The claim that the government should curtail speech which offends religious sensibilities is a form of practical reasoning. It involves a conclusion about what someone ought to do under specific circumstances. The agent considers the available options for action and assesses the reasons which support or negate each option. Reasons are normatively significant because they determine behaviour when certain conditions obtain.[3] Thus, the claim entails the assertion that the fact that some people are offended in their religious sensibilities by some communication is reason for the government to prohibit it.

Here, reason should be understood to mean normative reason. Reasons can perform an explanatory function if they provide an answer to the question why something happened or why it came to exist or what an agent's motivations are for doing something.[4] Normative reasons go beyond this function because, as Joseph Raz explains, 'they count in favour of that for which they are reasons. They have the potential to ... justify and require that which they favour'.[5] The existence of a normative reason to do something means that this is the right thing to do. Normative reasons also include a certain kind of explanation but this function is secondary because it depends on the normative relation between the fact and that which it favours.[6] In the claim about offensive speech, the fact of offence supports that for which it is a reason, namely state interference with communications which offend; offence is the normative reason which performs a justificatory function for the interference with speech. So, if

[3] Joseph Raz, *Practical Reason and Norms* (Oxford University Press 1999) 18–19.

[4] For a discussion of the distinction between the explanatory and motivational functions of reason see Maria Alvarez, *Kinds of Reasons: An Essay on the Philosophy of Action* (Oxford University Press 2010) ch 2.

[5] Joseph Raz, 'Reasons: Explanatory and Normative' in Joseph Raz, *From Normativity to Responsibility* (Oxford University Press 2011) 13, 18.

[6] ibid 19.

one asserts that offence explains, say, a legal rule criminalizing blasphemy, one may be saying that offence is the answer to the question 'why was blasphemy made a criminal offence by the legislature?' or one may be referring to the rightness of the legislature's action to criminalize blasphemy. It is the second sense of having a reason to prohibit offensive speech, reflecting the normative relation between the fact of offence and the prohibition, which is the subject of my discussion.

This normative relation can be expressed in terms of the value that underpins the relevant reason. The agent has reason to do something because by doing it he will realize a value. The value that will be realized by the agent's action is what makes it right for the agent to act in a particular way.[7] Raz notes that 'reasons for action track value'[8] and this creates a 'value-reason nexus':[9] the fact that the agent values something is a reason for action. Thus, to state what counts as a complete reason for acting in a particular way, one needs to state what is the value which underpins the reason and accounts for its normativity.[10]

The inference that the state ought to prohibit offensive speech is the conclusion of a syllogism which may be analysed as follows:

P1: respect for people's religious beliefs is a value;
P2: the prohibition of offensive speech can prevent offence to religious beliefs;
P3: therefore the law should prohibit offensive speech.

P1 is the operative reason which performs an evaluative function; P2 is an auxiliary reason which links the operative reason to the conclusion by identifying the act which there is reason to perform. Operative reasons express a practical critical attitude and auxiliary reasons link that attitude to a conclusion about what is the right thing to do.[11] We have not fully stated what behaviour is justified or required under certain circumstances unless we have identified the operative reason which justifies or requires such behaviour.

Asserting that offensive speech should be prohibited because it insults the listeners is akin to relying on an auxiliary premise. But the auxiliary premise cannot by itself justify or require the act identified in the conclusion, as its role

[7] Alvarez (n 4) 9; Joseph Raz, *Engaging Reason: On the Theory of Value and Action* (Oxford University Press 2002) 23.
[8] Joseph Raz, *Value, Respect, and Attachment* (Cambridge University Press 2009) 1.
[9] ibid 5.
[10] Raz, *Practical Reason and Norms* (n 3) 24–25.
[11] ibid 33–35. Raz calls the auxiliary reasons which perform this identification function 'identifying reasons'.

is to mediate between the operative premise and the conclusion as to what act there is reason to perform. An auxiliary premise can be a reason for action only by reference to the operative premise.[12] Therefore, the assertion that the law should ban offensive speech should be understood as being based on an operative premise that the protection of religious beliefs from offence is a value.

Even when stated that way, the claim for prohibition is not complete. It would be more accurate to say that offence is a *pro tanto* reason for prohibiting offensive messages. *Pro tanto* reasons are those that can be defeated by competing reasons.[13] This is an aspect of the fact that reasons have different strength or weight. When the agent considers the options available to her, there may be reasons which support conflicting courses of action. In such cases, the stronger or weightier reason will override one or more competing reasons.[14] We can then say that this undefeated reason which prevails over all others is the 'all things considered' reason which determines the agent's conduct.[15]

Those who think that offensive speech should be banned, and courts which have upheld legal provisions that do so, accept that there are reasons which support the opposite conclusion. The most important one is free speech.[16] They usually concede that the significance of uninhibited expression on religious matters for a liberal society is a fact which gives us reason to deny the protection of the law to those who take offence, their offence being a reason for prohibition. But they find that speech is overridden by the need to protect believers from offence in their religious sensibilities. Thus, they think offence to be a weightier or stronger reason which defeats any free speech considerations, and, thus, an all things considered reason for the prohibition.

A final distinction which bears on our understanding of the claim for prohibition of offensive speech relates to the agent for whom offence is a reason for action. Not all reasons for action apply to all agents; in some cases, facts are reasons for action only in relation to a specific agent so they are normatively

[12] John Gardner and Timothy Macklem, 'Reasons' in Jules Coleman and Scott Shapiro (eds), *The Oxford Handbook of Jurisprudence and Philosophy of Law* (Oxford University Press 2004) 440, 449.

[13] Alvarez, *Kinds of Reasons* (n 4) 12.

[14] Raz, *Practical Reason and Norms* (n 3) 25–28.

[15] Alvarez, *Kinds of Reasons* (n 4) 12.

[16] Speech is the most important but not the only reason. For example, a state may choose not to interfere with offensive communications because it would be too costly to investigate and prosecute the speakers who offend others. In this case, the reason which competes with offence is financial prudence, not free speech. My discussion is about free speech considerations.

significant as determinants of that agent's behaviour.[17] Further, even where the same reason applies to different agents, it may favour different courses of action for each agent. For example, the fact that a member of my family is ill is reason for me to call the doctor, and is reason for the doctor to prescribe appropriate medication. The illness is a reason which determines both my and the doctor's conduct but requires different actions. The thesis that the law should restrain speech which offends religious sensibilities concerns what the *state* has reason to do. This does not mean that offence may not be a reason for action for other agents such as individual citizens. The fact that another person will experience my criticism of the tenets of his religion as an insult to his religious sensibilities may, under certain circumstances, be reason for me to exercise self-restraint and temper my language or keep my mouth shut altogether. There is a distinction between what one has the right to do and what is the right thing to do.[18] Having the right to do X means that it is morally wrong for the state to use force to prevent me from doing X or punish me for having done X. However, it does not follow that because I have a right, it is always a good thing to exercise it. The existence of a right is not, as such, a reason to engage in the activity which the right protects, and there may be reasons not to engage in it. In the example of the devout, religious friend, not wanting to hurt his sensibilities may be reason not to exercise the right to speak in an offensive manner. The book does not address all the instances where offence may be a reason guiding an agent's conduct. My discussion is exclusively about the question of whether offence is a reason for the state to exercise its coercive power against those who offend through speech.

The assertion that the state should prohibit offensive speech entails that offence is a normative reason which justifies or requires the prohibition. Its normativity derives from the ultimate value of respect for religious convictions. It also entails that any competing reasons against prohibition, such as freedom of expression, are weaker than offence. And thus, the claim runs, the state has reason to exercise coercion against speakers whose communications offend others' religious sensibilities.

[17] In Nagel's well-known definitions, 'if a reason can be given a general form which does not include an essential reference to the person who has it, it is an *agent-neutral* reason ... If on the other hand the general form of a reason does include an essential reference to the person who has it, it is an *agent-relative* reason'. See Thomas Nagel, *The View from Nowhere* (Oxford University Press 1989) 152–53. Nagel presented an earlier formulation of this distinction in Thomas Nagel, *The Possibility of Altruism* (Princeton University Press 1979) 90 ff, where he used the terms 'objective' and 'subjective' reasons. Derek Parfit in *Reasons and Persons* (Oxford University Press 1984) 27, 143 suggested the terms 'agent-neutral' and 'agent-relative', which were adopted by Nagel in *The View from Nowhere.*

[18] See the discussion in Jeremy Waldron, 'A Right to Do Wrong' in Jeremy Waldron, *Liberal Rights: Collected Papers* 1981-1991 (Oxford University Press 1993) 63.

The Requirements of Public Reason

Having considered the structure of the claim for the prohibition of offensive speech, we can now turn to the question of what sorts of reasons can justify the exercise of the state's coercive power against speakers who offend. The question is important because reasonable people have different moral outlooks and disagree, often in deep and pervasive ways, about what is the right thing to do under certain circumstances. This is expressed not only in the realm of personal ethics but also in politics. Societies need rules which organize common life and make it possible for the community to function. What those rules will be, and which political institutions will make and enforce them, is the subject of political contestation. Given that individuals have different attachments and preferences and feel committed to different values, they will disagree on how state power should be used, and will compete in the political arena for institutional support of the moral viewpoint they favour. Those are disagreements about the values that public institutions should serve for every member of the political community.[19]

It is often said that political societies, when making rules which their members are expected to comply with, are bound by a public reason principle which requires that such rules be justifiable to all those whose life they purport to govern. Public reason is offered as an answer to the problem of political legitimacy. How can it be legitimate for society collectively to impose rules and institutions on individuals even when they do not share the values informing the choices of the majority? The suggestion is that the exercise of power is legitimate if it can be justified on grounds or reasons that people can be reasonably expected to find acceptable, even though they do not themselves endorse them. This does not mean that reasons are public only if they can actually persuade; it is enough if they can reasonably justify state action. The fact that an unreasonable audience may fail to be persuaded by an argument does not necessarily imply that the argument should be excluded from the range of acceptable public reasons.[20] Thus, when citizens argue about what rules are appropriate for regulating life in society, and when the state enshrines those rules in the law, they should invoke only arguments whose force does not depend (or does not depend exclusively) on a personal moral viewpoint about what constitutes a good life. In this section, I discuss

[19] Thomas Nagel, 'Moral Conflict and Political Legitimacy' (1987) 16 Philosophy and Public Affairs 215, 216.

[20] ibid 218.

aspects of public reason theory which are particularly relevant for the issue of offensive speech.

Justification and Coercion

While the idea of public reason has a long intellectual history,[21] it was the work of John Rawls which made it a prominent theme in contemporary moral and political philosophy. In *A Theory of Justice* it is part of the concept of a 'well-ordered society' based on the liberty and difference principles:

> a society is well-ordered when it is not only designed to advance the good of its members but when it is also effectively regulated by a public conception of justice. That is, it is a society in which (1) everyone accepts and knows that the others accept the same principles of justice, and (2) the basic social institutions generally satisfy and are generally known to satisfy these principles.[22]

This publicity requirement extends further than merely having principles of justice which are known to all members of society.[23] It is rather the locus where the reasoning processes of individuals meet, establishing 'the bonds of civic friendship'.[24] One of the duties they entail is to try, in good faith, to understand other people's points of view about a particular question and provide them with reasons based on a 'mutually acceptable conception of justice'[25] whenever a decision affects them. Our willingness to explain our position about the regulation of collective life using arguments our fellow citizens might find reasonable, matched by their reciprocal willingness to do the same, supports respect for others and enhances self-respect.[26] This effort to find a shared, as opposed to an exclusively personal, viewpoint which can legitimize the exercise of political authority is the element which defines our relation to one another in a liberal democracy.[27]

[21] Piers Norris Turner and Gerald Gaus (eds), *Public Reason in Political Philosophy: Classic Sources and Contemporary Commentaries* (Routledge 2018); Duncan Ivison, 'The Secret History of Public Reason: Hobbes to Rawls' (1997) 18 History of Political Thought 125.

[22] John Rawls, *A Theory of Justice* (rev edn, Harvard University Press 1999) 4.

[23] On publicity see Charles Larmore, 'Public Reason' in Samuel Freeman (ed), *The Cambridge Companion to Rawls* (Cambridge University Press 2006) 369–75.

[24] Rawls, *A Theory of Justice* (n 22) 5.

[25] ibid 297.

[26] ibid 155–56.

[27] Larmore, 'Public Reason' (n 23) 373 notes: 'What the publicity requirement really comes to ... is that each person's adherence to the principles of justice should turn on reasons that he understands others to have to affirm as well'.

Rawls links the public conception of justice, and the respect for persons it supports, to stability.[28] If a society is governed by utilitarian principles, individuals are unlikely to show allegiance to rules and institutions which require them to sacrifice their own prospects of a good life so as to maximize utility for the group as a whole. They would find it unreasonable to accept limits on their freedom and abandon their own projects and commitments to promote interests which they do not consider to be their own. And such a society, where citizens cannot psychologically identify with its basic structure, is not a stable one. On the other hand, in a society based on his conception of justice, it is publicly known that individuals are equals and their interests count independently of their potential to maximize public good. Therefore, they are more likely to view those principles of justice as their own principles, develop a commitment to them and act in accordance with them. This conception of justice, he argues, 'generates its own support'[29] and enhances the stability of social institutions.

Publicity is developed into a full public reason theory in *Political Liberalism*.[30] Rawls recasts his earlier thesis about what kinds of reasons can justify state action in a liberal and democratic society in terms of a political conception of justice: public reason is what legitimizes 'the exercise [of] final political and coercive power'.[31] There is a moral 'duty of civility'[32] to avoid 'appeal to comprehensive religious and philosophical doctrines-to what we as individuals or members of associations see as the whole truth'[33]- and try instead to explain to others our views about how common life should be organized invoking reasons which they can also accept. Later, Rawls took the view that comprehensive doctrines are acceptable in public discussion at any time if at a later stage public reasons are also given which can support whatever position one has adopted as a result of one's comprehensive doctrines. He described this revised approach as the 'wide view of public political culture' and the requirement for public reasons as the 'proviso' which legitimizes reliance on non-public reasons. [34]

The duty of civility applies to decisions about constitutional essentials and questions of basic justice. Constitutional essentials consist of two issues: first, the general form of government and the structure of the political process;

[28] For more on stability see Jon Garthoff, 'Rawlsian Stability' (2016) 22 Res Publica 285.

[29] Rawls, *A Theory of Justice* (n 22) 154.

[30] John Rawls, *Political Liberalism* (Columbia University Press 1996).

[31] ibid 214.

[32] ibid 217. The duty is moral and not legal because requiring citizens to express certain views and not others would violate their freedom of speech: John Rawls, 'The Idea of Public Reason Revisited' (1997) 64 The University of Chicago Law Review 765, 769.

[33] Rawls, *Political Liberalism* (n 30) 225.

[34] Rawls, 'The Idea of Public Reason Revisited' (n 32) 783–84. For an argument against this revision and in favour of the earlier position see Larmore 'Public Reason' (n 23) 386–87.

secondly, the basic rights and liberties of citizens.[35] In the former, there is space for considerable variation as several different arrangements will satisfy the essential requirements of liberal democracy—for example, the choice between a parliamentary or a presidential system or the division of power among the branches of government. In the latter, the scope for variation is much more limited because fundamental rights, such as freedom of speech and conscience, will have the same basic content in all regimes which claim to treat their citizens as free and equal persons.

Constitutional essentials and questions of basic justice do not exhaust all instances of necessary decision-making in a political community. When issues which fall outside those spheres are debated and decided on, the requirements of public reason do not apply and 'citizens and legislators may properly vote their more comprehensive views... they need not justify by public reason why they vote as they do'.[36] But, Rawls suggests, if those fundamental matters are at stake both public officials and citizens are expected to act within the bounds of public reason when they discharge their duties, advocate their views in the public forum and vote on elections. The main burden is on officers of the government and, especially, on judges who need to justify their decisions on the basis of the constitution and ordinary legislation.[37] But private individuals are also expected to think of themselves as if they were legislators and support the adoption of statutes which they find reasonable to enact for reasons which justify the criterion of reciprocity.[38] If citizens merely rely on their personal preferences, without trying to consider what decisions or policies are supported by the values of the political conception of justice, they have failed their moral duty of civility. In this sense, voting is not a personal matter for each voter.[39]

The inclusion of citizens' public advocacy and voting in the realm of public reason may appear excessive. But Rawls points out the link between participation in politics and the exercise of power over people: democracy implies 'an equal share in the coercive political power that citizens exercise over one another by voting and in other ways'.[40] Advocacy and voting need to be constrained by public reason because they constitute ways one exercises one's share of the power to regulate common life and coercively impose norms on

[35] Rawls, *Political Liberalism* (n 30) 227–28.

[36] ibid 235. The view that all political deliberation should be subject to the requirements of public reason even if no constitutional essentials and matters of basic justice are at stake is defended in Jonathan Quong, *Liberalism Without Perfection* (Oxford University Press 2010) ch 7.

[37] Rawls, *Political Liberalism* (n 30) 215–16. He considers the Supreme Court as the 'exemplar of public reason': 231–40.

[38] Rawls, 'The Idea of Public Reason Revisited' (n 32) 769.

[39] Rawls, *Political Liberalism* (n 30) 215, 219.

[40] ibid 217–18.

every member of the community. He contrasts this political, public power with non-public power, such as that exercised by voluntary organizations over their members, giving the example of churches.[41] In democratic states, church members freely accept their participation in the religious community and its authority over them on the basis of rules which have their source in religious doctrine. If they can no longer identify with the faith and its requirements, they are free to leave without having to worry that the government will coerce them to do otherwise. This is not possible when state authority is concerned because the government can coercively enforce compliance with rules enacted through the political process even if the individual does not identify with their content.

The role of coercion as the element which necessitates a public reason theory has been emphasized by Thomas Nagel[42] and Charles Larmore.[43] Their accounts are based on the Kantian idea of respect for persons as applied in the context of the political life. One aspect of respect is that people should be treated as ends, not means for achieving whatever aim the community is pursuing. This requires that, when the state is imposing on them an obligation to act in a particular way backed by the threat of coercion, they be offered grounds which they can reasonably accept as valid justifications for the obligation. It is not adequate to make them comply solely out of fear that they will be punished if they do not. In such a case, they are offered a reason to comply—avoid the harm of punishment—but they are still being treated as means because the state is not engaging with their reflective capacity as persons who can think about what rules are necessary for our common life and identify with them. Treating them with respect means that 'coercive or political principles be as justifiable to that person as they presumably are to us'.[44]

Justification for coercion over people is the theme which also underlies Robert Audi's account of public reason-giving. He focuses on the grounds on which the state can limit civil liberties and puts forward what he calls 'the principle of secular rationale: one should not advocate or support any law or public policy that restricts human conduct unless one has, and is willing to offer, adequate secular reason for this advocacy or support'.[45] This principle

[41] ibid 221–22.

[42] Nagel, 'Moral Conflict and Political Legitimacy' (n 19) 223–25; Thomas Nagel, *Equality and Partiality* (Oxford University Press 1991) 158–59.

[43] Charles Larmore, 'The Moral Basis of Political Liberalism' (1999) 96 The Journal of Philosophy 599, 607–08.

[44] ibid 608.

[45] Robert Audi, 'The Separation of Church and State and the Obligations of Citizenship' (1989) 18 Philosophy and Public Affairs 215, 279. He describes secular reason as 'one whose normative force, that is, its status as a prima facie justificatory element, does not (evidentially) depend on the existence of God (for example, through appeals to divine command), or on theological considerations (such as

favours the idea that resolution of questions about how individual liberty will be limited should be based on secular considerations.[46] The same may apply to non-liberty-restricting measures and policies but in such cases the obligation to adduce secular reasons is less stringent.

Jonathan Quong has criticized coercion-based rationales on the ground that coercive rules are not unique in calling for justification and that there are non-coercive arrangements which should also be subject to public reason constraints.[47] He gives two examples. The first is a country which is debating whether to make Catholicism the national religion, incorporate references to Catholic beliefs into official state documents, declare Catholic holidays to be national holidays, and subsidize the Catholic Church from the public purse. He argues that none of those measures interferes with individual liberty, yet the proposed policies are properly within the realm of public reason. The second is a society where citizens obey the laws even when they think they are mistaken or incoherent because they have internalized the obligation to be law-abiding. Thus, laws are not coercively enforced, nor is there need for the threat of coercion. His conclusion is that coercion cannot offer the moral basis for a public reason requirement.[48]

Quong is making an underinclusiveness objection: if the coercion-based argument for public reason cannot account for instances where public justification is required despite the lack of coercive enforcement, then coercion cannot ground an obligation to offer public reasons. We can leave aside questions about his conception of coercion and what counts as a restriction of liberty or whether the society where all citizens internalize the law without the need to consider the threat of sanctions is a plausible view of political life. Even if the argument from coercion is underinclusive and cannot explain all issues which require support with public political justification, it does not follow that coercion is not the main concern underlying public reason. Locating the need for such justification in the coercive nature of the state reflects what is perhaps the most important aspect of our experience of living with others in a

interpretations of a sacred text), or on the pronouncements of a person or institution qua religious authority' (page 278).

[46] ibid. Audi accepts that religious reasons can be introduced into public discussion if secular ones are also given: '[The secular rationale principle demands] that whatever other considerations one brings to the relevant contexts of advocacy or support, one put forward such advocacy or support only if one *also* has and is willing to offer adequate secular reason for the view in question' (emphasis in the original): 280. Rawls adopted this view when he revised his own earlier position to develop the wide view of public political culture and the proviso: Rawls, 'The Idea of Public Reason Revisited' (n 32) 783.

[47] Jonathan Quong, 'On the Idea of Public Reason' in Jon Mandle and David A Reidy (eds), *A Companion to Rawls* (Wiley Blackwell 2014) 265, 272.

[48] ibid 273. The alternative he prefers is justice.

political society: the government can deprive people of their property, liberty and life (where the death penalty exists) to ensure compliance with rules enacted through a majoritarian political process without them having a right of exit when they disagree with the law. Rawls actually alludes to the fundamental importance of this reality when he distinguishes the government from voluntary organizations which one can leave freely.[49] It is not that exiting a group one has joined voluntarily has no cost. It often involves great emotional costs for the departing member and may also provoke retaliation by the group in the form of shunning and shaming. But whatever power a voluntary group has over its members it is, as Rawls says, 'non-public' because it is ultimately subject to one's right of exit. No comparable right of exit from the power of political society exists for those who cannot identify with its laws and, thus, it is necessary to subject the exercise of coercive power to the rigour of public reason. Coercion may not be the only case where public justification is required but it is the paradigmatic such case.

Reasoning from Religious Beliefs

The exclusion of religious justifications from the realm of public reason has been met with criticism on various grounds.[50] The most potent and persuasive objection is a derivative of a broader criticism of the Rawlsian project, that of

[49] Rawls, *Political Liberalism* (n 30) 222. Rawls suggests that the only way to evade the authority of the government is to leave 'the territory over which it governs, and not always then'. Given the proliferation of immigration restrictions, even this option is becoming increasingly difficult, while there is no option to evade the coercive power of *a* government more generally.

[50] See eg Andrew F March, 'Rethinking the Public Use of Religious Reasons' in Tom Bailey and Valentina Gentile (eds), *Rawls and Religion* (Columbia University Press 2015) 97; Christopher J Eberle, 'Religion and War: Against the Standard View of Religion in Politics' in Tom Bailey and Valentina Gentile (eds), *Rawls and Religion* (Columbia University Press 2015) 29; Christopher J Eberle, *Religious Conviction in Liberal Politics* (Cambridge University Press 2002); Jeremy Waldron, 'Two-way Translation: The Ethics of Engaging with Religious Contributions in Public Deliberation' (2012) 63 Mercer Law Review 845; John Finnis, 'Political Neutrality and Religious Arguments' in John Finnis, *Religion and Public Reasons: Collected Essays Volume V* (Oxford University Press 2011) 103; Gerald F Gauss and Kevin Vallier, 'The Roles of Religious Conviction in a Publicly Justified Polity: The Implications of Convergence, Asymmetry and Political Institutions' (2009) 35 Philosophy and Social Criticism 51; Richard Ekins, 'Secular Fundamentalism and Democracy' (2005) 8 Journal of Markets and Morality 81; Michael J Perry, 'Why Political Reliance on Religiously Grounded Morality Does Not Violate the Establishment Clause' (2001) 42 William and Mary Law Review 663; Michael McConnell, 'Five Reasons to Reject the Claim that Religious Arguments Should be Excluded from Democratic Deliberation' (1999) 3 Utah Law Review 639; Steven Shiffrin, 'Religion and Democracy' (1999) 74 Notre Dame Law Review 1631; Nicholas Wolterstorff, 'The Role of Religion in Decision and Discussion of Political Issues' in Robert Audi and Nicholas Wolterstorff, *Religion in the Public Square: The Place of Religious Convictions in Political Debate* (Rowman and Littlefield 1997) 67.

incompleteness.[51] Rawls considered completeness to be an essential feature of public reason:

> Another essential feature of public reason is that its political conceptions should be complete. This means that each conception should express principles, standards, and ideals, along with guidelines of inquiry, such that the values specified by it can be suitably ordered or otherwise united so that those values alone give a reasonable answer to all, or to nearly all, questions involving constitutional essentials and matters of basic justice.[52]

The ordering of values cannot be made by reference to criteria external to public reason because this would turn political values into 'puppets manipulated from behind the scenes by comprehensive doctrines'.[53]

There are, however, several issues which concern constitutional essentials and questions of basic justice on which citizens trying to formulate a view within the realm of public reason will be deeply divided. Those are not disagreements between those who accept the core principles of constitutional democracy and those who support a competing political paradigm such as a dictatorship or theocracy. The disagreements arise within liberal democracy itself, among citizens who are broadly committed to a democratic form of government which respects individual rights. But while there is in the public political culture endorsement of those principles, and consensus that they should inform the decisions taken by officials and voters, there are serious disagreements about how they are to be applied.[54] For example, reasonable citizens can be expected to agree that freedom of religion or some redistribution of wealth through taxation are necessary components of a just society but might fail to find persuasive public reasons which others can also affirm when it comes to deciding whether the burqa should be banned in public or what is the appropriate level of income tax for the wealthy.

David Reidy has suggested that the failure to find answers to specific questions through public reasons may have two causes. First, there are issues—including human cloning, affirmative action, prostitution, and euthanasia—which

[51] Incompleteness can take two forms. Public reason may be indeterminate if it fails to provide a persuasive justification for selecting among different responses to a particular question; or it may be inconclusive if it provides several plausible answers without saying which one is the most reasonable. See Micah Schwartzman, 'The Completeness of Public Reason' (2004) 3 Politics, Philosophy and Economics 191, 194–98.

[52] Rawls, 'The Idea of Public Reason Revisited' (n 32) 777.

[53] ibid.

[54] John Horton, 'Rawls, Public Reason and the Limits of Liberal Justification' (2003) 2 Contemporary Political Theory 5, 13.

implicate conflicting values of approximately even weight.[55] As they concern constitutional essentials, the duty of civility requires citizens to reason exclusively from a public reason standpoint. This implies a need to prioritize values so as to identify the one which outweighs others and thus counts as the 'all things considered' reason for action. The ordering exercise must take place within public reason, with criteria which can be considered reasonable for the political conception endorsed by public reason. But for many citizens it will be impossible to identify a criterion for addressing this conflict without relying on their personal viewpoints of what counts as the ethical life. Even in the modified, wider conception of public reason, which admits of personal beliefs based on comprehensive doctrines, it is necessary to satisfy the proviso, i.e. supplement them at a subsequent stage with public reasons which support the position one takes in public debate as a result of one's comprehensive views. However, it is unrealistic to expect that citizens will not be indirectly relying on their comprehensive viewpoints when they perform that second reasoning exercise within the realm of public reason: they will tend to endorse a resolution of the conflict of values which supports the position they reached on the basis of their personal, non-public beliefs.

Secondly, there are cases, such as abortion, where making decisions requires the resolution of a preliminary issue.[56] Here the question is what the moral status of the foetus is. While it is possible for citizens to engage with each other's views in good faith, there seems to be no determinate answer which can be reached by reasons that all other citizens can be reasonably expected to affirm. In cases where public reason is silent or inconclusive, reliance on personal viewpoints is necessary for reaching a reasoned decision.[57]

This critique of Rawlsian public reason has important consequences for religious justifications for coercive laws. If the incompleteness objection is valid and there are at least some questions for which political public reason cannot provide an answer, then religious individuals can rely on personal reasons arising from comprehensive religious doctrines when debating those laws in public discourse without violating their duties as citizens. Does it follow, then, that they can legitimately advocate the punishment of those who insult a figure or a symbol which is considered sacred within their comprehensive religious

[55] David A Reidy, 'Rawls's Wide View of Public Reason: Not Wide Enough' (2000) 6 Res Publica 49, 64–68.

[56] ibid 69–70.

[57] By contrast, Schwartzman, 'The Completeness of Public Reason' (n 51) 209–14 argues than even if public reason is incomplete there are alternative decision strategies which make recourse to non-public reasons unnecessary.

view, presenting the fact of their offence as a valid reason for the exercise of state coercion? The answer depends largely on what are the issues which properly admit of reliance on comprehensive personal doctrines for their resolution.

Kent Greenawalt has developed an intermediate thesis between unlimited acceptance and strict prohibition of religious personal reasons in public debate.[58] He agrees with the Rawlsian line of argument that liberal democracy excludes certain grounds from being appropriately considered as reasons for state action and being invoked by citizens in the public domain. Discussion on matters pertaining to the organization of life in a political community should proceed from premises which are accessible and commonly shared. In contemporary pluralist countries, religious beliefs are unlikely to satisfy those criteria so public officials and citizens should strive to rely on secular rational arguments. Religious convictions are only a category of impermissible considerations as there are also secular personal viewpoints which are similarly excluded. Like Rawls', Greenawalt's theory excludes both religious and non-religious viewpoints which cannot be reasonably shared by all citizens.

The difficulty, Greenawalt continues, is that this test excludes too much: there will be many political issues for which citizens will not have adequate grounds to develop a reasoned view after all non-public reasons have been excluded. This is a variant of the incompleteness objection which, as we saw earlier, suggests that public political justifications cannot by themselves offer determinate answers to a number of issues where different values conflict. In those cases, he argues, it is acceptable to rely on non-rational arguments based on personal viewpoints about the ethical life. Thus, he considers that what makes abortion an intractable issue of public policy is the deep disagreement about to the moral status of the foetus, a question which features, directly or indirectly, in all arguments about the permissibility of abortion. He concludes that 'shared premises and publicly accessible reasons cannot resolve the points at which a fetus is entitled to particular degrees of moral consideration or what should be done in case of uncertainty'.[59] Similar questions of status arise in the areas of animal rights and environmental protection where it is necessary to consider

[58] For book-length, systematic treatments see Kent Greenawalt, *Private Consciences and Public Reasons* (Oxford University Press 1995) particularly ch 14 and Kent Greenawalt, *Religious Convictions and Political Choice* (Oxford University Press 1988) particularly chs 4 and 8. See also Greenawalt's articles 'Religion and Public Reasons: Making Laws and Evaluating Candidates' (2012) 27 Journal of Law and Politics 387; 'Religiously Based Judgments and Discourse in Political Life' (2007) 22 St John's Journal of Legal Commentary 445; 'Religious Grounds in Liberal Politics' (1993) 12 Criminal Justice Ethics 3; 'Religious Convictions and Political Choice: Some Further Thoughts' (1990) 39 De Paul University Law Review 1019; and 'Religiously Based Premises and Laws Restrictive of Liberty' [1986] Brigham Young University Law Review 245.

[59] Greenawalt, *Religious Convictions and Political Choice* (n 58) 126.

what conduct is required or permitted towards animals and the natural environment. While most reasonable people would agree that some moral duties are owed to animals which can experience pain and pleasure, specific questions about their legal protection are difficult to resolve without relying on one's personal views about life in our cosmos.[60] The inconclusiveness of public political reason is what legitimizes reliance on personal, non-public viewpoints. This includes personal religious convictions as it would be unfair to religious citizens to exclude religiously determined non-rational arguments but allow secular non-rational arguments: 'If all people must draw from their personal experiences and commitments of value to some degree, people whose experience leads them to religious convictions should not have to disregard what they consider the critical insights about value that their convictions provide'.[61]

He contrasts those cases with the issue of sexual acts between consenting adults. Here, relying on one's personal moral outlook, whether secular or religious, to argue for their prohibition would be incompatible with the mode of moral reasoning which liberal democracy requires: '[A] simple belief, whether religiously based or not, that acts are morally wrong is never an appropriate ground for prohibition; to support prohibition in a liberal society, one must be able to point to some genuine damage or danger to individuals or society'.[62] Placed in the context of a public reason theory, this principle means that the citizen who contemplates what sexual acts the law should prohibit must not rely on a view of sexual morality based on personal conceptions of the good life and the legislator must not rely on such views when establishing rules which apply to everyone. Therefore, the belief that homosexual acts or extramarital sex are sinful is not a morally relevant reason for their prohibition, as the incompatibility of an act with the teachings of a religion or the beliefs of a religious individual or group is irrelevant for the question how the state should treat it. While it is appropriate for a religious individual to arrange her own sexual life in a manner which conforms to her religious viewpoint, 'the curbing of these activities simply because they conflict with the religiously based convictions of others is unwarranted in any event'.[63] To the religious citizen who finds such activities an abomination we should, thus, reply that 'the aim to prevent an act condemned from a religious perspective is not a proper ground on which to legislate a prohibition'.[64]

[60] ibid 109–10.
[61] ibid 145.
[62] Greenawalt, 'Religiously Based Premises and Laws Restrictive of Liberty' (n 58) 259.
[63] Greenawalt, *Religious Convictions and Political Choice* (n 58) 91.
[64] Greenawalt, 'Religiously Based Premises and Laws Restrictive of Liberty' (n 58) 258.

I think that Greenawalt is correct that, when certain important conflicts of value cannot be resolved by secular rational arguments alone, the criterion for allowing or not reliance on religious grounds is the nature of the issue at stake. Speech which offends religious sensibilities and beliefs falls on the side of the line where such arguments are unacceptable. Offensive speech is more like consensual sex acts which a believer may find to be sinful and therefore in conflict with everything that he stands for in his life, and different from abortion or animal rights and environmental protection where the debate revolves around the moral status of the foetus or the proper place of the human race in the universe. The claim to punish a speaker who ridicules the dogma contained in a holy book or satirizes a venerated religious figure is determined by the religious nature of what is being talked about and aims at preventing an act which is considered wrong from a religious viewpoint. In this sense, the believer who advocates the prohibition of speech which offends what he holds to be sacred uses the same mode of moral reasoning as the believer who expects the state to prohibit gay or extramarital sex because it is a sin according to the teachings of his religion.[65] In both cases, they attempt to establish rules applicable to every member of the political community and use coercion to ensure compliance with them on the basis of a personal moral position which those citizens who do not share it cannot be reasonably expected to consider an appropriate basis for coercion.[66]

The exclusion of religious grounds from the reasons which can be relied on to support the exercise of state coercion does not mean that religious arguments, ideas and values should be excluded from public culture altogether. Rawls is clear that the political conception of justice requires justification based on commonly shared reasons in the context of the public political forum—the discourse of judges, the practice of government officials and legislators, and the speech of politicians.[67] In addition to that realm, there exists what he calls the

[65] As Greenawalt, *Religious Convictions and Political Choice* (n 58) 94 notes, '*if that kind of reason* [incompatibility with religious norms] *is not properly relied on with respect to consenting sexual acts, it is not properly relied upon with respect to any other social issues either*' (emphasis in the original).

[66] It may be objected that people who use religious arguments about abortion or animal rights are doing the same thing—trying to impose a personal moral standard which cannot be justified from an impartial viewpoint. Even if this objection is true, it does not bear on my argument here, as I am not trying to defend the permissibility of relying on religious premises in any area. Rather, my point is that one does not need to support the absolute exclusion of religious reasons from political debate to exclude them from the debate about religiously offensive speech; even an approach which is friendly towards them under certain circumstances, such as Greenawalt's, cannot tolerate them when it comes to offensive speech because they express merely a personal belief in the immorality of an act (i.e. insulting what one thinks is sacred). As explained above, Greenawalt clearly rejects reliance on beliefs about moral wrongness as a legitimate basis for state coercion.

[67] Rawls, 'The Idea of Public Reason Revisited' (n 32) 767; Rawls, *Political Liberalism* (n 30) 13–14.

'background culture' of civil society, which comprises all types of agencies and voluntary organizations such as churches, clubs, charities, universities, scientific or cultural associations, and so on. We can think of that sphere as our life outside the political institutions of the democratic state. Rawls notes:

> In a democracy, this culture is not, of course, guided by any one central idea or principle, whether political or religious. Its many and diverse agencies and associations with their internal life reside within a framework of law that ensures the familiar liberties of thought and speech, and the right of free association.[68]

The reference to the internal life of voluntary associations in civil society is important because it points to the limited nature of the obligation for public justification. One of the criticisms of public reason theory is that it impoverishes public discourse because it deprives it of the vitality, enthusiasm, and passion of ideas stemming from people's comprehensive doctrines and conceptions of the good, whether religious or secular.[69] While this is a real concern, it is significantly mitigated by the openness of the background culture where the constraints of public reason do not apply. Our experience in civil society takes up a much bigger part of our daily existence, and also our imagination and emotional life, than the part devoted to our role as citizens who deliberate and vote on public policy. The former is the space where we can express our personal view of what is a meaningful life and encounter the surprising and the unfamiliar in other people's viewpoints. Religiously inspired values and ideas have an equal claim to shape public culture as secular ones. This includes arguments about how one ought to behave in public and what is the morally required attitude toward those with whom we disagree as to how one should live. Thus, it is entirely appropriate for religious citizens publicly to assert the role of religion in their lives and their disapproval of profane or sacrilegious speech.

A possible worry is that it will not always be easy to delineate the proper realm of the background culture. When might spirited public advocacy of religious values and a religious way of life be considered an encroachment on the public political forum and, therefore, a violation of the duty of civility? Isn't there a danger that a commitment to public reason will lead us to draw the line in a way which leaves too little room for the expression of religious viewpoints

[68] Rawls, 'The Idea of Public Reason Revisited' (n 32) 768.

[69] Thus, Michael Walzer, 'Drawing the Line: Religion and Politics' (1999) Utah Law Review 619 offers qualified support for the involvement of faith groups and the employment of religious arguments in political debate provided that religious organizations cannot use the state's coercive power.

lest they undermine the political arena? I think there is no test which can yield a clear answer in every case, and Rawls does not say much on this point.[70] But there is a line which can be drawn with enough clarity and predictability: the advocacy of the exercise of state power. The citizens who argue that the government should proscribe certain acts and punish those who engage in them have left the area of the background culture of civil society and are within the public political forum where they should always be expected to rely on grounds which all other members of the community can accept.[71] We should thus ask those who are offended in their religious sensibilities by sacrilegious speech, and advocate its ban, to offer arguments which go beyond the fact that such speech is wrong from a religious perspective.

This exclusion does not necessarily imply an assessment about the reasonableness of the excluded beliefs as personal beliefs. There is a distinction to be made between justifications for individual belief and justifications for appealing to that belief to support the use of state coercion.[72] The exclusion is relevant only to the latter: it bars the citizen from relying on them to justify the claim for coercive measures over other citizens but it implies nothing as to whether he is justified in holding them as a personal matter. Objectivity in reasoning about political legitimacy does not require the religious citizen to stop believing in the truth of his personal convictions about what is sacrosanct and what is sinful; judged from the perspective of individual rationality they may be reasonable convictions. However, it requires him to refrain from using them in political debate about the exercise of state power and the form that political institutions should take, acknowledging that when seen from the perspective of individuals who do not share them, those convictions are not general truths.[73] It also requires legislators and other public officials not to rely on them when making decisions on public policy which will apply to all members of the community and can be coercively enforced. Therefore, it would be wrong to assume that when, in the debate about offensive speech, we discount arguments in favour of prohibition if they are based on personal religious beliefs, we show

[70] He does say that there is an intermediate space between the public political forum and background culture, which he calls the 'non-public political culture', mainly consisting of the mass media: Rawls, 'The Idea of Public Reason Revisited' (n 32) 768 fn 13.

[71] Gauss and Vallier, 'The Roles of Religious Conviction' (n 50) 62–65 argue that it is wrong to think that there is in public deliberation symmetry between the reasons in favour of coercive laws and reasons against them. The requirement for public justification that all can accept applies where citizens are advocating the use of coercion over others. Therefore, religious citizens cannot legitimately claim that the liberty of others should be restricted on the basis of grounds arising from their religious doctrine. But they can employ religiously based arguments in political discourse to argue against laws that violate their liberty of conscience.

[72] Nagel, 'Moral Conflict and Political Legitimacy' (n 19) 229.

[73] ibid 230.

disrespect or contempt towards those beliefs. It is logically possible to, and we should, respect them as expressions of an individual's ethical viewpoint, while at the same time denying them any normative force in the domain of political justification.

Since religiously based reasons cannot legitimize state coercion against those who offend religious sensibilities, the sincerity of those relying on such reasons is irrelevant for the question of whether the state should interfere. In other words, sincerity of belief is not a substitute for impartial reasoning in the public political forum. Most of us may often have the tendency to exaggerate the impact of unpleasant events and experiences. The person who claims that he cannot sleep at night because the local bookshop sells a book attacking sacred truths of his religion and expects the state to confiscate it may be overstating his case, or he may not. Either way, the truthfulness of his feelings is irrelevant because the religious beliefs on which his claim is based in the first place cannot be part of political argument about legitimate coercion in a liberal democracy. In excluding reliance on them, we are not denying the religious citizen's truthfulness—indeed, it is proper to acknowledge that he honestly holds the beliefs he says he holds and that the offence he takes when they are attacked is sincere—but only their use for the resolution of conflicts of value in the political arena.[74]

If an offence principle which can legitimize limitations of liberty does exist, it cannot be based on any particular conception about what is sacred and what is sinful. If we are to silence those offending the listeners' or viewers' religious sensibilities we need to look for an impartial public standpoint from which to do so, a standpoint which reasonable citizens in a liberal democracy can be expected, if not to embrace, at least to accept as legitimate. In the chapter which follows I will discuss whether such an impartial justification exists for the prohibition of offensive speech.

[74] Cf Waldron's view that while religious reasons may fail to persuade and be rejected in political deliberation, they can be legitimately invoked and citizens have an obligation to engage with them in good faith and try to understand them. See Waldron, 'Two-way Translation' (n 50) 845.

3
Responses to Offensive Speech

The view that it is morally legitimate for the state to silence speakers who offend, attack, or ridicule religious beliefs implies that the fact of offence is a normative reason performing a justificatory function for the prohibition. The problem with such a claim is that it relies on a personal viewpoint about the ethical life which is subjective to the offended person, while we would normally require the state to exercise coercion and restrict liberty for reasons which all reasonable citizens can be expected to find acceptable.

A way to address the problem is to try to reformulate the argument on secular grounds which could be acceptable to all citizens, whether religious or not. The revised claim involves an appeal to the moral and legal right to freedom of religion, and goes like this: freedom of religion guarantees a cluster of more specific rights such as choosing a religious affiliation, preaching the doctrine, worshiping, organizing in communities, and so on. One such specific right is the right to be free from offence to one's religious sensibilities. When the government bans profanity and sacrilege, it is giving effect to the right to religious freedom. The protection of a fundamental right is a normative reason which can justify the exercise of state coercion. Thus, speech may be limited so as to protect religious freedom.

Despite its reliance on religious freedom, the argument is secular in the sense that it can be accepted by everyone, regardless of his or her personal viewpoint on what life is worth living. Even atheists, agnostics, or those who are positively hostile to religion can be reasonably expected to agree that religious freedom is an important right and that a society which respects it and makes it possible for its members to enjoy it is better and more just than one which persecutes or suppresses religious expression. This position does not depend on a particular view about the existence of God, the truth of a religious book or doctrine, or the sanctity of a religious figure. Put differently, sound public political values support a right to freedom of religion, so state coercion to give effect to that right can, in principle, be justified in a way which satisfies the requirements of public reason. The blasphemer who is silenced is not treated with disrespect

Offensive Speech, Religion, and the Limits of the Law. Nicholas Hatzis, Oxford University Press. © Nicholas Hatzis 2021.
DOI: 10.1093/oso/9780198758440.003.0004

because the government's action is justifiable by objective reasons which even he can be expected to find acceptable.

The reformulated secular justification for banning offensive communications stands or falls depending on whether a right to be protected from religious offence is part of the cluster of specific rights protected by the right to freedom of religion. This is the question I explore in this chapter. In order to show how normative considerations about speech, religion, and offence feature in constitutional practice, I compare the approaches of the United States Supreme Court and the European Court of Human Rights (ECtHR). Cases on offensive speech figure prominently in American constitutional jurisprudence and have provided the Supreme Court with the opportunity to set out general principles on free speech protection. Similarly, the offensive speech cases decided by the Strasbourg Court have been influential in the development of the Court's conception of freedom of expression under Article 10 of the European Convention on Human Rights (ECHR).

Prohibiting Offence

The ECHR provides the classic example of a human rights document which has been interpreted to permit suppression of speech that offends religious sensibilities. The ECtHR has held that, notwithstanding the importance of free expression for a modern democratic society, the government is justified in restricting and even punishing through criminal law certain forms of sacrilegious speech. This principle was put forward by the Court in 1994 in *Otto-Preminger-Institut v Austria*.[1] The applicant was a non-profit association for the promotion of audiovisual art whose activities included operating a cinema in Innsbruck. It had scheduled to show a film called *Das Liebeskonzil*, which was based on a play written by the German author Oskar Panizza in 1894. The play and the film satirized the Christian religion and portrayed God, Jesus, and the Virgin Mary in a disrespectful and offensive manner.[2] At the request of the local diocese of the Roman Catholic Church, the public prosecutor brought criminal proceedings against the director of the Otto Preminger Institute based on a provision in the Penal Code which punished an individual whose behaviour was 'likely to arouse justified indignation, disparages or insults a person who, or an object

[1] (1995) 19 EHRR 34.

[2] Following the publication of his play, Panizza was sentenced to imprisonment and the play was banned by the German authorities.

which, is an object of veneration of a church or religious community established within the country, or a dogma, a lawful custom or a lawful institution of such a church or religious community'.[3] A court ordered the seizure of the film before it had been shown in the organization's cinema. The criminal prosecution was later discontinued. The Institute argued that the seizure of the film was a violation of Article 10 of the Convention[4] but the complaint was rejected.

The first question for the Strasbourg Court was whether the seizure served a legitimate aim. In the Convention system, national authorities can generally restrict rights only in order to serve one of the aims listed in the Convention itself and only if such restriction is necessary in a democratic society. Article 10(2) states that interferences with free speech may be imposed

> in the interests of national security, territorial integrity or public safety, for the prevention of disorder or crime, for the protection of health or morals, for the protection of the reputation or rights of others, for preventing the disclosure of information received in confidence, or for maintaining the authority and impartiality of the judiciary.

Which of those aims can justify the seizure of a film which is satirical of a religion's deity?

The Court repeated, first, the statement it had made in *Kokkinakis v Greece*[5] that religious freedom is one of the foundations of a democratic society and added that religious people must put up with some hostility towards their faith. It held, however, that

> [T]he manner in which religious beliefs and doctrines are opposed or denied is a matter which may engage the responsibility of the State, notably its responsibility to ensure the peaceful enjoyment of the right guaranteed under Article 9 (art. 9) to the holders of those beliefs and doctrines. Indeed, in extreme cases the effect of particular methods of opposing or denying religious

[3] *Otto-Preminger-Institut v Austria* (n 1) para 25.

[4] Article 10 of the ECHR reads: '1. Everyone has the right to freedom of expression. This right shall include freedom to hold opinions and to receive and impart information and ideas without interference by public authority and regardless of frontiers. This article shall not prevent States from requiring the licensing of broadcasting, television or cinema enterprises. 2. The exercise of these freedoms, since it carries with it duties and responsibilities, may be subject to such formalities, conditions, restrictions or penalties as are prescribed by law and are necessary in a democratic society, in the interests of national security, territorial integrity or public safety, for the prevention of disorder or crime, for the protection of health or morals, for the protection of the reputation or rights of others, for preventing the disclosure of information received in confidence, or for maintaining the authority and impartiality of the judiciary'.

[5] (1993) 17 EHRR 397.

> beliefs can be such as to inhibit those who hold such beliefs from exercising their freedom to hold and express them.[6]

The Court did not give any examples of 'extreme cases' where opposition to religious doctrines prevents those who hold them from exercising their religion, not did it examine whether opposition expressed in the form of speech (as opposed to actions) raises any special issues. What followed was another general statement to the effect that freedom of religion guarantees to believers that their feelings will be respected:

> The respect for the religious feelings of believers as guaranteed in Article 9 (art. 9) can legitimately be thought to have been violated by provocative portrayals of objects of religious veneration; and such portrayals can be regarded as malicious violation of the spirit of tolerance, which must also be a feature of democratic society.[7]

The conclusion was that the seizure of the film aimed at protecting 'the right of citizens not to be insulted in their religious feelings by the public expression of views of other persons'.[8]

Having concluded that the interference with free speech pursued the legitimate aim of protecting the right of believers not to be offended in their beliefs, the Court examined whether it was necessary in a democratic society. It stated that there is a general principle that amongst the duties speakers have is

> an obligation to avoid as far as possible expressions that are gratuitously offensive to others and thus an infringement of their rights, and which therefore do not contribute to any form of public debate capable of furthering progress in human affairs.
>
> This being so, as a matter of principle it may be considered necessary in certain democratic societies to sanction or even prevent improper attacks on objects of religious veneration . . .[9]

In applying that principle to the facts of the case, the Court asserted that the issue was one of a conflict between the right to disseminate those highly critical views about Christianity and the right of Christians to avoid offence. In Tyrol,

[6] *Otto-Preminger-Institut v Austria* (n 1) para 47.
[7] ibid.
[8] ibid.
[9] ibid para 49.

the Court continued, 87 per cent of the population were Roman Catholics, and the Austrian authorities were well within their powers when they decided to prioritize protection of religious sensibilities over free speech.

Ian Leigh has pointed out that the text of Article 9 of the ECHR does not refer to 'respect for religious feelings' or the 'peaceful enjoyment' of religion. Reading those terms into the text sets in motion a mode of thinking about how religion should be referred to publicly, which affects the interpretation of both freedom of religion (Article 9 ECHR) and freedom of expression (Article 10 ECHR): only a particular way of speaking about religious matters is acceptable and enjoys the protection of the Convention. The result is the creation of a 'protective perimeter around religious beliefs'.[10] This approach became evident in the ECtHR's decision to uphold a blasphemy law in *Wingrove v United Kingdom*.[11] The applicant was the director of an 18-minute video film which portrayed St Teresa of Avila as having erotic fantasies involving the body of Jesus. The British Board of Film Classification refused to issue a certificate which was necessary in order for the film to be distributed in any way, stating that its content would establish the common law offence of blasphemy. The ECtHR summarily concluded that the interference with the director's freedom of expression pursued the legitimate aim of protecting the rights of those who would be outraged by the content of the video. In relation to the question of whether the interference was necessary in a democratic society, the Court cited *Otto-Preminger-Institut* but shifted the emphasis from Article 9 to Article 10(2), which states that the exercise of the right to free speech carries with it 'duties and responsibilities'.[12] It held that individuals have a duty to 'avoid as far as possible an expression that is, in regard to objects of veneration, gratuitously offensive to others and profanatory'.[13] Given the lack of consensus among the Member States of the Council of Europe as to whether blasphemy laws are necessary and appropriate for the regulation of offensive speech, it was impossible to say that the English law in question which allowed for prior restraint was unnecessary in a democratic society. While restrictions on political expression would be scrutinized strictly, national authorities enjoyed a wider margin of appreciation in relation to restrictions on speech that was likely to offend people's beliefs 'within the sphere of morals or, especially, religion'.[14]

[10] Ian Leigh, 'Damned If They Do, Damned If They Don't: The European Court of Human Rights and the Protection of Religion from Attacks' (2011) 17 Res Publica 55, 65.

[11] (1996) 24 EHRR 1.

[12] See Leigh (n 10) 60.

[13] *Wingrove v UK* (n 11) para 52.

[14] ibid para 58. For a discussion in agreement with the Court's approach see Malcolm D Evans, 'From Cartoons to Crucifixes: Current Controversies Concerning the Freedom of Expression and

When *Otto-Preminger-Institut* was decided it appeared to be a slightly odd and poorly reasoned Chamber judgment which was not representative of the Court's overall approach to freedom of expression. *Wingrove* affirmed its relevance and the Court subsequently applied the same approach in *IA v Turkey*.[15] This time the claimant was an author who had published a book discussing his philosophical and religious views, which the Turkish authorities found blasphemous. The public prosecutor initiated criminal proceedings and the applicant was sentenced to two years' imprisonment which was commuted to a US$16 fine. Relying on *Otto-Preminger-Institut* and *Wingrove*, the Court affirmed the rule that national authorities may legitimately curtail speech in order to protect those who may feel deeply offended by what was said about their religion. The book in question contained, the Court said, a particularly offending passage: 'God's messenger broke his fast through sexual intercourse, after dinner and before prayer. Muhammad did not forbid sexual intercourse with a dead person or a live animal'.[16] In the Court's opinion this was 'an abusive attack on the Prophet of Islam',[17] which justified the prosecution and conviction of the author.

This line of cases was recently affirmed in *ES v Austria*.[18] The applicant had given a public seminar which the Austrian courts interpreted as potentially implying that the Prophet Muhammad was a paedophile. She was convicted of 'publicly disparaging an object of veneration of a domestic church or religious society, namely Muhammad, the Prophet of Islam, in a manner capable of arousing justified indignation'.[19] The ECtHR found the conviction to be compatible with the Convention. The part of the judgment where the Court announces the 'general principles' which it considers relevant for the case starts with its usual mantra that freedom of speech is a very important right, and continues:

> As paragraph 2 of Article 10 recognises, however, the exercise of the freedom of expression carries with it duties and responsibilities. Amongst them, in the context of religious beliefs, is the general requirement to ensure the peaceful

the Freedom of Religion Before the European Court of Human Rights' (2011) 26 Journal of Law and Religion 345, 347–352.

15 (2007) 45 EHRR 30.
16 ibid para 29.
17 ibid.
18 (2019) 69 EHRR 4.
19 ibid para 12. The Court held that conviction served two legitimate aims: the protection of religious feelings and the prevention of public disorder and maintenance of peace. I discuss the point about disorder caused by speech in ch 5.

> enjoyment of the rights guaranteed under Article 9 to the holders of such beliefs including a duty to avoid as far as possible an expression that is, in regard to objects of veneration, gratuitously offensive to others and profane. Where such expressions go beyond the limits of a critical denial of other people's religious beliefs and are likely to incite religious intolerance, for example in the event of an improper or even abusive attack on an object of religious veneration, a State may legitimately consider them to be incompatible with respect for the freedom of thought, conscience and religion and take proportionate restrictive measures. In addition, expressions that seek to spread, incite or justify hatred based on intolerance, including religious intolerance, do not enjoy the protection afforded by Article 10 of the Convention.[20]

What the Court offers here is an amalgam of references to different concepts—peaceful enjoyment of religion, respect, offence, intolerance, hatred—without any analysis of their normative ramifications. It is as if the Court is aware of the lack of reasoning in the judgment and is trying to fill the gap by putting together a haphazard compilation of ideas which appear to be relevant to the issue of offensive speech. This is then followed by the inevitable reference to the wide margin of appreciation enjoyed by the state before the conclusion is reached that the applicant's criminal conviction was necessary in a democratic society.

A notable feature of the judgment is that it teems with references to the judgments of the national courts, to which the ECtHR defers without any real critical assessment. The role of the Strasbourg Court is to form an independent view of the merits of the case instead of merely saying that the Convention has not been violated because a national court said so. This independent assessment is missing from the judgment. The reader is left with the impression that the ECtHR is so embarrassed at its own ruling that democracy requires

[20] ibid para 43 (internal citations omitted). Recently, the Court reached a different conclusion in *Tagiyev and Huseynov v Azerbaijan* App no 13274/08 (5 December 2019). The first applicant had written an article discussing Eastern and Western values and the role of religion in their development and making remarks critical of Islam, and the second applicant was the editor of the newspaper where the article was published. They were convicted of incitement to religious hatred and hostility and sentenced to three and four years imprisonment respectively. The domestic courts had reached this conclusion relying on a report prepared by a government expert on religious affairs who had analyzed the article in order to establish whether it constituted incitement. The ECtHR held that the article was not hate speech, which is not protected under the Convention, but a contribution to a debate about religion in society. Therefore, like *Otto-Preminger-Institut*, the case was about the conflict between free speech and religious freedom. It found a violation of article 10 because the national courts had relied exclusively on the report, without forming their own independent view of the article as a whole. The lack of judicial analysis, combined with the severity of the penalties, meant that the conviction was not necessary in a democratic society. Thus, while finding a violation of the Convention on the facts of the case, the Court affirmed its established approach to religiously offensive speech.

the conviction of a peaceful speaker, that it avoids speaking in its own voice. It withdraws into silence, letting the Austrian courts occupy the scene. The result is that after reading the judgment we know a great deal about how the Austrian judges thought but almost nothing of substance about the thinking of the Strasbourg judges.

The 'Conflict of Fundamental Rights' Model

The ECtHR has constructed its reasoning in the cases concerning offence to religious sensibilities around the core premise that such cases involve a conflict of two fundamental rights protected by the Convention: free speech and freedom of religion. The latter was interpreted as including a right to be protected from offence to one's religious beliefs or sensibilities. It follows that when the state silences a speaker whose views may be offensive to believers it has a prima facie defence that it does so in order to protect the 'rights of others', a limitation to the right to freedom of expression expressly referred to in the Convention. There are three steps in the European Court's reasoning:

(1) Freedom of religion includes a right to not be offended in one's religious sensibilities.
(2) Speech which offends religious sensibilities violates that right.
(3) Therefore, state coercion may be used to prevent speakers from violating the believers' right to not be offended.

The immediate effect is that prevention of offence is elevated to the status of a fundamental right; it is not merely a legitimate state interest similar to national security or public order or the authority of the judicial system which may necessitate limitations on free expression but an autonomous right which operates at the same level as free speech.[21] This transformation of offence-prevention from a limitation on speech to a free-standing right is of crucial importance for the Court's argumentative strategy. We have already seen that Article 10(2) of the Convention allows for restrictions on freedom of expression only for

[21] The main difference between something being a legitimate state interest which can justify limitations on rights and an independent right which may conflict with another right is the structure of the limitation enquiry. In cases concerning state interests, we start with a presumption in favour of the right and ask whether the interest relied on by the state is sufficiently compelling to override the right. When two rights are in conflict there is no presumptive priority of either of them. This distinction, however, does not appear to have any practical consequences for the outcome of Convention cases since the ECtHR treats legitimate interests and other rights in the same manner.

the 'legitimate aims' listed therein; those aims include some specified state interests (national security, territorial integrity or public safety, the prevention of disorder or crime, the protection of health or morals, the prevention of the disclosure of information received in confidence, the protection of the authority and impartiality of the judiciary) and a more general aim, that of the 'protection of the reputation or rights of others'. A state measure which interferes with speech may be saved in Strasbourg only if it pursues either one of the listed state interests or the general aim of protecting the reputation or rights of others. Since prevention of offence to religious sensibilities is not listed in Article 10(2), the only way to bring cases concerning offensive speech within its scope is to claim that such speech violates some right that people have. Thus, when the state silences offensive communications it can argue that it did so in pursuance of the legitimate aim of protecting the rights of others. Otherwise, the Court would have been obliged to hold that the restriction did not pursue an acceptable aim under the Convention and find a violation at the first stage of its assessment. By saying that protection from offence is a fundamental right covered by the Convention, it allows national authorities to pass easily the 'legitimate aim' hurdle and the resolution turns on whether the facts of a specific case show that the restriction was necessary in a democratic society.

The ECtHR has never explained why freedom of religion includes a right for believers not to be offended in their religious sensibilities.[22] It has never discussed whether such a right might be supported by principles of political morality underlying the ECHR or whether it fits within the rights-protection scheme established by the Convention. In *Otto-Preminger-Institut*, the judgment which set the tone for the subsequent development of the Court's case law on offensive speech, all we can find is an assertion that the censorship of the film had as its purpose to 'protect the right of citizens not to be insulted in their religious feelings by the public expression of views of other persons'.[23] A similar formulation was adopted in *IA v Turkey*:

> The issue before the Court therefore involves weighing up the conflicting interests of the exercise of two fundamental freedoms, namely the right of the applicant to impart to the public his views on religious doctrine on the one hand and the right of others to respect for their freedom of thought, conscience and religion on the other hand.[24]

[22] Eric Barendt, *Freedom of Speech* (Oxford University Press 2006) 192.
[23] *Otto-Preminger-Institut v Austria* (n 1) para 48.
[24] *IA v Turkey* (n 15) para 27.

In both cases, it is taken for granted that the right not to be offended exists and the issue is presented as one of a conflict between two fundamental rights.

The next step is what the Court describes as 'weighing up'. The Court weighs speech and freedom of religion in the factual context of the specific case and strikes the balance. The function of balancing, properly understood, is not to yield an uncontroversial, correct answer with mathematical precision but to identify the morally relevant reasons which the decision-maker should take into account and the way they should be applied to the facts of a case; then, he needs to exercise his own judgment.[25] While it is always possible to think that a decision is erroneous in relation to how the facts of a case were assessed, if the decision-maker has identified correctly the morally relevant considerations the decision is not illegitimate. In *Otto-Preminger-Institut*, *Wingrove*, *IA*, and *ES*, the Strasbourg Court held that offensive speech may be restricted and that the speaker may be held criminally liable for upsetting the religious sensibilities of believers. What this conclusion implies is that the fact of offence gives the state reason to interfere with free expression, a reason which is stronger, and thus supersedes any competing reasons against interference and in favour of free speech. Offence is treated as the 'all things considered' reason, which justifies the prohibition. This conclusion is only made possible by the Court's earlier assertion that not being offended is part of the right to religious freedom; that assertion performs the logically prior function of identifying the morally relevant reasons for the resolution of those cases. Once those reasons have been identified, the Court assesses their relative strength and concludes that offence overrides free speech.

It is possible to criticize the ECtHR for the way it weighed the reasons for and against prohibition of offensive speech. That would be a criticism directed against the conclusion that the fact of offence is a morally relevant reason which *overrides* the competing facts that are reasons to prioritize freedom of expression. But that objection leaves intact the Court's logically prior assertion that offence is a morally relevant reason for the state to exercise its coercive power to silence the speaker.[26] Saying that the Court was mistaken in the relative weight it assigned to offence and free speech implies that it failed to perform the exercise correctly, but it was right to balance one against the other because both are morally relevant reasons stemming from the right to free expression and free exercise of religion, respectively. This latter point needs to be explored further. The weighing up exercise is necessary only if there is a right

[25] See the discussion in ch 1.

[26] George Letsas, 'Is There a Right not to Be Offended in One's Religious Beliefs?' in Lorenzo Zucca and Camil Ungureanu (eds), *Law State and Religion in the New Europe* (Cambridge University Press 2012) 239, 247 ff.

to be protected from offence to religious sensibilities, which the Court thinks is self-evident. But if no such right exists, there is no conflict of fundamental rights which needs to be resolved through balancing. Put in other words, if it is not morally permissible for offence to count as a reason justifying state coercion the Court has made the logically prior mistake of relying on inappropriate considerations; it has failed to perform correctly the identification function of the balancing test. Therefore, before we ask whether offence can indeed override speech, we need to examine whether offence is a morally relevant reason for restricting speech in the first place.

A Right-based Claim to Be Protected from Offence?

Freedom of Religion

The ECtHR's construction of the right to freedom of religion includes a right not to be offended in one's religious sensibilities. The form it takes in the Court's jurisprudence reflects Hohfeld's analysis of rights as 'claims'. Hohfeld argued that rights, properly understood, have the concept of duty as their 'invariable correlative'.[27] While in legal discourse we often use the term 'right' to describe entitlements that are privileges, powers, or immunities, rights 'in the strictest sense' are only those which correspond to duties.[28] Therefore, he explained, 'if X has a right against Y that he shall stay off the former's land, the correlative (and equivalent) is that Y is under a duty toward X to stay off the place'.[29] Those rights in the strictest sense, namely the ones which have duties as their correlative, he called 'claims'.

The legal right not to be offended, as described in the jurisprudence of the ECtHR, is a right in the strict sense as it gives rise to a correlative duty of the speaker not to offend. The content of the right not to be offended is that 'a particular state of affairs shall obtain':[30] the religious individual has a right against the film-maker or the author not to be caused offence. The absence of

[27] Wesley Newcomb Hohfeld, 'Some Fundamental Legal Conceptions as Applied in Judicial Reasoning' (1913) 23 Yale Law Journal 16, 31 ('Recognizing, as we must, the very broad and indiscriminate use of the term, "right," what clue do we find, in ordinary legal discourse, toward limiting the word in question to a definite and appropriate meaning. That clue lies in the correlative "duty," for it is certain that even those who use the word and the conception "right" in the broadest possible way are accustomed to thinking of "duty" as the invariable correlative.). The feature of correlativity in Hohfeld's theory is discussed in Pavlos Eleftheriades, *Legal Rights* (Oxford University Press 2008) ch 6.

[28] Hohfeld (n 27) 30. For a discussion of Hohfeld's distinction between rights in the strict sense and privileges and powers see Judith Jarvis Thomson, *The Realm of Rights* (Harvard University Press 1990) 43 ff.

[29] Hohfeld (n 27) 32.

[30] Thomson (n 28) 38.

offence is the state of affairs that shall obtain as a result of the relevant right. Thus, speakers are under a duty not to cause offence; this is the moral significance of the believer's right not to be offended.[31] It follows that, if the ECtHR is right that religious freedom includes a right not to be offended, when the speaker does offend the listener's religious sensibilities he infringes a right of the listener's understood as a claim in Hohfeld's sense.

Rights in general can ground duties when the right-holder's interests are sufficient reason for holding another person to be under a duty.[32] But the assertion that A has a right does not provide a full account of the normative basis for holding another person B to be under a duty. It is an intermediate step in a reasoning process about how one ought to act when a practical question arises, grounding a requirement that B behave in a particular way in A's interest. The ultimate reason for holding B to be under a duty is the value underpinning the right, which, thus, links duties and values.[33] So, in the cases discussed above, the claim is that believers have a right to be protected from offence because there is a value of respect for religious sensibilities which grounds a right-based duty on speakers not to offend religious sensibilities.

We have seen that Joel Feinberg described offence to sensibilities as 'profound offence'. What distinguishes it from attacks on the senses, which he called 'offensive nuisances', is that it is cognitively mediated: one takes offence not at what one perceives with one's senses, such as a smell or noise, but rather at what one perceives to be the meaning of the offensive act. Judith Jarvis Thomson has used the term 'belief-mediated distress' to describe a range of unpleasant belief-mediated feelings such as insult, disappointment, embarrassment, anger, moral indignation, and so on.[34] Offence to religious sensibilities belongs to the same group: it is profound offence which comes about because we have certain beliefs which a certain type of expression upsets. It is a form of belief-mediated distress. If we have a claim not to be caused such distress, and others have a correlative duty not to act in a way which causes such distress, the state has reason to intervene when we fail to discharge that duty. Rights, when they exist, can be reason for state action.

The problem with the view that there is a valid claim to be protected from offence to religious beliefs is that it is based on the significance those beliefs have for the religious individuals who feel offended. Offence is caused because a venerated religious figure is referred to with disrespect or contempt or because an object which has religious significance is desecrated. A claim that the

[31] ibid 43.
[32] Joseph Raz, *The Morality of Freedom* (Oxford University Press 1984) 166.
[33] ibid 180–81.
[34] Thomson, *The Realm of Rights* (n 28) 250–51.

offender should be silenced is an expectation that the state will coercively impose an obligation of respect towards those religious values even on members of the political community who do not share them. The only way to justify the application of the law's coercive force in those cases is to appeal to the personal beliefs of those offended against the personal beliefs of those who wish to engage in the offensive communication.[35]

We are therefore back to the problem of justifying state coercion over some citizens on the basis of the personal comprehensive viewpoints of others. The fact that the claim for prohibition is now mediated through the right to religious freedom does not help its proponents because it is still based on the importance that a religious figure or object or belief has in the comprehensive personal doctrine of believers. Those who were outraged at the Danish cartoons and the bishop who asked for the prosecution of the director of the Otto Preminger Institute expressed their particular moral viewpoints which were based on their religious beliefs about the sanctity of the central figures in their respective religions. As personal viewpoints, which are significant for the lives of those who hold them, they command respect, but they do not give rise to a moral right to be protected from offence because they lack an objective, impersonal justification which all reasonable citizens—including those who hold competing viewpoints—may be expected to find acceptable.

This partial nature of religious beliefs makes them inappropriate as a basis for the imposition of general rules of conduct in a liberal democracy. A commitment to a religious life is only one of the many possible conceptions of the good life, and there are many different ways of pursuing this choice.[36] It is this particular conception which valorizes the beliefs and practices that make up the religious way of life. Different conceptions of the good life will attribute value to alternative, often directly competing, ideas, commitments, and practices. Challenging the orthodoxy of a religion or the value of religion in general is, for the person holding this moral outlook, as valuable as adopting and promoting the religious life is for the believer. Where the state silences the former so as to protect the latter's view of the ethical life from offence, it coerces her to attribute value to a way of life which she cannot identify with or even directly opposes. This is a worry, of course, only for those who believe that there are many different worthwhile modes of life and that the state cannot legitimately use its power to coerce acceptance of a specific conception of the good life. The problem disappears if one thinks that there is only one type of life worth living

[35] As mentioned above, another reason is the protection of public order. This is discussed in ch 5.

[36] Letsas, 'Is There a Right Not To Be Offended?' (n 26) 255.

and that this is reason for the state to interfere coercively with personal choices. But most people would reject that view and would find it intolerable to live in such a state.

In a system of morality which allows for the development of various personal outlooks on the ethical life, what one finds offensive depends on what beliefs and practices one endorses as part of one's conception of how one should live. Where communications which insult religious sensibilities are concerned, it is the believer's view of the sacred which is at stake. Protecting that view by state coercion treats the sacred not as a personal value which operates in the context of a subjective moral outlook but as a moral viewpoint to which all reasonable citizens are expected to relate. The law, then, becomes an instrument for silencing any opinion that a religious group may find offensive.[37]

Offence as a Limit on Freedom of Expression

The view that prohibiting the expression of offensive opinions is a proper function of the law has been consistently and convincingly rejected in First Amendment jurisprudence. In *Texas v Johnson*[38] the plaintiff, who had burned a flag during a political demonstration protesting governmental policies, had been convicted under a Texas law which prohibited the desecration of a venerated object. Many people who had witnessed the burning testified that they had been seriously offended. The Supreme Court held that this was expressive conduct which fell within the scope of the First Amendment, and that the law in question was 'not aimed at protecting the physical integrity of the flag in all circumstances, but is designed instead to protect it only against impairments that would cause serious offense to others'.[39] Thus, what was targeted by the prohibition was not the act of desecration itself but its communicative impact on those who identified with the ideals, such as nationhood and national unity, embodied in the flag. The Court, applying a strict scrutiny test, held that, although the state had a legitimate interest in trying to preserve the flag as a national symbol it was not justified in silencing speech which undermined the message the flag conveys: 'If there is a bedrock principle underlying the First

[37] Robert Post, 'Religion and Freedom of Speech: Portraits of Muhammad' (2007) 14 Constellations 72, 80.

[38] *Texas v Johnson* 491 US 397 (1989).

[39] ibid 411. Texas conceded that the statute was designed to catch intentionally offensive conduct.

Amendment, it is that the government may not prohibit the expression of an idea simply because society finds the idea itself offensive or disagreeable.'[40]

While *Texas v Johnson* was the first case where the Court dealt explicitly with the question of whether the government can prohibit the desecration of the flag in order to protect the symbolism it carries, a series of earlier cases had established the rule that the flag does not belong to a special category which can escape First Amendment scrutiny.[41] The issue of offence to sensibilities was discussed in *Street v New York*.[42] The case concerned a conviction under a New York law which made it a crime 'publicly [to] defy or cast contempt upon [an American flag] by words ...'.[43] The plaintiff had publicly burned a flag and said that 'If they did that to Meredith, we don't need an American flag' and 'We don't need no damn flag' as a protest upon hearing that James Meredith, the first African American student at the University of Mississippi, had been shot. Justice Harlan found that the trial record indicated that the plaintiff's words had probably been an independent cause of his conviction, and confined his opinion to the narrow point whether it was constitutional to punish speech which was contemptuous of the flag. He stated that one of the interests the government could invoke for punishing Street was the protection of the sensibilities of the passers-by who might be shocked by what he had said about the flag.[44] In the present case, he continued, the element of shock was absent:

> Except perhaps for appellant's incidental use of the word 'damn' ... any shock effect of appellant's speech must be attributed to the content of the ideas expressed. It is firmly settled that under our Constitution the public expression

[40] ibid 414. Following the judgment, Congress enacted the Flag Protection Act 1989 which criminalized the destruction of the flag in any way. The Act was struck down in *United States v Eichman* 496 US 310 (1990) and a subsequent effort to amend the Constitution was unsuccessful. See Frank I Michelman, 'Saving Old Glory: On Constitutional Iconography' (1990) 42 Stanford Law Review 1337; Geoffrey R Stone, 'Flag Burning and the Constitution' (1989) 75 Iowa Law Review 111.

[41] *West Virginia State Board of Education v Barnette* 319 US 624 (1943) (compulsory flag salute and pledge unconstitutional); *Smith v Goguen* 415 US 566 (1974) (conviction for treating the flag in a contemptuous manner by wearing pants with a flag sewn to their seat unconstitutional); *Spence v Washington* 418 US 405 (1974) (conviction for improper use of the flag by affixing on it a peace symbol unconstitutional).

[42] 394 US 576 (1969).

[43] ibid 580.

[44] The other interests mentioned by Justice Harlan as possible justifications of limiting offensive speech were the prevention of the advocacy of unlawful conduct (which was irrelevant here), the prevention of a breach of peace caused by inflammatory words which would provoke the listeners to attack the speaker under the 'fighting words' doctrine of *Chaplinsky* (Street's words were disrespectful but not inherently inflammatory) and the need to ensure that people show proper respect for the flag (incompatible with the First Amendments which guarantees the free expression of defiant or contemptuous opinions).

> of ideas may not be prohibited merely because the ideas are themselves offensive to some of their hearers.[45]

The origin of Justice Harlan's reference in *Street* to the protection of sensibilities can be traced back to *Chaplinsky v New Hampshire*, where the Supreme Court had held that the government may legitimately punish communications which are 'insulting ... which by their very utterance inflict injury or tend to incite an immediate breach of the peace'.[46] The injurious insults, whose prevention the *Chaplinsky* Court considered a legitimate state interest to be balanced against speech, are reformulated in *Street* as shock to sensibilities.[47] But even this broad construction of the *Chaplinsky* doctrine which gives the state considerable discretion in deciding how to restrict offensive speech, does not cover shock caused by the content of the message.

The Supreme Court revisited the *Chaplinsky/Street* approach to offensive messages in *Cohen v California*.[48] The appellant had been convicted for wearing a jacket bearing the words 'Fuck the Draft' while being inside a courthouse under a statute which criminalized 'maliciously and wilfully disturb(ing) the peace or quiet of any neighbourhood or person by offensive conduct'.[49] Justice Harlan explained that what was targeted by the conviction was the offensiveness of the message, as the defendant had not engaged in any other form of conduct. Given that the substance of his opinion could not serve as a legitimate basis for punishment, the state could only attempt to regulate the manner in which it was expressed. Here the words used were not obscene, as the erotic element of obscenity was lacking; they did not qualify as fighting words because they were not inherently likely to provoke violence; and individual privacy was not an issue as they were not directed to anyone in particular. Rather, the issue was

> whether California can excise, as 'offensive conduct,' one particular scurrilous epithet from the public discourse, either upon the theory of the court below that its use is inherently likely to cause violent reaction or upon a more general assertion that the States, acting as guardians of public morality, may properly remove this offensive word from the public vocabulary.[50]

[45] *Street v New York* (n 42) 592.

[46] *Chaplinsky v New Hampshire* 315 US 568, 572 (1942). The Court described those words as 'fighting words'.

[47] Mark C Rutzick, 'Offensive Language and the Evolution of First Amendment Protection' (1974) 9 Harvard Civil Rights-Civil Liberties Law Review 1, 14–15.

[48] *Cohen v California* 403 US 15 (1971).

[49] ibid 16.

[50] ibid 23.

The Court answered the question in the negative. With regard to the likelihood of violent reaction, it noted that there was no evidence that a large number of citizens were ready to assault physically whoever happened to offend their sensibilities in a manner similar to Cohen's. In relation to the public morality interest, it held that the First Amendment did not allow the government to remove from public discourse words that others may find offensive. In explaining the rule, Justice Harlan offered one of the most memorable expositions of free speech values:

> The constitutional right of free expression is powerful medicine in a society as diverse and populous as ours. It is designed and intended to remove governmental restraints from the arena of public discussion, putting the decision as to what views shall be voiced largely into the hands of each of us, in the hope that use of such freedom will ultimately produce a more capable citizenry and more perfect polity and in the belief that no other approach would comport with the premise of individual dignity and choice upon which our political system rests.
>
> To many, the immediate consequence of this freedom may often appear to be only verbal tumult, discord, and even offensive utterance. These are, however, within established limits, in truth necessary side effects of the broader enduring values which the process of open debate permits us to achieve. That the air may at times seem filled with verbal cacophony is, in this sense not a sign of weakness but of strength. We cannot lose sight of the fact that, in what otherwise might seem a trifling and annoying instance of individual distasteful abuse of a privilege, these fundamental societal values are truly implicated.[51]

Thus, *Cohen*, on the one hand, requires a narrow approach to *Chaplinsky* whose rule should be confined to face-to-face communications which are inherently likely to provoke violence and, on the other hand, and in contrast to *Street*, makes no reference to the protection of 'sensibilities' as a legitimate aim for the use of state coercion.[52] Given that Justice Harlan was the author of both *Street* and *Cohen*, the omission is significant. After *Cohen*, the *Chaplinsky* doctrine remains relevant only for speech which causes a breach of the peace and does not apply to impersonal communications to the broader public. Thus, while the government may legitimately act to prevent violence or protect the

[51] ibid 24.
[52] Rutzick (n 47) 21–22.

privacy rights of citizens, it cannot suppress speech because it upsets or offends their beliefs and sensibilities about any matter. The effect of *Cohen* is that 'the Constitution does not permit prohibition based on the offensiveness of language alone'.[53]

The idea that offensive utterances cannot be constitutionally proscribed by reason of their offensiveness was extended in *Hustler Magazine v Falwell*.[54] The case concerned a very offensive satirical article about the fundamentalist minister and political commentator Jerry Falwell published in *Hustler* magazine. The article was based on a parody of a well-known advertisement for Campari featuring various celebrities discussing their 'first time', the latter phrase implying the first time they had drunk Campari but also the first time they had had sex. It was supposedly an interview with Falwell revealing that his first time was with his mother while they were both drunk. A disclaimer was added by the magazine stating that this was 'fiction' and 'a parody—not to be taken seriously'.[55] Falwell sued successfully for intentional infliction of emotional distress,[56] but the Supreme Court reversed.

Writing for a unanimous court, Chief Justice Rehnquist held that a public figure could not recover damages for that tort by reason of an offensive publication unless he could show that it contained 'a false statement of fact which was made with actual malice',[57] the test which the Court had previously established in *New York Times v Sullivan*[58] in relation to the defamation of public officials. Of particular importance for the issue of offensive speech is the Court's rejection of the argument that where the publication is particularly 'outrageous' it should not benefit from the protection of the First Amendment:

> If it were possible by laying down a principled standard to separate the [outrageous publication from traditional political cartoons], public discourse would probably suffer little or no harm. But we doubt that there is any such standard, and we are quite sure that the pejorative description 'outrageous' does not supply one. 'Outrageousness' in the area of political and social

[53] Kent Greenawalt, 'Insults and Epithets: Are They Protected Speech?' (1990) 42 Rutgers Law Review 287, 301.

[54] 485 US 46 (1988).

[55] ibid 48.

[56] He failed in his two other claims for libel and invasion of privacy.

[57] *Hustler Magazine v Falwell* (n 54) 56. For a criticism of the Court's reasoning see Paul A LeBel, 'Emotional Distress, the First Amendment, and "This Kind of Speech": A Heretical Perspective on *Hustler Magazine v Falwell*' (1989) 60 University of Colorado Law Rev 315 (arguing that it is constitutionally possible for the tort for intentional infliction of emotional distress to have a more expanded role but agreeing with the outcome of *Falwell* on the facts).

[58] 376 US 254 (1964).

> discourse has an inherent subjectiveness about it which would allow a jury to impose liability on the basis of the jurors' tastes or views, or perhaps on the basis of their dislike of a particular expression. An 'outrageousness' standard thus runs afoul of our longstanding refusal to allow damages to be awarded because the speech in question may have an adverse emotional impact on the audience.[59]

On this view, outrageous publications which inflict emotional distress are protected not because they make a contribution to public debate in the same manner that traditional political satire does, but because outrageousness does not offer a principled test for the purposes of constitutional adjudication. If it were to be used to distinguish protected from non-protected messages, the constitutionally privileged area for speech that the First Amendment carves out would be threatened. It is, therefore, the concern to maintain the integrity and open character of public discourse which motivates the judgment.[60] As the Court explained, the opinion reflects the fact that it is 'necessary to give adequate "breathing space" to the freedoms protected by the First Amendment'.[61]

The Value of Offensive Speech

Reading the judgments of the ECtHR in *Otto-Preminger-Institut*, *Wingrove*, *IA*, and *ES* against *Texas v Johnson* and *Cohen* can shed light on the flaws of the ECtHR's approach. All of them concerned the expression of views about politics, religion, national identity, and art in a manner which some audiences would have found offensive but the communications were impersonal and not addressed to a specific individual; they did not violate any of the listeners' legal rights such as privacy or property; and they were peaceful. *Falwell* goes even further as it involved offensive speech directed against a particular individual with the intention of causing him distress. Where the Supreme Court excluded mere offence from the range of permissible justifications for governmental prohibition of speech, the ECtHR created a free-standing fundamental right to be protected from offence. Those two approaches reflect radically different views about freedom of expression. The Supreme Court's jurisprudence boils down to a rejection of belief-mediated distress as a reason which can justify

[59] *Hustler Magazine v Falwell* (n 54) 55.

[60] Robert C Post, 'The Constitutional Concept of Public Discourse: Outrageous Opinion, Democratic Deliberation, and *Hustler Magazine v Falwell*' (1990) 103 Harvard Law Rev 601.

[61] *Hustler Magazine v Falwell* (n 54) 56.

state coercion. This, as we will see in Chapter 5, is explained by the need to keep public debate open to all members of the political community and all competing viewpoints about what is good in politics or religion or art. True, some speech will insult or undermine beliefs which others hold dear. But this is the consequence of embracing a political morality which puts 'the decision as to what views shall be voiced in the hands of each of us'.[62]

The Supreme Court's emphasis on the 'choice upon which our political system rests'[63] is indicative of the personal value that speech has for each individual.[64] The views we contribute to the public forum will reflect our own moral outlook and our conception of the good life. As each person attributes value to different beliefs and practices, one's exercise of one's right to free speech will engage those beliefs and practices with which one identifies. Thus, speech expresses in the public sphere a choice of life, which is validated by its public portrayal. The effect is recognition 'of a plurality of valuable ways of life' and the 'generation of novel, valuable forms of life'.[65]

The protesters in *Cohen* and *Texas v Johnson*, the author in *IA*, the filmmakers in *Otto-Preminger-Institut* and *Wingrove*, and the speaker in *ES* found value in challenging certain attitudes in their societies; communicating their message was an expression in the public forum of their choice of ethical ideals, a choice which forms, according to the Supreme Court, the foundation of a political system. As religious individuals may not be expected to have found value in the kind of art created by the various applicants before the ECtHR, the latter should not be expected to have found value in a religious way of life and the conception of the sacred this life entails.[66] It is this divergence of views about the good and the ethical values that public institutions should embrace in a 'diverse' and 'populous' society that calls for the 'powerful medicine' of free speech.[67] The alternative vision, espoused by the ECtHR, is to turn the necessarily subjective experience of what counts as offensive for some citizens into

[62] *Cohen v California* (n 48) 24.

[63] ibid.

[64] Rutzick, 'Offensive Language' (n 47) 19. For a discussion of the societal value of offence in the context of public discourse see ch 4 below.

[65] Joseph Raz, 'Free Expression and Personal Identification' in *Ethics in the Public Domain: Essays in the Morality of Law and Politics* (Oxford University Press 1995) 146, 155.

[66] Letsas, 'Is There a Right Not to Be Offended?' (n 26) 255.

[67] My argument here has some affinities but is ultimately based on different premises from the argument about the accommodation of extreme speech developed in Maleiha Malik, 'Extreme Speech and Liberalism' in Ivan Hare and James Weinstein (eds), *Extreme Speech and Democracy* (Oxford University Press 2009) 96, 109 ff. Malik argues that a liberal democracy has good reasons to attempt to engage with extremists by creating space for the expression of extreme speech which is incompatible with basic liberal values and challenges the consensus around a liberal political identity. My argument is that allowing speech which offends religious sensibilities and, therefore, challenges commonly accepted norms about the sacred to be communicated in public space is itself an expression of those liberal political values.

a reason for suppressing the speech of others through the invention of a right not to be offended. The result is that, in pluralist and diverse societies, like societies in contemporary Europe, almost all speech is at risk of being prohibited because someone might find it insulting. In other words, 'there is no way of securing freedom of expression if we also maintain that there is a right not to be offended'.[68]

The ECtHR practically ignored the value that the offensive speech had for the speakers in the cases concerning offence to religion.[69] By contrast, it overemphasized the importance of the beliefs of the various religious majorities. In *Otto-Preminger-Institut*, the censorship of the film was justified as necessary to protect the feelings of the 'overwhelming majority of Tyroleans'[70] who were 87 per cent Catholics; in *IA*, the Turkish government had asserted in support of the conviction that in Turkey the majority of the population were Muslims and the Court accepted that the disrespectful references to the Prophet of Islam could legitimately be considered as 'unwarranted and offensive attacks'[71] on the believers themselves; and, in *Wingrove*, the potentially blasphemous character of the film was enough for the Court to justify prior restraint under a law which protected the Christian religion in a predominantly Christian country.[72] As an empirical statement, what the Court says about the religious sensitivities of those majorities is probably true. We can reasonably assume that a number of Christians and Muslims, possibly a large one, would have been upset had they seen the films which were at stake in *Otto-Preminger-Institut* and *Wingrove* or read the book in *IA*, respectively. Clearly, a very large number of Muslims felt offended by the Danish cartoons or by the knowledge that they had been published even if they had not seen them themselves. Given that irritation, insult, and offence are unpleasant mental states, those people are better off if the speech which causes them is suppressed. But it does not follow, as the ECtHR wrongly thought, that this is reason for the state to silence coercively the offensive expressions. Rights are aspects of one's status as an equal member of the moral community. Their function is to limit the ways in which public

[68] Baroness O'Neill of Bengarve, 'Freedom of Expression and Freedom of Religion' Theos Annual Lecture 2015 https://www.theosthinktank.co.uk/research/2015/10/19/freedom-of-religion-and-freedom-of-expression.

[69] Leigh, 'Damned If They Do" (n 10) 70, attributes this to the Court's more general failure to appreciate the importance of artistic speech. A case which demonstrates this failure is *Müller v Switzerland* (1991) 13 EHRR 212, where the Court upheld the confiscation of the applicant's paintings which depicted sexual scenes and his conviction for showing obscene material on the basis of the national authorities' determination that they offended 'the sense of sexual propriety' (para 18).

[70] *Otto-Preminger-Institut v Austria* (n 1) para 56.

[71] *IA v Turkey* (n 15) para 29.

[72] *ES v Austria* (n 18) is, thus, different in this respect because it concerned the sensibilities of a religious minority. I discuss whether this justifies offensive speech bans in ch 6.

institutions may pursue their aims. They guarantee a core of inviolability for every person, whose interests should count independently and not merely as a part of the overall sum of general good in a community.[73] Respecting this inviolable core will sometimes make it more difficult to promote an aggregate good but this is the inevitable consequence of a moral system which attributes value to certain rights independently of their contribution to (or even frustration of) an increase in the overall amount of good, happiness, or well-being. Freedom of expression belongs to that inviolable core because it is one of the characteristics that define us as thinking beings who are able to form opinions of their own. The ability to express them is of fundamental importance for their formation, which is a collective enterprise. In making our views public we influence the other members of our community and in turn we are influenced by theirs.[74]

The link between communication and thought has been recently explored in detail by Seana Shiffrin, who offers an account of free speech based on the interests of speakers and listeners *qua* thinkers.[75] She argues that communicating the content of our minds and gaining access to the mental content of others is a prerequisite for our development as moral agents capable of understanding the requirements of morality and discharging important aspects of moral relationships with others. Speech is the epistemic medium for overcoming the opacity of the human mind and accessing others' mental content, without which it is impossible to reflect on the human condition. Freedom of speech, she continues, consists of 'two related and mutually dependent freedoms':[76] freedom of thought and freedom of communication. By communicating our thoughts, i.e. by exercising free speech, we give specific expression to our moral agency as a unique characteristic of our humanity. Unlike other free speech theorists, Shiffrin does not rely on a distinction between the interests of speakers and listeners, nor does she anchor the value of free speech to its contribution towards the achievement of a desirable outcome. Rather, what supports a robust protection for free communication of ideas is the fact that 'the individual mind and its free operation ... is valued and treated with respect'.[77]

Shiffrin's thinker-based account of speech offers important insights into the issue of the wrongness of censorship of sacrilegious communications. Such communications are the externalization of mental content: they impart the

[73] Thomas Nagel, 'Personal Rights and Public Space' (1995) 24 Philosophy and Public Affairs 83, 85–87.
[74] ibid 96–97.
[75] Seana Shiffrin, *Speech Matters: On Lying, Morality, and the Law* (Princeton University Press 2014).
[76] ibid 79.
[77] ibid 85.

speaker's thoughts to others and form part of his moral outlook. At the same time, they provide listeners with access to the speaker's mind and allow them to relate and react to his views, and reflect critically on their own. Censorship interrupts this link between autonomous moral agents. The judgments in *Cohen* and *Texas v Johnson* echo this moral significance of free expression for human beings. Recall the Supreme Court's statement in *Cohen* that 'no other approach would comport with the premise of individual dignity' than denying the government the power to decide what views should be heard in public discussion and leaving that instead in the hands of the citizens. Suppression of speech merely because it is offensive undermines 'individual dignity' precisely because the possibility to speak our minds is an aspect of our status as thinking beings who are equal members of the moral community. Although expressed in terms different from those used by Shiffrin, a core concern underlying both judgments is the effect of governmental coercion on the thinking capacity of moral agents. It is the recognition of that status which underlies the rule in *Texas v Johnson* that 'government may not prohibit the expression of an idea simply because society finds the idea itself offensive or disagreeable'.

The possibility to think free from coercion (and this possibility is severely undermined if we cannot express our thoughts) is a prerequisite not only for artistic creation but also for reflection about our own lives—our choices, motives, desires, and relationships. Examining, and revising, even modestly, who we are depends on us not being forever tied to established, and usually rigid, patterns of thought. As Howard Jacobson has aptly noted, we need to distance ourselves from 'the false seriousness of belief systems, conviction, ideology, thinking what it's right to think'[78] before we can open up to the prospect of the unexpected, of novel ideas and ways of life, which without a free speech regime can never come within our sight. The legal right to free speech supports that endeavour.

The European Court of Human Rights was wrong to conclude that freedom of religion includes a right to not be offended in one's religious sensibilities and beliefs. There is no moral right to be protected from offence and there is nothing in the European Convention on Human Rights to suggest that such a right can be derived from its guarantee of religious freedom. It is wrong, then, to think of cases of religiously offensive speech as conflicts between freedom of

[78] Howard Jacobson, 'Artistic Creation Frees Us from "Right-Thinking"' *The Guardian* (20 June 2015) https://www.theguardian.com/artanddesign/2015/jun/20/howard-jacobson-artistic- creation-frees-us-from-right-thinking.

religion and freedom of expression. Such cases involve only one fundamental right: free speech. While the state may have a number of legitimate interests which can justify restrictions, protecting people from feeling offended by a communication is not one of them. As the Supreme Court's First Amendment jurisprudence demonstrates, offence as such is never a reason justifying the suppression of speech.

4

Religious Speech in Public Discourse

So far, I have argued that there is no moral right to be protected from cognitively mediated distress caused by offence to one's beliefs and sensibilities and that it is a mistake to interpret religious freedom as including a more specific right for believers to be free from the unpleasant feeling they experience when they encounter insulting speech. This is not the position of the European Court of Human Rights (ECtHR), which has repeatedly upheld this right, affirming rulings of national courts which punish speakers who upset the religious sensibilities of listeners.

As we saw in Chapter 1, Joel Feinberg has argued that a liberal conception of the law can accommodate a properly delineated offence principle without turning into moralism. His theory rests on two mediating criteria—the seriousness of the offence and the reasonableness of the offending conduct—which are balanced against each other. The function of the balancing exercise is not to produce a mathematically correct answer in each case but to pick out the morally relevant factors and ascribe them their appropriate weight. Thus, it identifies the conditions under which the fact of offence is a reason for state action. Where those conditions obtain, offence is a reason supporting the use of governmental coercion to punish the offence-giver.

The ECtHR's judgments in offensive speech cases make use of the balancing method, often in a nebulous manner which obscures rather than elucidates the reasoning. In addition to affirming the right not to be offended, those judgments have a further dimension: they imply a particular understanding of the character of public discourse, which affects the way the scales come down for or against the prohibition of offensive speech. In this chapter, I will attempt to flesh out this understanding and explore how it is relevant for the application of an offence principle.

Offensive Speech, Religion, and the Limits of the Law. Nicholas Hatzis, Oxford University Press.
DOI: 10.1093/oso/9780198758440.003.0005

Gratuitous Offence and Debate on Matters of Public Interest

The ECtHR tried to rationalize its judgment in favour of the censorship of the offensive film in *Otto-Preminger-Institut v Austria* by stating that among the responsibilities incumbent of speakers

> in the context of religious opinions and beliefs may legitimately be included an obligation to avoid as far as possible expressions that are gratuitously offensive to others and thus an infringement of their rights, and which therefore do not contribute to any form of public debate capable of furthering progress in human affairs.[1]

There are two points made in this excerpt. First, gratuitous offences are taken, without any further explanation, to constitute an infringement of the believers' right to not be offended, which, in turn, presupposes that such a right exists. Secondly, and this is the issue I would like to explore here, gratuitous offences, the Court says, do not make a contribution to a public debate which can further progress in human affairs.

This idea is at the heart of the Court's perspective on religiously offensive speech: some communications which insult religious sensibilities are deemed unworthy of protection because they do not contribute to a public debate. Put differently, if the message is offensive it needs to satisfy a 'contribution-to-a-public-debate' requirement in order to claim the protection of the European Convention on Human Rights (ECHR). That requirement, then, is one of the qualifying criteria for the application of an offence principle which can legitimize the suppression of speech under the Convention, in the sense that if no such contribution is made it becomes morally legitimate to silence the speaker.

Public Deliberation

The privileged position of speech among other human activities and its special place in constitutions and human rights documents and the case law of courts (in short, the free speech principle) is often justified by the role free expression plays in the deliberative process on matters of public interest in a democratic state. This is a consequentialist conception of freedom of speech which emphasizes its importance for the conduct of public affairs. By allowing all views to be

[1] (1995) 19 EHRR 34 para 49.

heard in the debate we make it more likely for citizens to understand what is at stake in each case and reach a correct decision, while at the same time recognizing them as equal members of the political community who can influence public life. The other side of the coin is the function that speech performs as a check on the power of the government.[2] Even where there are institutional checks and balances, officials may act in ways which are illegal or arbitrary; free expression is essential for exposing those who abuse the power entrusted to them by the state for serving the interests of the people.

The judicial tradition which attributes the special status of free speech to its public affairs function starts with the judgment of Learned Hand in *Masses Publishing Co v Patten*.[3] The Espionage Act 1917 authorized US postal authorities to exclude from the mail publications which were likely to impede the war effort and interfere with recruitment. *The Masses*, a socialist, anti-war journal, had published a number of cartoons and articles which criticized the government's war policy, the draft, and the treatment of conscientious objectors. When the Postmaster General of New York City, invoking the Act, refused to accept that issue of the journal for posting, the editors sought injunctive relief invoking the First Amendment. Learned Hand held that the Act should be construed to catch only communications which advise the listeners to violate the law; even very harsh and aggressive criticism of governmental policies which stops sort of such advocacy cannot be suppressed. His judgment was based on an understanding of freedom of expression as the legitimizing factor of government in a democratic polity.[4] He stated that the publication fell 'within the scope of that right to criticize either by temperate reasoning, or by immoderate and indecent invective, which is normally the privilege of the individual in countries dependent upon the free expression of opinion as the ultimate source of authority';[5] there is, he continued, a 'normal assumption of democratic government that the suppression of hostile criticism does not turn upon the justice of its substance or the decency and propriety of its temper'.[6] Hand's test, based on the content of the message at issue, did not gain momentum and was soon overshadowed by the 'clear and present danger' test for subversive advocacy, based on the likely consequences of the message, which was developed subsequently by Justice Holmes in *Schenck*,[7]

[2] Vincent Blasi, 'The Checking Value in First Amendment Theory' (1977) 2 American Bar Foundation Research Journal 521.

[3] 244 F 535 (SDNY), rev'd, 246 F 24 (2nd Cir 1917).

[4] See generally Vincent Blasi, 'Learned Hand and the Self-Government Theory of the First Amendment: *Masses Publishing Co v Patten*' (1990) 61 University of Colorado Law Review 1.

[5] *Masses Publishing Co v Patten* (n 3) 539.

[6] ibid 540.

[7] *Schenck v United States* 249 US 47 (1919).

Frohwerk,[8] and *Debs*.[9] However, Hand' s main contribution was not the test itself but the reasoning he put forward to support it.[10] Government by consent means that citizens always have the right to criticize public policies and officials, even where they do so in a manner which goes beyond the usually accepted limits of propriety and decency, violating norms of respect. In *Masses*, for the first time, freedom of expression derives its meaning from democratic theory; hence its function as 'the ultimate source of authority' and the very high protection afforded to it by law.

The most influential academic exposition of that view is Alexander Meiklejohn's book *Free Speech and Its Relation to Self-Government*.[11] His theory rests on a distinction between public and private speech. The former is speech which contributes to the process of self-government, which, Meiklejohn argues, is the core principle of American democracy; it includes political communications in the strict sense, as well as debates on the general welfare of society. This is the only form of speech covered by the First Amendment, which offers it full and unqualified protection because it would be incompatible with democratic self-government to allow officials to decide which views should be heard. By contrast, speech which lacks this political and public dimension is private and falls outside the scope of the First Amendment. Therefore, it enjoys the same constitutional protection with other private activities, and can be overridden by reasons of public interest.[12] The justification of free speech from democracy underlies the Supreme Court's judgment in *New York Times v Sullivan*,[13] where it was held that a public official cannot succeed in a libel suit for false statements relating to his official conduct unless he can demonstrate that the defamatory statement was made with actual malice. Justice Brennan justified the rule by relying on the 'profound national commitment to the principle that debate on public issues should be uninhibited, robust, and wide-open, and that it may well include vehement, caustic and sometimes unpleasantly sharp attacks on government and public officials'.[14] Harry Kalven immediately pointed out the link between the Supreme Court's reasoning in

[8] *Frohwerk v United States* 249 US 204 (1919).

[9] *Debs v United States* 249 US 211 (1919).

[10] Blasi, 'Learned Hand and the Self-Government Theory of the First Amendment' (n 4) 5.

[11] Alexander Meiklejohn, *Free Speech and Its Relation to Self-Government* (Harper Brothers 1948).

[12] For contemporary support of the view that the First Amendment is about the furtherance of political discourse in order to reach the best decisions about public matters see James Weinstein, 'Participatory Democracy as the Central Value of American Free Speech Doctrine' (2011) 97 Virginia Law Review 491; Cass R Sunstein, *Democracy and the Problem of Free Speech* (Free Press 1995); Owen M Fiss, Free Speech and Social Structure (1986) 71 Iowa Law Review 1404.

[13] 376 US 254 (1964).

[14] ibid 270.

New York Times v Sullivan and the democratic theory of freedom of expression.[15] Although this is not the whole meaning of the First Amendment, its central meaning is to abolish seditious libel and, therefore, protect fully the uninhibited criticism of public officials. 'The democratic necessities of free speech'[16] are the momentum driving the judgment which, Kalven says, 'literally incorporated Alexander Meiklejohn's thesis that in a democracy the citizen as ruler is our most important public official'.[17]

An instrumental justification of freedom of expression as a means to achieve an end is at its most potent in the domain of politics. Democratic government requires a free debate on public matters and individuals have an interest in being able to participate in it, even in large communities where their speech may not have a discernible impact, because it affirms their status as equal citizens. But in politics speech has even greater value as a public good, necessary for maintaining a democratic regime and checking abuses of power by officials. Even those individuals who rarely or never exercise their right to speak publicly have an interest in living in a democracy which recognizes a free speech right and protects it through a legal right to freedom of expression.[18] This is why democratic theory arguments in support of freedom of expression have been historically very influential in the development of the law. The ECtHR alluded to this perspective on speech rights when, in *Otto-Preminger-Institut v Austria*, it referred to a 'public debate capable of furthering progress in human affairs',[19] as opposed to gratuitous offence which makes no such contribution. Besides, it has interpreted the ECHR as offering very strong protection to political speech and subjected national measures which restrict political expression to scrutiny similar to the one applied by the US Supreme Court.[20] Speech on other matters of public importance also receives comparably strong protection.[21] In the

[15] Harry Kalven Jr, 'The *New York Times* Case: A Note on "The Central Meaning of the First Amendment"' [1964] Supreme Court Review 191.

[16] ibid 209.

[17] ibid.

[18] Joseph Raz, 'Free Expression and Personal Identification' in *Ethics in the Public Domain: Essays in the Morality of Law and Politics* (Oxford University Press 1994) 146, 149–53.

[19] *Otto-Preminger-Institut v Austria* (1995) 19 EHRR 34 para 49.

[20] See eg *Karácsony v Hungary* (2016) 42 BHRC 1; *Jerusalem v Austria* (2003) 37 EHRR 25; *Incal v Turkey* (1998) 29 EHRR 449; *Castells v Spain* (1992) 14 EHRR 445. Also, in *Lingens v Austria* (1986) 8 EHRR 407 the Court held that politicians need to tolerate even harsh criticism and can claim in defamation under more limited circumstances compared to private individuals. The judgment does not go as far as *New York Times v Sullivan* but shares with it a concern to protect political speech, even when it is insulting or outrageous.

[21] See eg *Kuliś and Różycki v Poland* App no 27209/03 (6 October 2009) (criticism of a company's advertising campaign); *Selisto v Finland* (2004) 42 EHRR 144 (medical malpractice); *Tierfabriken v Switzerland* (2001) 34 EHRR 159 (cruelty to animals); *Bergens Tidende and Others v Norway* (2000) 31 EHRR 430 (conditions in a plastic surgery clinic); *Bladet Tromso and Stensaas v Norway* (1999) 29 EHRR 125 (seal hunting); *Hertel v Switzerland* (1998) 28 EHRR 534 (dangers from the use of microwave ovens); *Thorgeir Thorgeirson v Iceland* (1992) 14 EHRR 843 (police brutality).

ECtHR's logic, the protection of religiously offensive speech is contingent on the distinction between gratuitous and non-gratuitous offence. Insulting communications can be protected, despite the fact that they upset moral or religious sensibilities, if they contribute something serious to public debate and, by definition, such contribution cannot be made by gratuitous insults.

When is Offence Gratuitous?

The distinguishing factor between gratuitous offence and other offensive messages is the style and the words used by the speaker to express her ideas. In *Otto-Preminger-Institut v Austria* the Court stated that 'the manner in which religious beliefs and doctrines are opposed or denied is a matter which may engage the responsibility of the State';[22] in *Wingrove v United Kingdom* it referred to the fact that English blasphemy law does not prohibit all criticism of the Christian religion but 'it is the manner in which views are advocated rather than the views themselves which the law seeks to control';[23] and in *IA v Turkey* it emphasized that the book did not merely contain criticism of Islam, but was (in the Court's view) 'an abusive attack on the Prophet of Islam'.[24] If the Danish cartoons had been prohibited by law and the case had reached Strasbourg, the Court would probably have concluded that they were gratuitously offensive and that the prohibition was compatible with the Convention. The rule, then, is that believers should put up with criticism that is sober and temperate, even if the substance of the opinion is offensive, but have a valid claim to be protected from criticism expressed in insulting or immoderate terms.[25]

Are the style and words chosen by the speaker morally significant for the question whether offensive speech should be suppressed? Feinberg believed that while the substantive content of speech is always privileged and the government is never justified to prohibit it because others are offended, 'the offensiveness of the manner of expression, as opposed to its substance, may have sufficient weight in some contexts'[26] so as to count in favour of prohibition. It is unclear, however, whether by 'manner of expression' he meant the choice of words or something like the content-neutral 'time, place, and manner'

[22] *Otto-Preminger-Institut v Austria* (n 19) para 47.
[23] *Wingrove v United Kingdom* (1996) 24 EHRR 1 para 60.
[24] *IA v Turkey* (2007) 45 EHRR 30 para 29.
[25] Robert Post, 'Religion and Freedom of Speech: Portraits of Muhammad' (2007) 14 Constellations 72, 80.
[26] Joel Feinberg, *Offense to Others* (Oxford University Press 1985) 44.

restrictions which, under the First Amendment, the government may apply to speakers seeking access to public fora such as streets and parks.[27] Typical examples of such restrictions are noise and traffic regulations which do not restrict speech on the basis of the substance of the message but for the attainment of a further objective. Non-content-based restrictions are subject to intermediate scrutiny and will pass constitutional muster if they are narrowly tailored to achieve a significant governmental interest (unrelated to the substance of the message) and leave open alternative channels for communication.[28]

Certainly, Meiklejohn thought that the style and words the speaker uses are relevant for the issue whether his message is constitutionally protected. His vision of the public discourse which the First Amendment was meant to protect and promote was that of a traditional American town meeting where people come together not merely to talk or exchange views in the abstract but to discuss in an orderly manner how to act on issues of general concern:

> The meeting has assembled, not primarily to talk, but primarily by means of talking to get business done. And the talking must be regulated and abridged as the doing of the business under actual conditions may require. If a speaker wanders from the point at issue, if he is abusive or in other way threatens to defeat the purpose of the meeting, he may be and should be declared 'out of order'. He must then stop speaking, at least in that way. And if he persists in breaking the rules, he may be 'denied the floor' or, in the last resort, 'thrown out' of the meeting. The town meeting, as it seeks for freedom of public discussion of public problems, would be wholly ineffectual unless speech were thus abridged. It is not a Hyde Park. It is a parliament or congress. It is a group of free and equal men, cooperating in a common enterprise, and using for that enterprise responsible and regulated discussion. It is not a dialectical free-for-all. It is self-government.[29]

[27] The following passage implies that he probably meant 'time, place, and manner' requirements which aim to protect peace and tranquillity: 'Some statutes ... do receive a warrant even from our highly restricted version of the offense principle. Some of these are worded in such a general and imprecise way that they leave it to the courts, in effect, to apply the offense principle in their own way, as for example, Section 415 of the California Penal Code which prohibits "maliciously and wilfully disturbing the peace or quiet of any neighborhood or person ... by tumultuous or offensive conduct". The statute proceeds to list various examples including loud and unusual noise, challenging to a fight, running a horse race for wager or amusement on a public street, firing a gun, and using "any vulgar language within the presence or hearing of women or children in a loud and boisterous manner". The clause about "women and children" would not do well by the extent of offense standard, however': Feinberg, *Offense to Others* (n 26) 46. Vulgar language which might offend a section of the population, Feinberg says here, does not qualify for prohibition under his offence principle.

[28] *Clark v Community for Creative Non-Violence* 468 US 288 (1984).

[29] Meiklejohn, *Free Speech and Its Relation to Self-Government* (n 11) 23.

Meiklejohn's imagery in this excerpt is captivating. On the one hand, there is Hyde Park, this paradigmatic venue of unregulated speech that is nothing more than a 'dialectical free-for-all'; the reader almost hears voices talking indiscriminately, without any sense of direction or purpose. On the other hand, there is a parliament or congress, the archetypal forum of rational discussion where the body politic reflects on the course of action that will serve the wider good. If we have to choose a blueprint for fashioning public debate the scales seem to come down unquestionably in favour of the latter. That is because speech, according to Meiklejohn, serves an aim, namely the efficient conduct of public affairs and the 'voting of wise decisions'.[30] It is this common enterprise that matters and, therefore, takes precedence over one's need to express oneself; about the latter, the First Amendment 'has no concern'.[31] Once the issue is presented in those terms, admitting that people may be silenced when what they have to say does not contribute to the common aim comes almost naturally.

Meiklejohn's view of the role of the moderator of the town meeting is revealing. The moderator is the one who ensures that order is kept and that discussion progresses in a way which serves the objective of self-government; it is not a choice for him, but a duty to suppress speech which might undermine its achievement. Speakers who are 'abusive' must be declared out of order and, if necessary, thrown out of the town meeting. The implication must be that religiously offensive speech which insults listeners and causes resentment and divisiveness in the political community can be proscribed unless it is necessary for the making of an informed, 'wise decision' on a topic properly brought before the meeting. This is an unlikely possibility, given Meiklejohn's view that disorderly and abusive speech frustrates the purpose of the meeting. We cannot know what he would have thought of the communications which were at issue in the cases decided by the ECtHR but it is possible that, while he would have acknowledged that religion is a proper topic for public discussion, he would have agreed, in principle, with the Court's view that speech which offends religious sensibilities is acceptable only if it is a serious contribution which promotes collective understanding and correct decision-making.[32] If not, it is merely gratuitous insult with very little weight in the balancing exercise for and against censorship. Under this view of freedom of expression, one's

[30] ibid 25.
[31] ibid 94.
[32] This does not necessarily mean that he would have also agreed with the European Court of Human Rights that the communications in *Otto-Preminger-Institut* (n 19), *Wingrove* (n 23), and *IA* (n 24) made no contribution to public debate.

choice of words in conveying an otherwise protected message is legitimately taken into account by the regulator.

The Government as Regulator of Public Discourse

In modern societies the regulator of public discourse is, of course, the government.[33] Robert Post has used the term 'managerial' authority to describe the government's power to administer its own institutions. This authority is not subject to the usual First Amendment constraints which apply to governmental regulation of private expressive activity. Here, speech rights are subordinate to institutional logic and structures, and communication can be regulated in ways which maximize the potential for achieving the aims of each institution. Managerial authority may require courts to defer to the judgment of officials about the need to regulate speech insofar as this is necessary for achieving institutional objectives.[34] The town meeting model which Meiklejohn puts forward as the appropriate standard for public discourse is regulated by such managerial authority. The meeting is not an open forum but a democratic institution set up for the citizens to decide how public affairs should be conducted. Speech has instrumental value, and can be managed, limited, and suppressed so as to allow the institution to perform its functions.[35] Meiklejohn sees public discourse covered by the constitutional guarantee of freedom of expression as a very extended town meeting with the role of the moderator played by the government, which, through law, ensures an orderly and productive debate.

[33] This is not to imply that private actors such as media corporations do not exercise control over public discourse. They clearly do, but only the government can use the coercive power of the law.

[34] Robert Post, 'Between Governance and Management: The History and Theory of the Public Forum' (1986) 34 UCLA Law Review 1713, 1775. Obviously, what speech properly falls within the government's managerial authority will not always be clear, as the judgment in *Walker v Texas Division, Sons of Confederate Veterans* 576 US 200 (2015) shows. Texas offers car drivers the option to ask for specialty licence plates of their own design subject to the approval of the Department of Motor Vehicles. The department refused a request to issue licence plates featuring the Confederate battle flag. In an opinion by Justice Breyer, the Supreme Court held that the refusal did not violate the First Amendment because licence plates are governmental speech and, therefore, not subject to the rule against viewpoint discrimination. The state cannot compel an individual to endorse its messages, but when it engages in expressive activity of its own, it can decide the content of its speech. Justice Alito, joined by Chief Justice Roberts and Justices Scalia and Kennedy, dissented, considering that the plates included some governmental speech (the name of the State of Texas and the numbers identifying the vehicle) but that the messages added to the custom-made plates were private speech, and that the department had rejected the request for a Confederate flag because many citizens would have found the message it conveyed offensive.

[35] Robert Post, 'Meiklejohn's Mistake: Individual Autonomy and the Reform of Public Discourse' (1993) 64 University of Colorado Law Review 1109, 1113.

An example of what such a debate looks like can be found in the judgment of the ECtHR in *Giniewski v France*.[36] The applicant was a journalist who had published an article arguing that the way certain doctrines of the Christian religion were presented by the Catholic Church was anti-Semitic and had prepared the ground for the ideas that led to the Holocaust. A Christian religious association brought criminal and civil proceedings against him, claiming that the article was defamatory of the Christian community.[37] The civil claim was upheld by the French courts, which awarded damages to the association. The ECtHR held that the applicant's right to free speech had been violated. It referred to its earlier judgments on religiously offensive speech but distinguished the present case because the article was not gratuitously offensive or insulting. Clearly, it contained phrases which could offend, shock, or disturb Christians but it enjoyed the protection of the Convention because it dealt with an important issue of public concern and made a contribution to the relevant debate. The position was explained as follows:

> The Court considers, in particular, that the applicant sought primarily to develop an argument about the scope of a specific doctrine and its possible links with the origins of the Holocaust. In so doing he had made a contribution, which by definition was open to discussion, to a wide-ranging and ongoing debate without sparking off any controversy that was gratuitous or detached from the reality of contemporary thought ... By considering the detrimental effects of a particular doctrine, the article in question contributed to a discussion of the various possible reasons behind the extermination of the Jews in Europe, a question of indisputable public interest in a democratic society. In such matters, restrictions on freedom of expression are to be strictly construed. Although the issue raised in the present case concerns a doctrine upheld by the Catholic Church, and hence a religious matter, an analysis of the article in question shows that it does not contain attacks on religious beliefs as such, but a view which the applicant wishes to express as a journalist and historian. In that connection, the Court considers it essential in a democratic society that a debate on the causes of acts

[36] (2007) 45 EHRR 23.

[37] They referred, in particular, to the following excerpt from the article: 'The Catholic Church sets itself up as the sole keeper of divine truth ... it strongly proclaims the fulfilment of the Old Covenant in the New and the superiority of the latter ... Many Christians have acknowledged that scriptural anti-Judaism and the doctrine of "fulfilment" [*accomplissement*] of the Old Covenant in the New led to anti-Semitism and prepared the ground in which the idea and implementation [*accomplissement*] of Auschwitz took seed': *Giniewski v France* (n 36) para 14.

> of particular gravity amounting to crimes against humanity should be able to take place freely.[38]

This is as good an example as one can find in the ECtHR's case law of what constitutes a worthwhile contribution to public discourse: there must be a debate about a genuine matter of public interest; the speaker must be seeking to further the understanding of the topic under discussion; and the message must be phrased in terms which are not abusive. If those criteria are met, the fact that some people may take offence cannot justify the use of state coercion to silence the speaker. The Court did not doubt that many Christians could be offended by the article but since the language used was sober and the communication was part of a serious ongoing debate about a very important matter of general interest the offence was not gratuitous and believers had no right to be protected from it. Therefore, this was a case where the conditions for offence to count as reason for the state to suppress speech were not satisfied.

Giniewski may lack the eloquence of Justice Brennan's opinion in *New York Times v Sullivan* and express the commitment to freedom of expression in less robust terms but the perspectives of the two cases are similar. Meiklejohn's view of speech as the instrument for dealing with public affairs in a democracy and his town meeting model of public deliberation are the best way of understanding *Giniewski*, especially when contrasted with *Otto-Preminger-Institut*, *Wingrove*, *IA*, and *ES*. In the former, the speaker had used moderate language to contribute, in an orderly manner, to a debate on a matter of public interest, the epitome of legally protected public speaking. In the latter, the suppression of speech was deemed to be compatible with the Convention because the films, the book, and the lecture did not fit the town meeting model.

As discussed in the previous chapter, in those cases the ECtHR ignored the value that religiously offensive speech had for the creators of the films and the author of the book. This was partly because in the Court's perspective of public discourse—orderly and serious discussion *à la Meiklejohn*—this aspect is irrelevant for its balancing exercise. Recall that Feinberg's offence principle balances the seriousness of the offence against its reasonableness, the latter being assessed by, among others, the importance of the offensive conduct for the offence-giver and for society. Unlike Feinberg, the Court was willing to ascribe

[38] ibid paras 50–51 (internal citations and cross-references omitted).

weight only to speech with societal value, and no such value could exist in profane and provocative communications.

Another View of Public Discourse: Legitimacy, Plurality and Change

The ECtHR conceives of public discourse as a space for highly regulated, sober discussion on important public matters subject to the managerial power of the government. An alternative view also starts from the societal value of free expression and its role in democracy but understands this value differently, and reaches different conclusions about the role of the government and the limits on its power over public discourse.

The justification for free speech from democratic theory invariably links speech rights to the ideal of self-government which requires that citizens are themselves authors, through the democratic process based on majority rule, of the laws which apply collectively to everyone. Self-government, however, does not exhaust the full spectrum of freedom we expect the law to guarantee. We also expect it to create for everyone a space for personal liberty which is beyond the reach of the majority which happens to prevail in the political game at any given time.[39] In addition to its aspect as popular self-government through the political process, democracy is also a substantive ideal of political morality.[40] When assessing whether a particular decision regulating the life of our political community is correct we do not restrict ourselves to the examination of the process by which the decision was made but also refer to substantive values (such as equality, freedom, autonomy, and so on), which such decisions are meant to serve. If they do not do so, we can fairly claim that they are not democratic in the true sense of the word, despite the fact that they have been arrived at through an impeccable decision-making procedure.[41] Constitutions, and supranational human right documents where they apply, typically embody such substantive values and perform the function of

[39] See Frank I Michelman, 'Law's Republic' (1987) 97 Yale Law Journal 1493, 1500–502. Michelman argues that the tension between those two aspects of modern constitutionalism can be resolved by using republican constitutional thought to reconceptualize the relationship between law, politics, and democracy in a way which both enhances individual liberty and promotes collective self-government through the inclusion in the political community of persons who had been excluded in the past.

[40] See generally Ronald Dworkin, *Is Democracy Possible Here? Principles for a New Political Debate* (Princeton University Press 2006); Frank I Michelman, 'Brennan and Democracy' (1998) 86 California Law Review 399.

[41] Post, 'Religion and Freedom of Speech' (n 25) 75.

limiting the authority of the self-governed political community to decide the content of its laws.

If self-government is viewed as authorship of decisions by every member of the political community as individuals, we need to explain how this ideal can be realized through the law-making process, which is by nature collective and majoritarian, and how we can expect individuals to identify with decisions of which they disapprove or even find abhorrent.[42] Where a serious discrepancy exists between collective will, formed and expressed through majoritarian political processes, and individual autonomy, it is difficulty to claim that each individual is, morally speaking, self-governing. Post has suggested that it is possible to bridge the gap through a 'responsive interpretation' of the constitution which guarantees that constitutional doctrine is informed by the values and ideals of the political community.[43] Given the cultural diversity in today's pluralist societies and the deep disagreements about the moral values that the state should embrace, this responsive version of democratic politics focuses on the importance of processes for making decisions about public issues. It is those processes, as exemplified by public discourse, that need to be as responsive and inclusive as possible, so as to ensure that individual citizens can experience their outcome as a personal exercise in self-government.[44]

The responsive model of political authority has affinities with public reason theories discussed in Chapter 2. Public reason requires that decisions about the regulation of common life be made on the basis of reasons which everyone can be reasonably expected to accept, so they cannot arise from personal viewpoints about what kind of life is worth living. Legislators and other officials, as well as individual citizens, are expected to invoke public political values when they enter public debate instead of relying on comprehensive doctrines, whether religious or secular, which others cannot be expected to embrace. The

[42] Michelman, 'Brennan and Democracy' (n 40) 403.

[43] Robert Post, *Constitutional Domains: Democracy, Community, Management* (Harvard University Press 1995) 18.

[44] Despite being cast in procedural terms, Post's theory of democracy rests on normative foundations which have substantive content. The existence of an ongoing, uninhibited public discourse is a foundational prerequisite of responsive democratic politics and is itself beyond debate. Therefore, it functions as the substantive standard against which the rightness of political decisions is assessed. See Michelman, 'Brennan and Democracy' (n 40) 407. See also Frank I Michelman, 'Must Constitutional Democracy be "Responsive"?' (1997) 107 Ethics 706. Besides, Post himself acknowledges that the responsive version of democracy is informed by considerations of respect for individual agency and autonomy, which is itself a substantive principle of political morality. See eg Post, *Constitutional Domains* (n 43) 197: 'When [the law] attempts to organize social life based on the ... principle that persons are autonomous and independent, it instantiates the social form of responsive democracy'); ibid at 187: 'Responsive democracy is therefore ultimately grounded on a respect for individuals seen as free and equal persons' (internal quotation marks and citations omitted).

possibility for this sort of democratic deliberation is a requirement for public reason.[45]

The role of free speech in the responsive model is to mediate between the collective will and individual autonomy by creating a safe, inclusive public discourse space where an uninhibited dialogue can take place. Public discourse is what happens not only in the traditionally designated fora of political debate, such as legislative assemblies, parliaments, and local government organs, but also in civil society groups, voluntary organizations, newspapers and other publications, the internet, and any other instrument of expression.[46] The aim is to make it more likely for citizens to identify, at least to some extent, with their government.[47] This does not mean that they will agree with every decision produced by democratic politics and embrace every exercise of governmental authority; nor should we expect them to do so. But by keeping public discourse open to all viewpoints and moral ideals, a political community makes it possible for individuals to participate in the making of societal attitudes and decisions about how state power should be used, which, in turn, allows them to relate even to those outcomes of the political process with which they disagree, and discern, even in them, a trace of their own moral agency.

Marketplaces—of Ideas and Communities

Public discourse can perform this mediating function if it is inclusive and pluralistic. Post suggests that it ought to be understood as creating not only a 'marketplace of ideas', a metaphor whose intellectual origins are in Justice Holmes' dissent in *Abrams v United States*,[48] but also a 'marketplace of communities',[49] where the state remains neutral in relation to the viewpoints expressed. If offensive speech were to be suppressed to protect people belonging to a particular religious, or political, or other group from being insulted, the state would

[45] Jonathan Quong, 'On the Idea of Public Reason' in Jon Mandle and David A. Reidy (eds), *A Companion to Rawls* (Wiley Blackwell 2014) 265, 266.

[46] This is a difference between public deliberation theories and Rawlsian public reason. In the former, the public sphere encompasses all expressive activities of civil society. For Rawls, the public political forum where the requirements of public reason apply is much more limited, and discourse within civil society structures is part of background culture and not subject to the justification conditions of public reason. For more on this see Evan Charney, 'Political Liberalism, Deliberative Democracy, and the Public Sphere' (1998) 92 American Political Science Review 97 and the discussion in ch 2 above.

[47] Post, 'Meiklejohn's Mistake' (n 35) 1114–16; Post, 'Religion and Freedom of Speech' (n 25) 75–76.

[48] 250 US 616 (1919). Holmes did not use the phrase 'marketplace of ideas' but rather spoke of 'free trade in ideas' and 'the competition of the market': *Abrams v United States* 630.

[49] Robert Post, 'The Constitutional Concept of Public Discourse: Outrageous Opinion, Democratic Deliberation, and *Hustler Magazine v Falwell*' (1990) 103 Harvard Law Review 601, 632.

be using its force to embed the standards of propriety of that group and impose them on society. This would undermine the open and inclusive character of public discourse and negate its role as an element of legitimization of democratic decision-making.

The marketplace metaphor has been influential in free speech theory and practice but it is not obvious what idea it was supposed to convey. Vincent Blasi has argued that the emphasis on the social function of speech as a mechanism for the ascertainment of truth similar to the market mechanisms based on demand and supply—an emphasis generated by the way the metaphor has been commonly understood—is misplaced.[50] There is no such thing as a perfect market in real life, as every market is affected by distortions and failures. Therefore, it would be odd to think that there exists a perfect market in ideas which the constitution should privilege for the sake of seeking the truth. Moreover, it is inappropriate to treat ideas and opinions in the same way as goods and services because the respective processes by which they are produced and disseminated are substantially different.[51] The justification for a robust free speech theory cannot rest on the assumption that there is a competitive marketplace of ideas where truth will eventually beat falsehood and emerge victorious.

Instead, Blasi argues, the metaphor makes more sense if it is linked to a rejection of moral absolutism and the acceptance of the need for change. Holmes was a sceptic who, while acknowledging that there is value in the intellectual effort of truth-seeking, did not believe in absolute truths.[52] This view was coupled with a belief that constitutional interpretation cannot be blind to the fact that evolution and social change are inevitable.[53] Speech performs the vital function of challenging embedded beliefs and practices and triggers the process of reshaping a community's morality and social structure. Thus, the intellectual foundations of Holmes' theory of free expression can be traced in his repudiation of dogmatism and stagnation in favour of a way of thinking which subjects all ideas to criticism and embraces the prospect of change. An open and inclusive public discourse both legitimizes the exercise of democratic authority and sustains the conditions in which society can cast a critical eye on itself and revise its self-understanding.

[50] Vincent Blasi, 'Holmes and the Marketplace of Ideas' [2004] Supreme Court Review 1.

[51] ibid pt IV.

[52] The answer to the question how much of a sceptic Holmes was, and whether his scepticism undermines his approach to free speech, is not clear. See the discussion in Blasi, 'Holmes and the Marketplace of Ideas' pt V.

[53] ibid 34: '[Holmes] thought that change is both inevitable and endurable ... his approach to constitutional interpretation depended on an attitude, if not a theory, about change.'

The idea that all value judgments are subject to debate and change is not exclusively Holmesian or American. The ECtHR has also indicated, albeit less robustly and consistently than the Supreme Court, that provocative *political* (but not religious) speech which questions even the most fundamental values a society has come to embrace cannot be excised from public discourse. *Lehideux and Isorni v France*[54] concerned the conviction of the applicants, who were active in the Association for the Defence of the Memory of Marshal Pétain, of the offence of publicly defending the crimes of collaboration. Their prosecution was triggered by the publication of an advertisement, written and paid for by the association, in the newspaper *Le Monde*. The text portrayed Marshal Pétain in a positive light. It stated that the French people 'rightly saw him as their saviour' as he had saved 'two million prisoners of war', protecting them 'against German omnipotence and barbarism' in an era marked by 'Nazi atrocities and persecutions'. It also adopted the so-called 'double-game' theory, i.e. that Pétain agreed in Montoire (where he met Hitler in October 1940) to collaborate with Nazi Germany while he was secretly in contact with Britain and the United States preparing the liberation of France. Finally, the advertisement omitted any reference whatsoever to the anti-Semitism and the racial laws of the Vichy regime which resulted in thousands of Jewish people being sent to concentration camps in Germany. The applicants' defence was that they had not praised collaboration with the enemy but were trying to generate a debate about the role of Pétain with the aim of having the judgment which convicted him to death in 1945 overturned. The French criminal courts stated that they could not take sides in the historical controversy but held that the advertisement was not a contribution to a debate about history but a fully-fledged *apologia* for Pétain and his regime.

The ECtHR found that the conviction was a violation of the applicants' free speech rights under Article 10 of the ECHR. It noted, as the French government had done, that this was a 'page of the history of France', which 'remains very painful in the collective memory, given the difficulties the country experienced in determining who was responsible, whether isolated individuals or entire institutions, for the policy of collaboration with Nazi Germany'.[55] While the views expressed by the applicants were likely to bring back memories of 'past sufferings', the lapse of time meant that the law should leave more room for open discussion: every country, the Court remarked, 'must make [an effort] to debate its own history openly and dispassionately'.[56] The fact that the text

[54] (2000) 30 EHRR 665.
[55] ibid para 55.
[56] ibid.

omitted reference to events which were common knowledge was relevant but not determinative. The association had been constituted lawfully under French law and the authorities had never questioned the legality of its aim which was to defend Pétain's memory.

One of the most interesting aspects of the judgment is the way it dealt with the French government's submission that the advertisement fell outside the scope of free speech protection because its content was incompatible with the very liberties the Convention was meant to protect. The government relied on Article 17 of the Convention:

> Nothing in [the] Convention may be interpreted as implying for any State, group or person any right to engage in any activity or perform any act aimed at the destruction of any of the rights and freedoms set forth herein or at their limitation to a greater extent than is provided for in the Convention.

The European Commission on Human Rights, which had heard the case at the admissibility stage, had taken the view that Article 17 was not applicable as the publication had not advocated racial hatred or any act which could undermine Convention rights. The Court did not pronounce on that point separately but incorporated it in its analysis of the substantive guarantees that Article 10 of the Convention offers to free expression. It drew a distinction between 'clearly established historical facts' and facts which are part of 'an ongoing debate among historians'.[57] The Holocaust, a crime against humanity, belongs clearly in the former category and its 'negation or revision would be removed from the protection of Article 10 by Article 17'.[58] By contrast, the role of Pétain and the interpretation of his acts as head of the Vichy government were still part of a historical debate which included conflicting theories. What the applicants had done was to take sides by supporting a particular view, which, although undoubtedly favourable to Pétain, was not a piece of revisionist history similar to Holocaust denial.[59]

[57] ibid para 47.

[58] ibid.

[59] The Court has relied on art 17 in cases where it classifies the expression at stake as hate speech, holding that it falls outside the scope of the right to freedom of expression protected by art 10 of the Convention. Those applications are declared inadmissible. See eg *Belkacem v Belgium* App no 34367/14 (20 July 2017) (extremist speech against non-Muslims); *M'Bala v France* App no 25293/13 (20 October 2015) (Holocaust denial); *Pavel Ivanov v Russia* App no 35222/04 (20 February 2007) (anti-Semitism); *Norwood v United Kingdom* (2005) 40 EHRR SE11 (anti-Muslim speech); *Garaudy v France* App no 65831/01 (24 June 2003) (Holocaust denial); *Glimmerveen and Hagenbeek v Netherlands* (1982) 4 EHRR 260 (racial hatred).

A similar issue arose in relation to political party membership in *Redfearn v United Kingdom*.[60] The applicant was a bus driver for a private firm which provided transport services to local authorities. He was mainly responsible for transporting people with mental disabilities, the majority of whom were of Asian origin. No complaints had ever been made about his work and his supervisor, who was also of Asian origin, had nominated him for an award. A local newspaper identified the applicant as a candidate for the British National Party (BNP) in the local elections. Two trade unions and some employees took issue with the applicant's continued employment, given the BNP's racist agenda. When the applicant was elected as a local councillor, his employer summarily dismissed him, stating that his employment would give rise to considerable anxiety among passengers, undermine the firm's reputation, and possibly lead to the loss of the contract with the local council. The applicant claimed that the dismissal was incompatible with both Article 10 and Article 11 (freedom of association) of the ECHR. The Court examined only the complaint under Article 11 (but in the light of free speech principles of Article 10) and found a violation of the Convention.

The Court noted that the applicant's conduct had never been inappropriate and that the complaints against him were about problems that might arise in the future. While restrictions on an employee's freedom of association could be acceptable in certain cases, a fair balance had to be struck between such rights and the need to protect other employees and the public. The applicant was dismissed on account of his political beliefs and affiliation, a ground which, under domestic law, could not serve as the basis for an unfair dismissal claim. Thus, domestic courts never had the chance to examine the particular circumstances of the case and perform this balancing exercise, so as to assess whether the employer was justified in dismissing the applicant.

What is notable for the purposes of our discussion is that, although the BNP's racist views go against the most fundamental values the Convention stands for, the Strasbourg Court did not exclude them from the range of political beliefs that the Convention protects. Borrowing from its case law on freedom of expression, the Court held that 'Article 11 is applicable not only to persons or associations whose views are favourably received or regarded as inoffensive or as a matter of indifference, but also those whose views offend, shock or disturb'.[61] The crucial distinction, which tipped the balance in favour of the applicant,

[60] (2013) 57 EHRR 2.
[61] ibid para 56.

was that between belief and action.[62] What Article 11 protects is having those morally reprehensible beliefs, and associating with others who share them;[63] acting upon them is clearly not protected. *Redfearn* affirms that strand in the Court's jurisprudence, of which *Lehideux and Isorni* is the prime example, that includes within the scope of the Convention some very insulting political beliefs and ideas. In other words, the offensiveness of a political opinion as such is not a reason for prohibiting its expression. In such cases, a weighing up of the competing interests is required, with national authorities enjoying a wide margin of appreciation.

I suggest that the best way of understanding *Lehideux and Isorni* and *Redfearn* is through the metaphor of the marketplace of communities and ideas. Both concerned viewpoints about history and politics which are not merely outside mainstream opinion but deeply offensive and objectionable. In both cases, the Court found a violation of the Convention, but the underlying concerns were different. In the former, the plural character of public discourse ensures a safe space for an open debate on controversial historical facts; this is part of a reflective process on a community's past and the way its current identity has emerged. In the latter, the Court was concerned with the evil of thought control and the possibility of penalizing people not for how they behave to others but for what they think in their minds;[64] here, the inclusiveness of public discourse was an affirmation of the basic equal status of all citizens in the deliberative process, which mediates between individual autonomy and collective power and legitimizes the exercise of democratic authority.

Lehideux and Isorni does not offer to controversial political speech the level of protection it enjoys under the First Amendment. However, it recognizes the need to maintain the possibility of challenging even very deeply held views about societal values. The Vichy regime is a very dark page in modern French history. Questions about the role of Pétain and the extent to which ordinary citizens collaborated with the Nazis have been part of historical debate for many years. Those discussions strike at the heart of the view French people have of themselves and their nation's history. Supporting Pétain may not be revisionism of the same scale as Holocaust denial but it is certainly very controversial and, for many people, very painful. There seems to be no reason for a constitution or a human rights charter to protect such speech other than the need to leave open the possibility of challenging society's most deeply

[62] George Letsas, '*Redfearn v United Kingdom*: Even Racists Have the Right to Freedom of Thought', UK Const L Blog (13 November 2012) (http://ukconstitutionallaw.org).

[63] The Court emphasized that the BNP and its activities were legal under domestic law.

[64] Letsas (n 62).

held views and treasured values. The ECtHR would not subscribe to Thomas Emerson's view that

> democratic society should tolerate opinion which attacks the fundamental institutions of democracy [because] suppression of any group in a society destroys the atmosphere of freedom essential to the life and progress of a healthy community. It is not possible for a society to practice both freedom of expression and suppression of expression at the same time.[65]

However, in its admonition to European countries to maintain an open debate about their history we can discern at least some elements of the same concern about the possibility of change which motivates much of the First Amendment case law and scholarship. The project of revisiting and reshaping our communal identity and morality can be undertaken only in a public environment which affords speech a high level of protection.

The Constitution as an Instrument for Change

The question at the beginning of this chapter was what is the ECtHR's conception of public discourse and how it matters for religiously offensive speech. We saw that the distinction between gratuitous and non-gratuitous offence, which runs through its case law on religious offence, reflects an understanding of public discourse similar to Meiklejohn's town meeting model, which is subject to the broad managerial power of the government. A competing, and more convincing, view considers public discourse as the locus of a deliberative process in which all citizens have an equal claim to speak, even if the content of their speech is morally repugnant, abusive, or insulting.

Is there a plausible argument that the *constitution* ought to give effect to the second, speech-protective version of public discourse? The answer depends on how we understand the function of the constitution in representative democracy grounded on majority rule. Frank Michelman has suggested that contemporary constitutional doctrine can resolve its most persistent puzzle—reconciling popular majoritarian government with respect for individual liberty under law—through a dialogic normative process (described as 'jurisgenerative') within the political community, a process which is both

[65] Thomas Emerson, *The System of Freedom of Expression* (Random House 1970) 51, 53.

self-reflective and self-revisionary so as to ensure that the community does not become tied to a static moral consensus informed by the moral preferences of a majority.[66] His project rests on a reinterpretation of republican constitutional theory which makes the acceptance of social plurality a necessary condition for the normative character of democratic politics and constitutional adjudication.[67] Democracy, properly understood, does not provide the majority with the right to exclude any group from the identity-formation procedure of a political community which aspires to be both self-governed and governed by law.

This aspect of Michelman's argument can help to explain why a marketplace of communities with a claim to be allowed a public voice is necessary. If what generates rules which can properly count as law is a normative dialogue, we have reason to structure it in a way which is responsive to the 'deep and conflictual diversity of social experience'.[68] Participation in the dialogue can trigger a process of self-reflection and, eventually, self-revision—we may come to question the elements that make up our identity and inform the values we expect the state to embrace through law. That self, 'whose identity and freedom consist, in part, in its capacity for reflexively critical reconsideration of the ends and commitments that it already has and that make it who it is'[69] can evolve only in conditions where 'plurality of perspectives' [70] is guaranteed. By accepting the prospect of change as an element of constitutional function we are extending to everyone membership in the project of communal identity-formation. And a robust commitment to free speech is indispensable for this pluralist and inclusive vision of constitutional function.

We have now a view of how the concepts of plurality and change combine to justify constitutional protection for a version of public discourse which is not defined by the norms and sensibilities of any particular group. If one of the reasons the constitution privileges free expression is that it fosters and promotes the possibility for change, it is reasonable to think of constitutional guarantees of free speech as creating a marketplace of communities which is free from state regulation that favours one community over the others. In this protected space for public discourse the character and moral outlook of the body politic are formed and revised through the contribution of all groups and their

[66] Michelman, 'Law's Republic' (n 39) 1493.

[67] ibid 1504: 'In republican thought, the normative character of politics depends on the independence of mind and judgment, the authenticity of voice, and—in some versions of republicanism—the diversity or plurality of views that citizens bring to the debate of the commonwealth' (internal quotation marks and citations omitted).

[68] ibid 1506.

[69] ibid 1528.

[70] ibid 1526.

competing visions of public life. Thus, suppressing messages because a particular group finds them offensive falls foul of the constitutional rules on freedom of expression because it embeds in public discourse and immunizes from challenge the values of that group, preventing those who do not share them from trying to put forward an alternative vision of common identity.

To accept that all communities and all moral viewpoints have an equal claim of access to public discourse means that by censoring religiously offensive speech the government excludes certain individuals or groups from the main vehicle of participation in collective decision-making and formation of communal identity.[71] In the democracy-based justification for free expression discussed above, what we are interested in is the link that speech creates between one's moral agency and autonomy and the collective will. Participation in public discourse allows one to challenge orthodox ideas and contribute to the shaping of an alternative moral outlook, instead of merely being a passive subscriber to established truths. This project is thwarted when offensive speech is silenced because it is deemed incompatible with what some listeners think are necessary standards of propriety.

It follows that the town meeting model of free speech, which entails the exercise of managerial governmental authority over public debate, is ill-suited for the analysis of cases of religiously offensive communications. What is offensive to religious sensibilities necessarily depends on what each religious group considers sacred and how intensive a criticism of its doctrines it can tolerate; where offensive speech is prohibited the state endorses the standards of a specific religion. The town meeting model can accommodate this practice because it offers unqualified protection to all substantive viewpoints since this is required for democratic self-government of the people, but allows for limitations in the words, tenor, and style the speaker uses to convey her views, and treats the state as the moderator which can restrict or fully suppress messages which, because of the form in which they are expressed, disrupt the orderly discussion of matters of general importance.

However, there is no neutral distinction between the substance of speech on the one hand, and its function in public discourse and the procedure for regulating the debate on the other.[72] Claims (usually put forward in procedural terms) about the appropriate structure of public discourse, the standards

[71] Post, 'Meiklejohn's Mistake' (n 35) 1116; Eric Barendt, *Freedom of Speech* (Oxford University Press 2006) 20: '[G]overnment should not be permitted to delimit the contours of public discourse; otherwise it could privilege the speech of some individuals by ruling the contributions of others, as it were, out of bounds.'

[72] Post, 'Meiklejohn's Mistake' (n 35) 117.

of propriety that should be applied and the proper role of free expression are normative in character and constitute themselves part of the debate. Any relevant rules that the state may impose embody a value judgment about what the moral outlook of the community should be, and, therefore, must be treated in the same way as substantive opinions. The lack of a neutral point outside public discourse from which to judge the appropriateness of the style in which opinions are expressed within it, means that a theory of free speech based on democracy and collective decision-making can only succeed in its democratic aspirations if it protects both substance and form. Thus, to go back to the ECtHR, the distinction between gratuitously offensive speech, which can be silenced, and non-gratuitously offensive speech, which those who feel insulted must tolerate, is untenable.

Limits on Governmental Regulation of Public Discourse

If we reject the version of public discourse as a very extended town meeting model subject to the managerial authority of the government (the view of Meiklejohn and the ECtHR in its case law on religious offence) in favour of a plural and inclusive public space which legitimizes the exercise of democratic authority and supports the conditions for change, two important limitations on the power of the government to regulate speech follow.

Substance and Style of Expression

First, constitutional and human rights documents ought to be interpreted as protecting both the substance of the message and the words used by the speaker to convey it. Justice Harlan explained the rationale in *Cohen v California*, the case concerning the anti-war protestor who wore a jacket with the words 'Fuck the Draft' inside a courthouse in Los Angeles:

> [W]e cannot indulge the facile assumption that one can forbid particular words without also running a substantial risk of suppressing ideas in the process. Indeed, governments might soon seize upon the censorship of particular words as a convenient guise for banning the expression of unpopular views.[73]

[73] 403 US 15 (1971) 26.

The rule was reaffirmed in *Texas v Johnson* (on flag burning) where the respondents had argued that it was the manner of expression, and not the content, which triggered Johnson's conviction. While criticism of the flag with words or deeds was acceptable, its outright destruction was not. The Supreme Court dismissed this argument, reiterating that the fact that 'the government may not prohibit expression simply because it disagrees with its message, is not dependent on the particular mode in which one chooses to express an idea'.[74]

This link between content and style had been drawn by the Supreme Court thirty years before *Cohen*, in *Cantwell v Connecticut*,[75] which concerned the use of very offensive words by a Jehovah's Witness against the Catholic Church. The Court held that 'exaggeration', 'vilification of men ... prominent in church or state', and 'even ... false statement' cannot be excluded from the scope of the First Amendment.[76] A commitment to an open public debate entails the 'probability of excesses and abuses', but those are risks 'essential to enlightened opinion and right conduct on the part of the citizens of a democracy'.[77] This, in turn, is necessary because 'in the realm of religious faith, and in that of political belief, sharp differences arise';[78] where diversity is the norm, the Court noted, democratic governance requires a public discourse which is open and inclusive.[79] The Court thus associates the need to protect offensive and inflammatory speech to notions of plurality, citizenship, and democracy. But the type of democratic polity it has in mind is different from the one envisaged in Meiklejohn's theory. The latter functions in a highly structured, highly regulated communicative environment where the law may be used to suppress speech which, because it is incompatible with generally accepted standards of propriety, has the potential to frustrate the decision-making process on matters of general interest. In the former, the constitution carves out a protected

[74] 491 US 397 (1989) 416. Cf *Virginia v Black* 538 US 343 (2003), which upheld the constitutionality of a Virginia statute criminalizing the burning of a cross with an intent to intimidate a person or group of persons. The Supreme Court ruled that such conduct did not merely communicate a message but was a 'true threat', namely the expression of an intent to commit an act of violence against an individual or a group. Thus, the basis for the prohibition was not the offensiveness of the message conveyed by cross burning but the intimidating character of this particular mode of expression which placed the victim in fear of physical harm or death. But the Court struck down the part of the statute which treated *any* cross burning as prima facie evidence that the cross burner intended to intimidate others. It noted that some cross burnings involve intimidation but others are an expression of political ideas without an intent to intimidate, and that the prima facie evidence provision blurred the line between the two, proscribing constitutionally protected political speech.

[75] 310 US 296 (1940).

[76] ibid 310.

[77] ibid.

[78] ibid.

[79] On the conception of public discourse in *Cantwell* see Post, 'The Constitutional Concept of Public Discourse' (n 49) 629–31.

area for expressive activities which covers both the substance and the form of speech, and thus includes offensive messages. It is within this area that public debate takes place and the moral character of the polity is determined through an ongoing process of evolution and change. *Cohen*'s prescription of 'free expression' as a 'powerful medicine' in a 'diverse and populous society' is part of a judicial tradition which goes at least as far back as *Cantwell* and has distinct affinities with Justice Holmes' sceptical intellectual attitude and its emphasis on the possibility of change.[80]

The argument of the government in the cases before the US Supreme Court was the same as the 'gratuitous offence' approach of the ECtHR: it relied on a distinction between temperate criticism which must be tolerated and outrageous acts of offence which violate standards of respect to suggest that the protesters could have said what they wanted to say in a more moderate manner. At a trivial level the argument is correct. The speakers could have used different words, words within the generally accepted notions of civility and propriety and therefore more palatable for the authorities and the audience. But those would not have been their words, and something of the force and impact of their message would have been lost.

Of course, there is nothing novel in the idea itself that style shapes content. Great works of art captivate our imagination because they persuade us that their way is the only way to get the message across. Gustave Flaubert obsessively looked for the word that it alone could express what he wanted to convey each time—the *mot juste*—this quest becoming for him the cornerstone of the creative process. But one does not need to be an artist to appreciate the connection between the means and content of expression. We know from our experience as communicative beings that our use of language shapes the substance of what we say. Whether we can externalize our thoughts successfully depends on the means we have for doing so. Words matter, and when some of them are no longer at our disposal, expressing the content of our minds becomes more difficult. Being allowed to choose our language is part of free expression and it ought to be part of the legal right to free speech.

The Procedure and Agenda of Public Discourse

Secondly, if public discourse is to remain open and inclusive and play its proper role in democratic self-governance it should be free from governmental regulation of its procedure and agenda. What topics are discussed and in what

[80] Lee C Bollinger, 'Free Speech and Intellectual Values' (1983) 92 Yale Law Journal 438, 470.

way they are discussed are not issues which occupy a neutral point, external to public discourse; they are value-laden and part of public discourse itself, in the sense that a community's attitude towards them depends on the public values it embraces and the communal moral outlook. In the context of the ECHR this means that national authorities should have a very limited margin of appreciation to decide what an acceptable public debate looks like and censor communications which do not fit the picture. The ECtHR's judgment in *Murphy v Ireland*[81] is a particularly telling example of its failure to appreciate the dangers inherent in allowing the government to decide which messages will be allowed in public discourse.

The case concerned an inoffensive, short advertisement which the Irish Faith Centre, a Bible-based Christian ministry in Dublin, wished to have broadcast by a private radio station. The advertisement read:

> What think ye of Christ? Would you, like Peter, only say that he is the son of the living God? Have you ever exposed yourself to the historical facts about Christ? The Irish Faith Centre are presenting for Easter week an hour long video by Dr Jean Scott PhD on the evidence of the resurrection from Monday 10th to Saturday 15th April every night at 8.30 and Easter Sunday at 11.30am and also live by satellite at 7.30pm.

The station agreed to broadcast it, but the Irish authority supervising radio and television prohibited the broadcast invoking a statutory rule providing that 'no advertisement shall be broadcast which is directed towards any religious or political end or which has any relation to an industrial dispute'.[82] The ECtHR held that it was more appropriate to examine the case under Article 10 of the Convention on freedom of expression and not Article 9 on religious freedom. Article 10 has a similar structure to Article 9; the first paragraph provides for a guarantee of free speech and the second is a limitation clause listing the grounds which national authorities may invoke to restrict expression, one of those grounds being 'the protection of the rights of others'. The government submitted that the aim of the prohibition was to protect the religious beliefs of those citizens who might be offended when they listened to an advertisement from a religious group different from the one to which they belonged. The

[81] (2004) 38 EHRR 13. See Andrew Geddis, 'You Can't Say "God" on the Radio: Freedom of Expression, Religious Advertising and the Broadcast Media after *Murphy v Ireland*' (2004) 2 European Human Rights Law Review 181.

[82] *Murphy v Ireland* (n 81) para 21.

structure of the argument is identical to the one in *Otto-Preminger-Institut v Austria*: speech can be restricted when it violates the rights of others and one of the rights people have is to not be offended by listening to religious advertisements on the radio. But how could this particular advertisement be considered offensive? Here comes the most important part of the argument: 'offensiveness' should be assessed against national standards of acceptability by the domestic authorities alone, because only they can interpret authentically the prevailing climate in the country. In the Convention language this translates into a claim that the government should be accorded a wide margin of appreciation to decide how much and what type of religious speech the Irish society could sustain: '[Since] ... the Irish population was unwilling to tolerate any religious advertising, then the State should be allowed to restrict such advertising'.[83] The fact that the advertisement at issue was not in the least offensive but merely informed the listeners about a religious meeting was, in the government's view, irrelevant: 'it was simply the religious nature of the advertisement that constituted sufficient justification for its restriction';[84] 'in the Irish context', the government went on, 'the fact of religious advertising was considered of itself to be potentially offensive'.[85]

The ECtHR held that the censorship of the applicant's religious message was compatible with freedom of expression principles. It distinguished *Murphy* from an earlier case, *Tierfabriken v Switzerland*,[86] where it had held that the refusal to broadcast a television advertisement concerning the treatment of animals violated Article 10 of the ECHR, on the basis that the latter concerned a matter of public importance and was therefore different from the religious communication at issue in *Murphy*. The core of the Court's reasoning was that in cases of religious speech the government has wide discretion to regulate the public forum:

> [A] wider margin of appreciation is generally available to the Contracting States when regulating freedom of expression in relation to matters liable to offend intimate personal convictions within the sphere of morals or, especially, religion. Moreover, as in the field of morals, and perhaps to an even greater degree, there is no uniform European conception of the requirements of 'the protection of the rights of others' in relation to attacks on their religious convictions. What is likely to cause substantial offence to persons of a

[83] ibid para 37.
[84] ibid para 38.
[85] ibid para 43.
[86] (2001) 34 EHRR 159.

> particular religious persuasion will vary significantly from time to time and from place to place, especially in an era characterised by an ever growing array of faiths and denominations. By reason of their direct and continuous contact with the vital forces of their countries, State authorities are in principle in a better position than the international judge to give an opinion on the exact content of these requirements with regard to the rights of others as well as on the 'necessity' of a 'restriction' intended to protect from such material those whose deepest feelings and convictions would be seriously offended. The Court therefore observes that it is this margin of appreciation which distinguishes the present case from the above-cited case of *Vgt Verein gegen Tierfabriken v. Switzerland.* In the latter case, the Court considered that the advertisement prohibited concerned a matter of public interest to which a reduced margin of appreciation applied.[87]

Both points made here are unconvincing. First, the Court appears to take the absurd view that animal welfare is more of a public interest issue than religion in relation to advertisements. This is presented as an axiomatic assertion, without any effort to substantiate it either with an empirical argument that people actually value more communications about how animals are treated in farms than communications about religion, or with a deontological argument that this is the view reasonable people are expected to take. Even if the Court's statement about *Tierfabriken* is to be interpreted as meaning that both animal rights and religion are matters of public interest but are subject to differing margins of appreciation, there is no effort to explain why this is so or which specific considerations justify the differential treatment and determine the intensity of the Court's review of the national measures in each case. Given that *Murphy* was an instance of content-based prior restraint—the most draconian interference with speech available to the state—very detailed reasoning was necessary. Instead, one has the impression that the Court is uneasy with the precedent of *Tierfabriken* which stands in the way of justifying the censorship in *Murphy*, so it makes this feeble attempt to distinguish it while, in truth, it just ignores it.

Secondly, the Court finds that the existence of an 'ever growing array of faiths and denominations' militates in favour of a wide governmental discretion, in the form of a margin of appreciation, to regulate public discourse. The margin of appreciation doctrine is a deference mechanism to the judgment of national

[87] *Murphy v Ireland* (n 81) para 67 (citations omitted).

authorities as to how the Convention should be applied in the domestic conditions of a country.[88] The Strasbourg Court uses it to reduce the tension between national and supranational interpretations of rights by accommodating in the Convention system national conceptions of their content.[89] The problem with *Murphy* is that the accommodation went too far. The Court accepted without any real scrutiny the contention that local circumstances made the censorship necessary, ignoring, in essence, both the content of the advertisement and the importance of the right at stake,[90] which itself has repeatedly been described as one of the 'essential foundations' of a democratic society.[91] Instead, it tried to justify its complete deference to national authorities by invoking the conditions of religious pluralism prevalent in contemporary societies. The perverse consequence of this approach is that the more diversity there exists, the more power the government has to silence speakers. But this is wrong: conditions of social, political, and religious plurality require an open and inclusive public discourse which is protected from state interferences aimed at excluding specific viewpoints, topics, or speakers. As the Supreme Court has held in *Cantwell*, *Texas v Johnson*, and *Cohen*, diversity of political opinions, religious persuasions, and ways of life requires the possibility of free expression in the public forum and the curtailment of state power to define what and how it can be said.

Murphy aptly demonstrates the point made by Kenneth Karst that it is a mistake to think of the state as a neutral 'moderator' of public discourse.[92] The government excised from the audiovisual media religious advertisements; this

[88] Gerald L Neuman, 'Human Rights and Constitutional Rights: Harmony and Dissonance' (2003) 55 Stanford Law Review 1863, 1884: 'The margin of appreciation doctrine combines several strands, but it results in a degree of deference to the state's evaluation of how a convention right applies to the state's particular circumstances.'

[89] ibid 1883–86.

[90] ibid1884: 'In part, the doctrine reserves the European Court's closer scrutiny for occasions when the importance of the right . . . justifies it.'

[91] Starting in *Handyside v United Kingdom* (1976) 1 EHRR 737 para 49. The form of margin of appreciation applied in *Murphy* was about deference to the national authorities as to what form of religious speech was acceptable in Irish society. This approach has been described by George Letsas as the 'structural' concept of the margin of appreciation (as opposed to the 'substantive' concept which addresses the relationship between individual rights and collective goals): George Letsas, *A Theory of Interpretation of the European Convention on Human Rights* (Oxford University Press 2007) 81.

[92] Kenneth L Karst, 'Equality as a Central Principle in the First Amendment' (1976) 43 University of Chicago Law Review 20, 40: 'The state lacks 'moderators' who can be trusted to know when 'everything worth saying' has been said, and the legislature lacks the capacity to write laws that will tell a moderator when to make such a ruling.' In fact, the Strasbourg Court has to some extent endorsed that view, holding that courts, both national ones and itself, should not be entrusted with that function either: 'It is not for this Court, nor for the nationals courts for that matter, to substitute their own views for those of the press as to what technique of reporting should be adopted by journalists. In this context the Court recalls that Article 10 protects not only the substance of the ideas and information expressed, but also the form in which they are conveyed': *Jersild v Denmark* (1995) 19 EHRR 1 para 31. *Murphy* proves the point that the Strasbourg Court itself should not be thought of as a moderator which knows when to put an end to public debate.

was content-based censorship of speech which should have been subjected to the strictest scrutiny by the ECtHR, especially since, in a country with a solid religious majority, it operated as an exclusion mechanism of smaller and non-mainstream religious groups which were prevented from using the most effective communication tools—radio and television—for accessing the general public. It is no answer to those objections to claim that differences about religion had been the cause of violent conflict on the island and therefore it was reasonable for the Strasbourg Court to defer to the judgment of national authorities completely as to what local conditions required. Such an argument might have been convincing if the Irish Faith Centre had intended to insult or attack the religious majority; but by no stretch of the imagination could the advertisement be described as an insult or attack. If the majority were provoked by the mere presence of a minority religious group in the audio-visual media and reacted violently, the appropriate response of the government would be to arrest and prosecute the rioters, not to silence the minority. Regrettably, this aspect of the case was not even discussed by the Court, which adopted the government's view that the mere fact of having the advertisement broadcast was an offence to the religious majority.

In *Otto-Preminger-Institut v Austria* and *Wingrove v United Kingdom* the ECtHR upheld the censorship of the two experimental films because they portrayed venerated figures of the Christian religion in a disrespectful manner and, therefore, were offensive for believers. In *Murphy* this line of reasoning was not available to the Court because the advertisement did not attack or insult another religious community or competing religious dogmas. Still, the Court stated that 'it is not to be excluded that an expression, which is not on its face offensive, could have an offensive impact in certain circumstances'.[93] Given that the advertisement merely provided information about the Centre's meetings, it follows that what the Court called 'offensive impact' stemmed from the fact that the religious majority was hostile to the presence of non-mainstream religious groups in the audio-visual media. The Irish High Court had been even more outspoken on this issue when it had upheld the prohibition considering that 'Irish people with religious beliefs tended to belong to a particular church so that religious advertising from a different church might be considered offensive and open to the interpretation of proselytism'.[94]

One aspect of the constitutional protection of free expression is a principle of *equal* liberty of expression, which plays a particularly significant role as a

[93] *Murphy v Ireland* (n 81) para 72.
[94] ibid para 73.

guarantee against content-based restrictions of speech: 'The equality principle, viewed as a barrier against content censorship, also implicitly underlies the elaborate first amendment doctrines that prohibit giving officials discretion to decide when speech shall be permitted and when it shall be punished or the speaker denied a licence.'[95] In *Murphy* the censorship of the applicant's message was upheld because the Court mistakenly allowed the government to exercise managerial authority over public discourse and decide itself what speech was acceptable. In doing so, it failed to guarantee to every citizen equal access to the process of collective identity-formation and, ultimately, the possibility to identify with the moral character of the community.

Personal Insults

In Chapter 1, I mentioned the distinction between attacks on religious beliefs and attacks on the believers themselves. The ECtHR consistently conflates the two, treating insults to religious doctrines and figures as if they were abusive attacks on the persons of the believers. This is evident even where the Court finds that freedom of expression has been violated. In *Giniewski*, in response to the Christians who had been insulted by the statement that some doctrines of the Catholic Church prepared the ground for the Holocaust, the Court noted that the article in question 'does not contain attacks on religious beliefs as such'[96] and therefore the offended readers had no claim to be protected from the distress they felt. The implication is that if it had contained attacks on Christian doctrine the outcome might have been different, because such attacks would have been interpreted as abusive to the believers themselves, who could then claim that their right not to suffer offence had been infringed.

The offensive speech cases before the ECtHR did not involve speech directed to a specific believer; the communications were impersonal, addressed to the public at large as works of art or statements of opinion about matters of public interest. Those who felt insulted were members of the group 'Christians' or 'Muslims'. But it is possible for religious or other insults to be expressed in a manner which is specific enough to count as a personal communication to an identifiable individual. If public discourse is construed in the manner I suggested in the previous section, how should those cases be treated?

[95] Karst (n 92) 29.
[96] *Giniewski v France* (n 36) para 51.

I should first explain what should not count as a personal insult through speech. In debates about the permissibility of offensive speech, it is often said that the beliefs are part of the identity of the person who holds them, an element which makes up who they are. Therefore, when they are ridiculed or abused, the believer herself is personally abused, although the speech takes an impersonal form, like the publication of a book or the showing of a work of art. In this approach, censorship of offensive speech is meant to protect the person who holds the beliefs which are criticized.

This use of identity politics, which merges the belief with the person of the believer, should be resisted. The invocation of identity cannot turn an attack on beliefs into a personal attack on the believer. When beliefs are treated as constitutive elements of one's personhood, the effect is that they are removed from the plane of everyday social interaction to the domain of fundamental interests which admit of no compromise. We reasonably expect that in our common life with others the elements of our humanity will be respected, and that where this is not the case the law will intervene to protect us. If a belief, opinion, preference, or choice is considered as part of who we are as human beings because we feel very strongly about it, it has a claim to this kind of protection from the law. But then social life becomes extremely difficult. Identity is a very expansive concept which can incorporate all kinds of religious, cultural, or political viewpoints; if we say that they should be protected from insulting speech as elements of people's identity, it will become impossible to speak publicly without our speech becoming an attack on someone.[97]

The rejection of the claim that attacks on beliefs are, via the concept of identity, also attacks on the believer has nothing to do with whether the complainants are sincere about their wounded feelings. Some of them may be exaggerating their claims so as to secure for themselves and their views more visibility and influence in public space under the protection of the law. Or they may be entirely honest that a particular issue, like religious devotion, is part of who they feel they are, and that they experience offensive speech as a personal affront. As mentioned previously in the book, sincerity is irrelevant for assessing whether the belief-mediated distress suffered by listeners is a reason to silence speakers.

The kind of offensive speech which can become a personal insult is a communication intentionally addressed to a specific individual with the aim

[97] Jeremy Waldron, *The Harm in Hate Speech* (Harvard University Press 2012) 131–36. For a defence of strong identity claims as reason to restrict offensive speech see Meital Pinto, 'What are Offences to Feelings Really About? A New Regulative Principle for the Multicultural Era' (2010) 30 Oxford Journal of Legal Studies 695 (suggesting, at 698, that 'in general, every individual has a *prima facie* right to be protected from all acts that offend the integrity of his or her cultural identity').

of pressuring or intimidating him. I will use two cases to demonstrate what I mean. The first arose in the context of a nuisance claim. During the miners' strikes in the mid-1980s, a number of miners in South Wales had decided to work. Large numbers of their colleagues picketed the gates of the collieries, which was an act protected by labour relations legislation. Some striking miners also picketed the homes of working miners and the premises of a college which one of them attended, using abusive language and, in some instances, making threats. The working miners were successful in obtaining an injunction against the picketing of their homes and the college. The court held that, although peaceful picketing at the place of work was lawful, demonstrations or picketing of workers' homes with the aim of pressuring them to strike constituted per se common law nuisance, even if it was peaceful.[98]

In the second case, the US Supreme Court upheld against a First Amendment challenge a city ordinance prohibiting the picketing of residential dwellings.[99] The claim was brought by anti-abortion activists who wished to picket the house of a doctor performing abortions. The Court stated that the ordinance prohibited picketing which targets a particular residence but not all picketing (such as general marching) in the streets of a residential area. Thus, it was a narrowly drafted law aiming at protecting residential privacy and left adequate alternative channels for communicating a message. Citing *Cohen v California*, the Court further noted that usually people would be expected to try to avoid speech they dislike but this is not possible when one's home is targeted because then the resident becomes a captive: 'The First amendment permits the government to prohibit offensive speech as intrusive when the captive audience cannot avoid the objectionable speech'.[100]

Both judgments rely on the difference between a generalized message, which may be unpleasant or offensive for the listeners but remains protected, and the targeting, through speech, of specific individuals. They also share a concern

[98] *Thomas and Others v National Union of Mineworkers* [1986] Ch 20, 65. The court also held that picketing at the workplace was unlawful if it was carried out 'in a manner that represents an unreasonable harassment of the working miners'.

[99] *Frisby v Schultz* 487 US 474 (1988).

[100] ibid 487 (internal quotation marks omitted). The case was distinguished in *Snyder v Phelps* 562 US 443 (2011). A fundamentalist Christian group had picketed the funeral of a marine protesting the tolerant attitude towards sin of American society and displaying signs against the Catholic Church, the Pope, and homosexuality. The group believed that God killed American soldiers as a punishment and had organized several hundreds of such pickets in the space of 20 years. The dead soldier's father successfully sued the group for intentional infliction of emotional distress. The Supreme Court found for the group. It held that the group's messages concerned public issues and were not a masked attack on the family over a private matter. The picket was peaceful, took place in a public space and had not interfered with the funeral.

about the availability of alternative ways for expressing the substance of the message so that the ideas at stake are not suppressed. Miners could picket the collieries to show their disagreement with their colleagues' decision not to strike and persuade them to change their minds, and the anti-abortion protesters could march in the neighbourhood to express their opposition to abortion. What decided the cases in favour of banning speech was the effect the mode of expression (individual targeting) had on the targeted listeners.

Consider now the case of an anti-religious group regularly picketing the home of a fundamentalist preacher, or following him around whenever he goes out.[101] This is not an impersonal communication in the context of a public debate on religion, like the speech involved in the judgments of the ECtHR. It is directed against him personally with the aim of putting pressure on him and causing him distress, so he is in a position similar to that of the working miners or the doctor performing abortions. This can be a form of offence which is profound and carried out in a way which assaults a core element of his moral identity. As I suggested in Chapter 1, this is the only instance where one can claim to be properly offended for the purposes of applying an offence principle which can lead to the legal prohibition of offensive speech. If those conditions are satisfied, it is legitimate to put offensive speech on the scales and, as suggested by Feinberg, perform the balancing exercise by looking at the reasonableness of the offensive conduct and the injury caused to the target of the offence. Which way the scales will come down will depend on the facts of each case and the circumstances prevailing in a particular society at the relevant time. But, in principle, this is an instance where it might be morally appropriate to proscribe offensive speech. In other words, offence is a *pro tanto* reason for the exercise of state coercion and may become the 'all things considered' reason justifying the prohibition.[102]

[101] I am assuming that their picket is carried out in a way which does not amount to a breach of privacy or trespass to property, or causes a breach of peace.

[102] Amnon Reichman, 'Criminalizing Religiously Offensive Satire: Free Speech, Human Dignity, and Comparative Law' in Ivan Hare and James Weinstein (eds), *Extreme Speech and Democracy* (Oxford University Press 2009) 331 discusses the Israeli case of *Suszkin v Israel* [1998] IsrSC 52(3) 289 concerning a woman who had entered an Arab area in Hebron carrying posters depicting the Prophet Muhammad as a pig, which she intended to glue on Muslims' houses. She was arrested by Israeli soldiers and subsequently convicted of attempting to outrage religious feelings. The Israeli Supreme Court affirmed her conviction. Reichman suggests (at 348–50) that a decisive factor in the judgment was that she would have targeted specific houses, and that had she addressed her offensive message to the general public, the outcome may have been different. Injury to religious sensibilities could justify the proscription of speech when the insult took an individualized form but not if the same poster had been published in a newspaper. While it is debatable whether her actions were direct enough to count as a personal insult, the distinction makes good sense.

I am not claiming that the application of this rule will always be uncontroversial. For example, when is speech direct enough to count as a personal communication to an identifiable individual? What if offence is directed at a very small group? Is it necessary for the target to have felt threatened or is distress enough? Does it matter how the target herself has behaved in the past or whether she is a private person or a public figure?[103] Those are questions without obvious answers but this does not mean that the principle itself is unintelligible. Despite the uncertainties, there is an obvious difference between the author who writes a book attacking Christianity or Islam and the anti-religious extremists who gather outside the house of a devout believer for regular picketing.[104]

So, to sum up. Offensive speech, no matter how distressing some listeners find it, should always be allowed in the context of public discourse which functions as a safe space for the expression of all viewpoints in a plural society. There is only one case where those offended have a claim to be legally protected from the unpleasant feelings offensive speech causes: when a communication is directed against them personally. Impersonal speech which assaults ideas, beliefs, doctrines, or holy figures is never an attack on individual believers, even if they feel that those elements are constitutive of their personality and identity. But when insults are intentionally addressed to an identifiable individual, the offence principle becomes applicable and, depending on the outcome of the balancing exercise, speech may be prohibited.

[103] In *Hustler Magazine v Falwell* 485 US 46 (1988) the US Supreme Court held that public figures cannot sue for the tort of intentional infliction of emotional distress unless they demonstrate that the defendant had made a false factual allegation with actual malice. See the discussion in ch 3 above. For an argument that the picketing of the private residences of public officials should be allowed subject to reasonable time, place and manner restrictions because it is an aspect of participatory democracy see Raphael Cohen-Almagor, *Speech, Media and Ethics: The Limits of Free Expression* (Palgrave 2001) ch.2.

[104] Of course, attacks on believers with means other than speech are always wrong and those targeted have a valid claim that the government take positive action to protect them. See eg *Members of the Gldani Congregation of Jehovah's Witnesses v Georgia* (2008) 46 EHRR 30 (failure of the authorities to investigate violent attacks against Jehovah's Witnesses by Orthodox extremists violates arts 3 and 9 of the Convention).

5
Blasphemy and Defamation of Religions

Historically, the customary response to profane speech has been to silence the speaker through the application of blasphemy laws. Contemporary practice in Western democracies has changed in many respects and the most severe of those laws have been repealed; however, versions of blasphemy prohibitions remain common.[1] Although this new generation of modernized blasphemy laws display some of the characteristics of their predecessors, a notable difference is that they no longer aim to protect only the established religion (where it exists) or the religion of the majority of the population; they are drafted in general terms and apply irrespective of the religious belief which is targeted by the criticism. An offshoot of blasphemy is the more recent concept of 'defamation of religion', particularly present in international law. Because blasphemy has developed a bad name for itself as an instrument for the persecution of dissidents, its proponents describe the revamped blasphemy offences in different words, perhaps in an attempt to make them look more anodyne. Defamation of religion is such an attempt to rename blasphemy.

Here, I look at how the free speech principles explored in Chapters 3 and 4 apply to this paradigmatic example of religious speech bans. The first part of the chapter discusses two important points in the evolution of blasphemy. First, while the blasphemy offence was initially triggered by the mere denial of the truth of Christianity, it later came to depend on the manner of expression, and only insulting or intemperate communications fell within its scope. Secondly, modern blasphemy laws in the Western world have expanded to protect not only the dominant religion but all religious beliefs and, in some cases, deeply held secular beliefs. Then I discuss two types of objections to blasphemy laws: that they are vague and impossible to enforce in a non-discriminatory manner; and that they are as such incompatible with a free speech principle. Finally, I address the argument that blasphemy bans are a necessary restriction

[1] US Commission on International Religious Freedom, 'Respecting Rights? Measuring the World's Blasphemy Laws' (2017); Paul Marshall and Nina Shea, *Silenced: How Apostasy and Blasphemy Codes Are Choking Freedom Worldwide* (Oxford University Press 2011); Jeremy Patrick, 'The Curious Persistence of Blasphemy' (2011) 23 Florida Journal of International Law 187.

Offensive Speech, Religion, and the Limits of the Law. Nicholas Hatzis, Oxford University Press.
DOI: 10.1093/oso/9780198758440.003.0006

on freedom of expression for the prevention of violence and the maintenance of public peace.

The Evolution of Blasphemy

The Common Law Offence

The English common law offence of blasphemy which was at stake in *Wingrove v United Kingdom*[2] protected only the established Church of England. In *Taylor's Case* in 1676 the court held that blasphemous communications were an offence not only to God but also to the state; since Christianity was the country's religion, disparaging its doctrines was equivalent to subversion of the civic order.[3] Respect of the official religion was thus linked to notions of good citizenship and law-abidingness, with dissidents being thought of as threats to both church and state. The crime of blasphemy required the publication of blasphemous material in written or oral form.[4] Initially, the style and the words used by the speaker were irrelevant: there was no need for the material to be insulting or profane, and even a denial of Christianity couched in temperate terms would satisfy the offence's *actus reus*.[5] Thus, a 1841 report on criminal law in England noted that 'any general denial of the truth of Christianity, without reference to the language or temper in which such denial is conveyed' was punishable.[6] Around the middle of the nineteenth century, however, the focus of blasphemy shifted to the manner of expression. It became acceptable to attack or deny the validity of Christian beliefs provided that the words used were temperate. In 1883, it was held that 'if the decencies of controversy are observed, even the fundamentals of religion may be attacked without the writer being guilty of blasphemy'.[7] Thus, the aim of blasphemy was no longer to defend the actual religious beliefs but to protect religious people from 'belief-mediated distress',[8]

[2] (1996) 24 EHRR 1. See the discussion in ch 3 above.

[3] *Taylor's Case* (1676) 1 Vent 293 ('Christianity is parcel of the laws of England ... to reproach the Christian religion is to speak in subversion of the law') cited in Russel Sandberg and Norman Doe, 'The Strange Death of Blasphemy' (2008) 71 Modern Law Review 971, 972. For a detailed discussion of the case in its historical context see Leonard W Levy, *Verbal Offence Against the Sacred, from Moses to Salman Rushdie* (The University of North Carolina Press 1995) 219.

[4] Sandberg and Doe (n 3) 972.

[5] Robert C Post, 'Cultural Heterogeneity and the Law: Pornography, Blasphemy, and the First Amendment' (1988) 76 California Law Review 297, 306.

[6] Commissioners on Criminal Law, Sixth Report (1841), 83 cited in Post, 'Cultural Heterogeneity and the Law' (n 5) 306–307.

[7] *R v Ramsay and Foote* (1883) 15 Cox CC 231, 238, cited in Sandberg and Doe (n 3) 973.

[8] Judith Jarvis Thomson, *The Realm of Rights* (Harvard University Press 1990) 250.

the unpleasant mental state caused by intemperate or aggressive speech which upset their beliefs and sensibilities.[9]

While there have been some suggestions that, on occasion, the law would cover other Christian doctrines which were also accepted by the established Church or even beliefs of non-Christian groups which were accepted by Christianity,[10] it was clear that whatever fell outside the scope of the Christian religion was not protected. This was confirmed in the *Choudhury*[11] case. The claimant had asked the magistrates' court to issue summonses again Salman Rushdie and the publishers of the book *The Satanic Verses* for the offence of blasphemy. When his application was refused on the grounds that blasphemy protected only the Christian religion he sought judicial review at the Divisional Court. It was held that the common law offence did not cover religions other than Christianity and that it would be improper for the court to extend it; since the law was clear, only Parliament could change it by statute.[12] The claimant then applied to the European Commission on Human Rights, claiming that the fact that the Muslim religion was not protected was a violation of his right to religious freedom under Article 9 of the Convention and that protecting Christianity only was a violation of Articles 14 and 9 of the Convention.[13] The Commission dismissed the application as inadmissible. It stated that the issue arising in the case was whether freedom of religion under the Convention included a right to 'bring any specific form of proceedings against those who, by authorship or publication, offend the sensitivities of an individual or of a group of individuals'[14] and concluded that there was no 'link between freedom from

[9] Robert Post, 'Religion and Freedom of Speech: Portraits of Muhammad' (2007) 14 Constellations 72, 77; Sandberg and Doe, 'The Strange Death of Blasphemy' (n 3) 973; Colin R Munro, 'Prophets, Presbyters and Profanity' (1989) Public Law 369, 372.

[10] Sandberg and Doe, 'The Strange Death of Blasphemy' (n 3) 973. See also Law Commission, 'Offences against Religion and Public Worship' Working Paper No 79 (1981) 82: 'Having regard to the authorities, it seems probable that at most other denominations are protected only to the extent that their fundamental beliefs are those which are held in common with the established Church.'

[11] *R v Chief Metropolitan Stipendiary Magistrate ex p Choudhury* [1991] 1 QB 429.

[12] Munro, 'Prophets, Presbyters, and Profanity' (n 9) 373 notes that a working party set up by the Archbishop of Canterbury to report on blasphemy recommended the creation of a new offence which would protect all religions.

[13] Article 14 reads: 'The enjoyment of the rights and freedoms set forth in this Convention shall be secured without discrimination on any ground such as sex, race, colour, language, religion, political or other opinion, national or social origin, association with a national minority, property, birth or other status.' The European Court of Human Rights has held that art 14 has no independent existence and has effect only in relation to the enjoyment of the substantive rights guaranteed by the Convention. See eg *EB v France* (2008) 47 EHRR 21 para 47. Protocol 12 now provides for a free-standing right to equal treatment which prohibits discrimination on any ground.

[14] *Choudhury v United Kingdom* App no 17439/90 (5 March 1991) (European Commission on Human Rights) para 1.

interference'[15] with the free exercise of religion and the applicant's complaints. Parliament abolished the offence of blasphemy in 2008.[16]

In the United States, prosecutions for blasphemy under state laws were common in the nineteenth century and continued until the 1920s.[17] At the time, the First Amendment to the federal Constitution was not applicable to the states[18] but state constitutions protected religious freedom in terms very similar to those of the First Amendment. Yet, when faced with constitutional challenges to blasphemy convictions, courts upheld them on the ground that not all religious speech was protected. An early case which proved very influential for the future development of the law was *People v Ruggles*,[19] which concerned a blasphemy prosecution for the statement that Jesus was a 'bastard' and the Virgin Mary a 'whore'. Relying on a series of English cases, the New York Supreme Court held that 'blasphemy against God, and contumelious reproaches and profane ridicule of Christ or the Holy Scriptures... are offences punishable by common law' because 'independent[ly] of any religious establishment or the rights of the church' they affect the 'essential interests of civil society'.[20] What was then Article 38 of the New York State Constitution provided that 'the free exercise and enjoyment of religious profession and worship, without discrimination or preference, shall forever be allowed in this state to all mankind' but also that 'the liberty of conscience hereby granted shall not be so construed as to excuse acts of licentiousness or justify practices inconsistent with the peace or safety of this state'.[21] This provision, the court continued, 'discarded religious establishment' and guaranteed 'a free and universal toleration, without any of the tests, disabilities, or discriminations incident to a religious establishment' but it was not meant to 'forbid judicial cognizance of those offences against religion and morality which ... are punishable because they strike at the root of moral obligation, and weaken the security of the social ties'.[22] While 'the free, equal, and undisturbed, enjoyment of religious opinion, whatever it may be, and free and decent discussions on any religious subject, is granted and secured',[23] the law will not protect 'malicious and blasphemous contempt'[24] of Christianity as this constitutes a 'gross violation of decency and

[15] ibid para 2.
[16] Criminal Justice and Immigration Act 2008, s 79(1).
[17] See the discussion in Note, 'Blasphemy' (1970) 70 Columbia Law Review 694.
[18] It was declared to apply to the states through the Fourteenth Amendment in *Gitlow v New York* 268 US 652 (1925).
[19] 8 Johns 290 (NY 1811).
[20] ibid 293–94.
[21] Cited in ibid 296.
[22] ibid 296.
[23] ibid 295.
[24] ibid 295.

good order',[25] which, in turn, undermines 'moral discipline' and 'those principles of virtue, which help to bind society together'.[26] Further, the New York constitution's guarantee of religious liberty did not mean that the government had

> to punish indiscriminately the like attacks upon the religion of Mahomet or of the grand Lama; and for this plain reason, that the case assumes that we are a christian people, and the morality of the country is deeply ingrafted upon christianity, and not upon the doctrines or worship of those impostors.[27]

The New York Supreme Court decided *Ruggles* under a constitutional provision which provided a degree of liberty far greater than that enjoyed by people in England at the same time, when members of religious groups other than the Church of England and atheists faced discrimination in relation to all aspects of public life.[28] Yet, there are three important similarities between the judgment in *Ruggles* and the English law of blasphemy. First, they both privilege the majority religion. The state constitution of New York protects everyone's equal right to practice their faith and prohibits an official establishment without, however, requiring equality across the board on all matters of religion. The social fact that the majority of people are Christians and that the values and attitudes adopted by society are influenced by Christianity is relied on to justify a legal rule which extends the protection of the law only to the dominant group. Thus, its values are supported by, and embedded in, the legal system. Secondly, in both cases the blasphemer is seen as a threat to social stability. Profanity and sacrilege are an insult to God but they are also understood to pose a more immediate risk of damage to societal norms which hold the community together and ensure its survival, so the government has a separate reason, based on civic order considerations and, therefore, at least on its face, secular in nature, to punish blasphemy. Thirdly, the emphasis is on the manner of expression and the words used rather than the substance of the communication. By 1811 the New York court had already taken the view that 'decent' discussion of religious issues was free as opposed to speech that was a 'gross violation of decency' and

[25] ibid 294.
[26] ibid 294.
[27] ibid 295.
[28] The year 1828 marks the beginning of a process towards religious equality. The Sacramental Test Act 1828 repealed the Corporation Act 1661 and the Test Act 1673, which required all those holding public office to receive the Holy Communion according to the rites of the Church of England, while the Roman Catholic Relief Act 1829 and the Jews Relief Act 1858 made it possible for Catholics and Jews to sit in Parliament. See the discussion in Julian Rivers, *The Law of Organized Religions: Between Establishment and Secularism* (Oxford University Press 2010).

thus fell outside constitutional protections, an approach which, as mentioned earlier, English courts would adopt towards the end of the century when it was established that the criterion for blasphemy was whether 'the decencies of controversy are observed'.[29]

A number of cases decided by other state courts upheld blasphemy laws on grounds similar to those invoked in *Ruggles*.[30] In 1897, even the Supreme Court stated at dictum that the First Amendment 'does not permit the publication of libels, blasphemous or indecent articles, or other publications injurious to public morals or private reputation'.[31] The first reported case striking down a blasphemy provision as incompatible with the First Amendment is *State of Maryland v West*,[32] decided by the Court of Special Appeals of Maryland in 1970. The state law at issue provided:

> If any person, by writing or speaking, shall blaspheme or curse God, or shall write or utter any profane words of and concerning our Saviour Jesus Christ, or of and concerning the Trinity, or any of the persons thereof, he shall on conviction be fined not more than one hundred dollars, or imprisoned not more than six months, or both fined and imprisoned as aforesaid, at the discretion of the court.

The court's analysis focused on the purpose of the statute. It was held that its purpose was 'to protect and preserve and perpetuate the Christian religion' and 'extend [to Christians] the aid comfort and support of the State'.[33] Given the wording of the statute and its historical origins, the court noted, it was impossible to read into it a secular purpose such as 'prevention of violence or breaches of the public peace' or protecting everyone's right to worship their God 'unmolested'.[34] Thus, the court held the law to be unconstitutional under the Religion Clauses of the First Amendment because it created this special link between the authority of the legal system and a specific religion by punishing

[29] *R v Ramsay and Foote* (1883) 15 Cox CC 231, 238 cited in Sandberg and Doe, 'The Strange Death of Blasphemy' (n 3) 973.

[30] Note, 'Blasphemy' (n 17) 704 ff.

[31] *Robertson v Baldwin* 165 US 275, 281 (1897). This was a habeas corpus case and the statement about blasphemy was made in the context of the discussion of the effect of the Bill of Rights. The Supreme Court found that the Bill of Rights embodied guarantees of freedom inherited from English law together with the recognized exceptions. The Court mentioned blasphemous articles as an example of such an exception to freedom of speech.

[32] 9 Md App 270 (1970).

[33] ibid 276.

[34] ibid 275–76.

sacrilegious speech only against Christianity, without discussing whether the free speech clause was also violated.

Robert Post has described the blasphemy offence as an example of assimilationist law. Such laws 'place the authority of legal sanctions behind the cultural perspectives of a dominant group'.[35] While in societies with a high degree of homogeneity assimilationist laws can be seen as an expression of generally accepted norms, where there is cultural heterogeneity they are a way to 'extend the values of a dominant group to a larger society'.[36] The offence of blasphemy was assimilationist in character both in its original form, with the focus being on the protection of the established order, and after it had been transformed into a mechanism of protection from offence and insult caused by profane speech. What changed is the social group whose values blasphemy imposed on society. Originally, the group was 'Christians holding allegiance to certain theological and doctrinal propositions' while later it was 'Christians holding allegiance to "the decencies of controversy" '.[37]

Transforming the aim of blasphemy meant that it was possible to dissent from the truth of the dominant religion provided that the manner of expression did not violate accepted standards of decency. The House of Lords explored in detail the reshaped blasphemy offence in *Bowman v Secular Society*,[38] a 1917 case concerning the question whether a legacy left to the Secular Society, whose aim was to promote secular beliefs among the citizens and the secularization of the state and, thus, was contrary to Christianity, could be enforced in English law. There was agreement among the judges that attack and denial of the doctrines of Christianity did not constitute blasphemy. Lord Sumner went further and stated that blasphemy had always had less to do with disrespect of God and more with the maintenance of social order. Since society's moral code, standards of conduct, and willingness to tolerate difference change, the crime of blasphemy evolves accordingly. The law punished the publication of blasphemous statements for

> their tendency to endanger the peace then and there, to deprave public morality generally, to shake the fabric of society, and to be a cause of civil strife. The words, as well as the acts, which tend to endanger society differ from time to time in proportion as society is stable or insecure in fact, or is believed by its reasonable members to be open to assault. In the present day meetings

[35] Post, 'Cultural Heterogeneity and the Law' (n 5) 299.
[36] ibid 300.
[37] ibid 309.
[38] [1917] AC 406.

> or processions are held lawful which a hundred and fifty years ago would have been deemed seditious, and this is not because the law is weaker or has changed, but because, the times having changed, society is stronger than before. In the present day *reasonable* men do not apprehend the dissolution or the downfall of society because religion is publicly assailed by methods not scandalous.[39]

It is, then, the reasonable person, this omnipresent and omniscient figure so often relied on by the law, who has changed. In 1917, there were, no doubt, many devout Christians who were offended by secularist ideas and considered them a threat to stability and order but their views were irrelevant for the definition of the crime of blasphemy. The approach remained assimilationist but the reasonable person was now the tolerant Christian who would not be scandalized by criticism or denial of the validity of his beliefs if it was expressed in sober language. Thus, whether the focus is on public order concerns or the insult inflicted on the believers, the determining factor is the manner of expression, and the standard endorsed by the law and applied uniformly across society is that of a subsection of the members of the dominant religion.

Expanding The Blasphemy Offence

This is the basis of one of the fundamental criticisms against blasphemy laws: they are underinclusive. They prohibit some sacrilegious communications but leave other similar speech unregulated because they are partial to the requirements of a particular religious doctrine, usually that of the majority of citizens. The force of law is used to shield the dominant religious group from aggressive criticism and sacrilegious speech, while minority and non-traditional groups are not accorded the same protection when their faith is attacked or ridiculed and the feelings of their adherents insulted.

A way of meeting that criticism is to argue for a general, across-the-board regulation of speech which is not linked to any particular religious group or faith. In international human rights law, the proposals for the adoption of measures to counter defamation of religion are examples of how such regulation might look. While the first draft resolution introduced before the United Nations Human Rights Commission in 1999 covered only the defamation of

[39] ibid 466–67 (emphasis added).

Islam,[40] a later draft extended the protection to all religions and was finally adopted by the Commission under the title 'Defamation of Religions'.[41] In subsequent years, several United Nations documents mentioned the term and, following the publication of the Danish cartoons in 2005, Muslim states campaigned vigorously for the adoption of a legally binding instrument.[42] Their efforts were resisted by Western states which were concerned about the effect on free speech, while a group of experts appointed to examine the need for additional international standards on the prevention of intolerance and racial discrimination concluded that 'religious intolerance combined with racial and xenophobic prejudices is adequately covered under international human rights instruments'.[43] A consensus was reached in 2011 and the Human Rights Council adopted Resolution 16/18 on combating religious intolerance and stigmatization without mentioning defamation of religion but without rejecting the concept explicitly either.[44] Similar resolutions on this issue were adopted in later years, the most recent one in 2015.[45]

At the level of national legal systems, blasphemy laws of various types are commonplace. A 2017 study by the US Commission on International Religious Freedom found that seventy-one countries around the world maintain blasphemy legislation.[46] In the West, examples include Austria, Germany, Italy,

[40] Commission on Human Rights Draft Resolution on Racism, 'Racial Discrimination, Xenophobia and All Forms of Discrimination' UN Doc E/CN.4/1999/L.40 (20 April 1999).

[41] Commission on Human Rights, Resolution 1999/82, UN Doc E/CN.4/Res/1999/82 (30 April 1999). For an argument that post-1999 Organisation of Islamic Cooperation Resolutions which emphasize the need to protect Islam demonstrate that the inclusive definition of 'defamation of religion' was a pragmatic move to reach consensus rather than a genuine attempt to protect all religions from insults see Robert C Blitt, 'The Bottom-Up Journey of "Defamation of Religion" from Muslim States to the United Nations: A Case Study of the Migration of Anti-Constitutional Ideas' (2011) 56 Studies in Law, Politics and Society, Special Issue Human Rights: New Possibilities/New Problems 121.

[42] It is beyond the scope of this book to provide a complete account of the defamation of religion saga. Useful discussions can be found in Lorenz Langer, *Religious Offence and Human Rights: The Implications of Defamation of Religions* (Cambridge University Press 2016); Robert C Blitt, 'Defamation of Religion: Rumors of Its Death Are Greatly Exaggerated' (2011) 62 Case Western Reserve Law Review 347; Marshall and Shea, *Silenced* (n 1).

[43] Human Rights Council, Intergovernmental Working Group On The Effective Implementation Of The Durban Declaration and Programme of Action, Complementary International Standards, UN Document A/HRC/4/WG.3/6 (27 August 2007) para. 130.

[44] Human Rights Council, Resolution 16/18 Combating Intolerance, Negative Stereotyping and Stigmatization Of, and Discrimination, Incitement To Violence and Violence Against, Persons Based On Religion or Belief, UN Document A/HRC/RES/16/18 (12 April 2011). Even after the adoption of the resolution member states of the Organisation of Islamic Cooperation argued that defamation of religions remained a valid concept in international human rights law and continued to call upon states to criminalize defamation of Islam. See the discussion in Blitt, 'Defamation of Religion' (n 42) 365–72.

[45] Human Rights Council Resolution 28/29, 'Combating intolerance, negative stereotyping and stigmatization of, and discrimination, incitement to violence and violence against, persons based on religion or belief' UN Document A/HRC/28/RES/29 (30 April 2015).

[46] US Commission on International Religious Freedom, Respecting Rights? Measuring the World's Blasphemy Laws (2017).

Switzerland, Spain, Denmark, Finland, Israel, Greece, New Zealand, and Canada. The common feature of those provisions is that they do not make reference to a specific religious dogma but protect all beliefs from insult and vilification, with Germany also protecting ideological and philosophical doctrines and Spain also criminalizing the disparagement of atheists and agnostics. While the frequency of enforcement varies considerably, there are recent cases which show the continuing relevance of blasphemy. For example, Irish police initiated an investigation against the actor Stephen Fry for making very critical comments about God in a television show in 2015 but no criminal charges were brought because not enough people were outraged by his comments.[47] Moreover, as discussed in Chapter 4, the European Court of Human Rights (ECtHR) has recently affirmed the criminal conviction of an Austrian citizen who had made disparaging remarks about the Prophet Muhammad.[48]

This new breed of inclusive blasphemy provisions in national legal systems do not protect only the established or majority religion. All religious faiths and religious communities are placed on an equal footing and, at least on its face, the law provides them with an equal claim to protection from ridicule and insult. I shall refer to this type of prohibition of speech as a 'general blasphemy law', as opposed to a blasphemy law which protects only one religious group or faith (or a limited number of faiths). The rest of this chapter explores the possible objections to general blasphemy laws.

General Blasphemy Laws: Vagueness and Enforcement

The first objection to general blasphemy laws is that they are usually worded in a way which does not specify with enough clarity what expression is prohibited or under what conditions the offence can occur. Legislators use concepts such as mockery, vilification, disparagement, and insult which are too vague to provide a clear standard of conduct. Moreover, since all religions engage in some criticism of other religions, which their adherents may find offensive or disparaging, the law needs to incorporate a seriousness, or another, similar, requirement, and prohibit only serious offence, otherwise there will be no room

47 Fiona Gartland, 'Stephen Fry will Not Be Prosecuted for Blasphemy' *Irish Times* (8 May 2017) https://www.irishtimes.com/news/crime-and-law/stephen-fry-will-not-be-prosecuted-for-blasphemy-1.3075938. Following a 2018 referendum which approved the amendment of the constitutional provision proscribing blasphemy, Ireland repealed its blasphemy law in 2019: Blasphemy (Abolition of Offences and Related Matters) Act 2019.

48 *ES v Austria* (2019) 69 EHRR 4.

for religious teaching and canvassing. Consider the example of the preacher who says that all those who do not subscribe to his religion are infidels or heretics who will burn in hell. Clearly, some listeners will find this unacceptable but is the statement disparaging or insulting enough to trigger the speaker's criminal prosecution? Coming up with an acceptable test and providing criteria and guidance to make the law predictable and certain is very difficult. As the US Commission on International Religious Freedom noted in its report, most blasphemy laws lack precision and do not satisfy the requirements of the principle of legality.

While vagueness and uncertainty are evils which should be avoided whenever a law interferes with citizens' liberty to conduct their lives as they choose, they are particularly problematic where the activity restricted is speech because of the potential chilling effect. When faced with a vague statute affecting free expression, individuals will probably prefer to play safe and avoid conduct which may be considered unlawful. In American constitutional jurisprudence a statute is void on vagueness grounds if 'it either forbids or requires the doing of an act in terms so vague that men of common intelligence must necessarily guess at its meaning and differ as to its application';[49] such a statute 'violates the first essential of due process of law'.[50] Procedural due process underpins the vagueness doctrine in that it requires the law to be drafted in terms which are clear and precise enough to allow citizens to understand its meaning and act accordingly. In essence, the law must provide 'sufficiently definite warning as to the proscribed conduct when measured by common understanding and practices'.[51]

The US Supreme Court has held that judicial scrutiny of allegedly vague provisions in First Amendment cases is stricter than in other contexts. In *Smith v Goguen*[52] it dealt with a Massachusetts flag-misuse statute which provided that 'whoever publicly mutilates, tramples upon, defaces or treats contemptuously the flag of the United States ... whether such flag is public or private property ... shall be punished by a fine of not less than ten nor more than one hundred dollars or by imprisonment for not more than one year, or both ...'.[53] When the defendant was charged with publicly treating the flag contemptuously because he wore a small cloth version of it sewn to the seat of his trousers he argued that the words 'treats contemptuously' were impermissibly vague.

[49] *Connally v General Construction* Co 269 US 385, 391 (1926).
[50] ibid.
[51] *Jordan v De George* 341 US 223 (1951).
[52] 415 US 566 (1974).
[53] ibid 568.

The Court agreed, observing that the casual use of the flag was a widespread phenomenon and that the state legislature had failed to draw a clear line between uses which were criminal and those which were not. In relation to the required standard of predictability it held that 'where a statute's literal scope, unaided by a narrowing state court interpretation, is capable of reaching expression sheltered by the First Amendment, the doctrine demands a *greater degree of specificity than in other contexts*'.[54] The Court's concern is with the danger posed for protected expressive activities by vague laws which, by failing to specify which acts are prohibited, lead citizens to be overcautious.

The idea was also explored in an earlier case, *Baggett v Bullitt*,[55] where the Court, in striking down as facially invalid two statutes which required teachers and other state employees to give a loyalty oath indicating that they were not involved in 'subversive activities', noted:

> We are dealing with indefinite statutes whose terms, even narrowly construed, abut upon sensitive areas of basic First Amendment freedoms. The uncertain meanings of the oaths require the oath-taker-teachers and public servants-to 'steer far wider of the unlawful zone' than if the boundaries of the forbidden areas were clearly marked. Those with a conscientious regard for what they solemnly swear or affirm, sensitive to the perils posed by the oath's indefinite language, avoid the risk of loss of employment, and perhaps profession, only by restricting their conduct to that which is unquestionably safe. Free speech may not be so inhibited.[56]

The concern with the chilling effect of vague provisions restricting speech explains why such provisions are usually declared invalid on their face: their pernicious effect is not limited to a specific unconstitutional application to a specific defendant but undermines a constitutionally protected liberty in general.

In the context of the European Convention on Human Rights, the elements of predictability and certainty are embodied in the requirement that any interference with a qualified right guaranteed in Articles 8 to 11 of the Convention be 'prescribed by law'[57] or 'in accordance with the law';[58] their architecture is

[54] ibid 573 (emphasis added). The Court, citing *United States v National Dairy Products Corp* 372 US 29 (1963), mentioned economic regulation as an example of an area where vagueness standards are less stringent than in First Amendment law.

[55] 377 US 360 (1964).

[56] ibid 372 (internal citation omitted).

[57] Articles 9 (freedom of religion), 10 (freedom of expression), and 11 (freedom of assembly). Article 1 of Protocol 1 (right to property) also states that an individual may be deprived of his possessions 'in the public interest and subject to the conditions provided for by the law'.

[58] Article 8 (private and family life).

identical, with a first paragraph spelling out what the protected right is, and a second containing an exhaustive list of grounds which may be relied upon by the state to limit it. It is in the second paragraph of those provisions that the Convention refers to the 'prescribed by law' requirement, thus making legal certainty a condition for the legality of the state's interference with a protected right.

The ECtHR explained the substantive content of the rule in *Sunday Times v United Kingdom*:[59]

> First, the law must be adequately accessible: the citizen must be able to have an indication, that is adequate in the circumstances, of the legal rules applicable to a given case. Secondly, a norm cannot be regarded as a 'law' unless it is formulated with sufficient precision to enable the citizen to regulate his conduct: he must be able—if need be with appropriate advice—to foresee, to a degree that is reasonable in the circumstances, the consequences which a given action may entail.

The ECtHR's scrutiny goes beyond the question of the mere existence of a legal rule authorizing the interference with a right guaranteed by the Convention. It is a qualitative test where the Court assesses the formulation and substance of the rule to ascertain that it gives adequate notice as to what is expected of citizens. The position was further clarified in *Malone v United Kingdom*:[60] 'in accordance with the law' does not merely refer back to domestic law but also relates to the quality of the law, requiring it to be compatible with the rule of law, which is expressly mentioned in the preamble to the Convention'. Predictability is, thus, a requirement of the rule of law which underpins the European human rights system as a whole.

In a liberal democracy, a general prohibition of religiously offensive speech needs to satisfy standards of certainty and predictability similar to those developed by the US Supreme Court and the ECtHR. This is a considerable challenge for legislators, prosecutors, and judges as blasphemy provisions need, at the same time, to remain open-ended so as to ensure genuine inclusiveness and protect all faiths and religious groups. For each group there will be different religious figures or doctrines considered particularly important and, therefore, requiring protection, and the law must provide guidance as to how far criticism and satire of those figures and doctrines can go before becoming unlawful

[59] (1979) 2 EHRR 245 para 49. See also *Silver v United Kingdom* (1983) 5 EHRR 347.
[60] (1984) 7 EHRR 14 para 67.

speech. The very broad wordings mentioned earlier in this chapter are inadequate because they do not include any standard whatsoever for speakers to rely on.

A second argument against a general blasphemy law is that it cannot be applied in a non-discriminatory manner. Even if it is drafted in neutral terms which can, in theory, protect all religions equally, it will be easier for large, mainstream religious groups to benefit from it because they are more powerful politically and can exercise pressure on those responsible for its application. On the contrary, offensive speech against small or non-traditional religions is unlikely to be curtailed because administrative agencies and prosecutors either do not feel pressure to take action, or the offensive communications come from mainstream religions, which usually view the newcomers with suspicion and hostility. In that scenario we have the worst of both worlds: traditional religions can use the law to silence their critics and can attack non-traditional ones with impunity.

The problem of unequal enforcement is exemplified by the first ever religious freedom case decided by the ECtHR under Article 9 of the Convention, which concerned another type of religious speech, canvassing and proselytism. In *Kokkinakis v Greece*[61] the ECtHR assessed a national law which prohibited 'improper' proselytism in neutral terms,[62] without reference to a specific religious group. In theory, it protected all religions and could have been applied against any person engaging in the conduct prohibited by the statute irrespective of his religion or the religion of the person he was trying to convert. In reality, it was systematically used to persecute religious minorities, and mainly Jehovah's Witnesses.[63] The government was unable to refer the Court to even a single prosecution for proselytism directed against members of minority groups or to cases where members of the dominant Christian Orthodox church were prosecuted for trying to convert members of other faiths. While the text of the law was facially neutral towards all religious groups, the history of its application showed that it was used exclusively to restrict the religious expression of

[61] (1994) 17 EHRR 397.

[62] The criminal offence of proselytism was defined as 'any attempt to intrude on the religious beliefs of a person of a different religious persuasion, with the aim of undermining those beliefs, either by any kind of inducement or promise of an inducement or moral support or material assistance, or by fraudulent means or by taking advantage of his inexperience, trust, need, low intellect or naivety': *Kokkinakis* (n 61) 404.

[63] The applicant in *Kokkinakis* provided the following data which was not disputed by the government: between 1975 and 1992 there were 4,400 arrests of Jehovah's Witnesses for proselytism; 1,233 of them were committed for trial and 208 were convicted: *Kokkinakis* (n 61) 399, 406.

minorities.[64] Thus, textual neutrality cannot as such address concerns about discriminatory enforcement.

A further example which demonstrates that the political power of religious groups is a major factor affecting the way their members are treated by the state are religious exemptions from neutral laws. For example, during the Prohibition, Congress exempted by statute the sacramental use of wine in Catholic and Protestant services. More recently, the differential treatment of mainstream and non-traditional religions was a central issue in *Employment Division Department of Human Resources of Oregon v Smith*,[65] one of the most important religious freedom cases in American constitutional jurisprudence. The case concerned the dismissal of a member of the Native American Church because he had ingested peyote at a religious ceremony. Peyote was prohibited by Oregon state law and, thus, the claimant was denied unemployment benefits because he was dismissed for work-related criminal conduct. Earlier Supreme Court case law had established the principle that where a neutral law burdens religion the government should grant an exception unless it can show that the law pursues a compelling state interest which cannot be served by less restrictive means.[66] In *Smith*, the Supreme Court changed course and, in a majority opinion by Justice Scalia, held that if the burden on religion is 'the incidental effect of a generally applicable and otherwise valid provision',[67] the Constitution did not mandate an exemption for believers.

Justice Scalia was not hostile to all religious exemptions as such. His point was that while they are not constitutionally required they are constitutionally permitted and, sometimes, even desirable, but they should be granted by the legislature, not by the courts. The problem with this view is that the political process tends to favour the interests of majority groups which are better placed to make their views heard in public debate and apply pressure on the executive and the legislature. Actually, Justice Scalia conceded that minority and non-traditional religions will be placed 'at a relative disadvantage' as their ability to lobby the authorities is limited, but he thought that this was 'an unavoidable consequence of democratic government'.[68] *Smith* is an example of such a disadvantage: Oregon had exempted the religious use of wine in localities where the

[64] For a discussion of neutrality in relation to proselytism and canvassing see Nicholas Hatzis, 'Neutrality Proselytism and Religious Minorities at the European Court of Human Rights and the US Supreme Court' (2009) 49 Harvard International Law Journal online 120.

[65] 494 US 872 (1990).

[66] Starting in *Sherbert v Verner* 374 US 398 (1963).

[67] *Employment Division, Department of Human Resources of Oregon v Smith* 494 US 872, 878 (1990).

[68] ibid 890.

use of alcohol was prohibited without providing a similar exemption for peyote in religious ceremonies of Native Americans.[69]

The two arguments considered in this section—vagueness and discriminatory enforcement—are separate but related, and mutually supportive. One of the effects of a vague statute is that the officials tasked with its application end up having impermissibly broad discretion which, in turn, gives rise to the danger of selective and arbitrary enforcement of the law.[70] The link between imprecise laws which restrict speech and arbitrary application has been emphasized by both the UN Human Rights Committee[71] and the US Supreme Court. The latter discussed the issue in *Smith v Goguen*, the Massachusetts flag-misuse statute case:

> We recognize that in a noncommercial context behavior as a general rule is not mapped out in advance on the basis of statutory language. In such cases, perhaps the most meaningful aspect of the vagueness doctrine is not actual notice, but the other principal element of the doctrine-the requirement that a legislature establish minimal guidelines to govern law enforcement. It is in this regard that the statutory language under scrutiny has its most notable deficiencies.[72]

The current state of the law was summarized in *Hill v Colorado*, where it was held that a statute is void on vagueness grounds if 'it fails to provide people of ordinary intelligence a reasonable opportunity to understand what conduct it prohibits' or where it 'authorizes or even encourages arbitrary and selective enforcement'.[73] Therefore, either lack of adequate notice or the danger of selective

[69] This differential treatment led Christopher Eisgruber and Lawrence Sager, who otherwise agreed with the conclusion that religious freedom does not imply a constitutional right to be exempted from neutral laws, to criticize the *Smith* Court for failing to ensure equal religious liberty for all citizens: Christopher L Eisgruber and Lawrence G Sager, *Religious Freedom and the Constitution* (Harvard University Press 2007) 95–96.

[70] For the development of the arbitrariness rationale in American law see Andrew E Goldsmith, 'The Void-for-Vagueness Doctrine in the Supreme Court, Revisited' (2002) 30 American Journal of Criminal Law 280, 286. A related point is that by banning selective enforcement of vague statutes courts maintain the separation of the executive from the legislature. See *Grayned v City of Rockford* 408 US 104, 108–109 (1972): 'A vague law impermissibly delegates basic policy matters to policemen, judges, and juries for resolution on an ad hoc and subjective basis, with the attendant dangers of arbitrary and discriminatory application' (citation omitted).

[71] United Nations Human Rights Committee General Comment 34, 'Article 19 Freedom of Opinion and Expression' UN Doc CCPR/C/GC/34 (12 September 2011) para 25.

[72] 415 US 566, 574 (1974). See also *Papachristou v City of Jacksonville* 405 US 156 (1972); *Kolender v Lawson* 461 US 352 (1983).

[73] 530 US 703, 732 (2000).

enforcement are sufficient reasons for declaring a statute unconstitutional on its face.

The dangers posed by vague standards and unequal enforcement are real and serious and would probably be enough to justify rejecting a general blasphemy law because of its potential to become an instrument of perpetuating the hegemony of mainstream groups. Still, those concerns aside, can a general blasphemy law be sustained in a legal system which adequately protects freedom of expression? Put differently, are there any intrinsic free speech objections whose force does not depend on arguments about drafting and application? To answer this question I will assume the existence of a law which is clear enough to satisfy the standards of predictability discussed above and a benign government which genuinely intends, and is able, to apply it even-handedly. In the following section I argue that such a law is incompatible with freedom of expression.

General Blasphemy Laws: Free Speech

Civility Norms

The objections against banning offensive speech discussed in previous chapters apply with equal force to general blasphemy laws. The argument for suppressing sacrilegious speech is based on the thesis that the legal right to freedom of expression, properly interpreted, protects criticism of religion which is expressed in a temperate and respectful manner but not communications which amount to 'particularly offensive statement[s] of contempt'.[74] It has been suggested that examples falling into the latter category include opinions 'hostile to religious beliefs … expressed with grossly disparaging character, form and circumstances', the use of 'evil swearwords', the 'sexualized presentation of religious content', and the 'shameless exaggeration in the assessment of a criticisable behaviour of a religious community'.[75] This approach to religious speech has been described by Jeremy Waldron as two-dimensional toleration: 'criticism and discussion between rival faiths is fine and unavoidable but two-dimensional toleration insists that it must be serious, earnest and respectful in character'.[76] Its basis is a reciprocal obligation; religious communities should tolerate

[74] Christian Hillgruber, 'Legal Limits of a Permissible Criticism of Religion' (2016) 17 German Law Journal 266, 272.

[75] ibid 273.

[76] Jeremy Waldron, 'Rushdie and Religion' in Jeremy Waldron (ed), *Liberal Rights: Collected Papers 1981-1991* (Oxford University Press 1993) 138.

criticism and critics should show respect to the religious beliefs or practices they criticize. Thus, the criterion for the constitutional protection of religious speech is the manner of expression, which, as we have seen, was the test applied under the traditional blasphemy laws which protected the majority religion.

Proponents of blasphemy laws are right to draw our attention to the importance of civility. Civility is a moral virtue and, under certain circumstances, can ground obligations to treat others in a certain way.[77] The problem is to extrapolate from this fact a rule that offensive religious speech should be subject to criminal prosecution. This view assumes that there is a clear distinction between the substance of public discourse about religion and the structure within which this discourse takes place. The former is protected by constitutional provisions on freedom of expression so speakers are entitled to communicate whatever substantive opinions they have on religion. By contrast, the way those opinions are expressed is subject to governmental regulation on the basis of certain civility norms which exclude modes of communication deemed to be 'particularly offensive'. Participants in public debate are not entitled to challenge such norms and if they transgress them they place themselves beyond the boundaries of the acceptable and should be subjected to criminal punishment.

However, 'there is nothing necessarily privileged about the norms of civility that we call moral seriousness'.[78] Assertions about how public debate should be conducted, what words and expressions are acceptable, which standards of propriety should be enforced are themselves part of the debate. Different people will have sometimes radically different ideas about what propriety requires and which communications meet those requirements because their moral viewpoints and their understandings of the ethical life differ. There exists no Archimedean point, situated outside public discourse, from which to assess how the discussion about any topic, including religion, should take place. The structure itself of public debate is part of what needs to be debated, challenged, and interpreted. Thus, there is no neutral, value-free distinction between the substance of the opinion and the manner the speaker chooses to express it.

The claim that the government should censor 'particularly offensive'[79] speech and punish blasphemers relies on a value judgment about what the moral outlook of the community should be and seeks to use the coercive force of criminal law to impose it on its member. It is not a neutral identification of

[77] Cheshire Calhoun, 'The Virtue of Civility' (2000) 29 Philosophy and Public Affairs 251.
[78] Waldron, 'Rushdie and Religion' (n 76) 139.
[79] Hillgruber, 'Legal Limits of a Permissible Criticism of Religion' (n 74) 274.

a prior set of commonly accepted rules on how to speak in public but one of the many viewpoints about the manner in which the collective formation of public opinion on religion should happen. What counts as abusive, offensive, insulting, sacrilegious or blasphemous is religiously determined; it will depend on each religious group's theological doctrine, history and willingness to tolerate criticism. What one religion might consider acceptable or tolerable, the other might find to be outrageously offensive and worthy of suppression. Even within the same religion, different groups can have disagreements about what their religion requires and what constitutes tolerable as opposed to outrageous criticism. Contributing those competing viewpoints to public debate is part of the ongoing political contest for the shaping of the character of the community.

Blasphemy as Pluralist Law

If the civility norms on which proponents of blasphemy laws rely are value laden, the question which arises is how this is relevant for assessing restrictions on religious speech in pluralist societies. Consider the judgment of Lord Scarman in *R v Lemon*,[80] the last successful prosecution for blasphemy in England. The case was about a poem published in the magazine *Gay News* which described homosexual erotic acts with the body of Christ after his death. The House of Lords upheld the conviction of the editor of the magazine, rejecting an argument that the common law offence of blasphemy required the showing of an intent to blaspheme: since its aim was 'to protect religious feelings from outrage and insult',[81] where the language used by the speaker was offensive, his intent was irrelevant. Lord Scarman started his judgment by calling for the extension by Parliament of common law blasphemy so as to protect all religious faiths:

> My Lords, I do not subscribe to the view that the common law offence of blasphemous libel serves no useful purpose in the modern law. On the contrary, I think that there is a case for legislation extending it to protect the religious beliefs and feelings of non-Christians. The offence belongs to a group of criminal offences designed to safeguard the internal tranquillity of the kingdom. In an increasingly plural society such as that of modern Britain it is necessary not only to respect the differing religious beliefs, feelings and practices

[80] [1979] AC 617.
[81] ibid 658.

> of all but also to protect them from scurrility, vilification, ridicule and contempt … When Macaulay became a legislator in India, he saw to it that the law protected the religious feelings of all. In those days India was a plural society: today the United Kingdom is also. I have permitted myself these general observations at the outset of my opinion because, my Lords, they determine my approach to this appeal. I will not lend my voice to a view of the law relating to blasphemous libel which would render it a dead letter, or diminish its efficacy to protect religious feeling from outrage and insult. My criticism of the common law offence of blasphemy is not that it exists but that it is not sufficiently comprehensive. It is shackled by the chains of history.[82]

Lord Scarman was suggesting the adoption of a general, inclusive blasphemy law. His reason was that the United Kingdom in the late 1970s had become a pluralist country, making it necessary to establish a framework that would allow different faiths to co-exist in a climate of mutual respect which could ensure societal peace. He placed blasphemy in the context of laws 'designed to safeguard the internal tranquillity of the kingdom'[83]: the implied assumption is that when citizens' religious feelings are offended by sacrilegious speech, the tensions that arise might undermine social order. Therefore, in political communities with a multitude of religions, it is inappropriate to reserve the protection of the law to only one of them, even if this is the faith of the majority of citizens and enjoys, for historical reasons, a special status in the legal system; protection from offence to religious sensitivities should become free from the 'chains of history' and develop according to contemporary pluralistic standards so as to alleviate the strain put on society by the inevitable differences between the way different religious groups perceive of the Divine and of themselves. Lord Scarman's ideas, with their emphasis on religious feelings and the need for comprehensive coverage of all religious groups, are a major element in the intellectual pedigree of the arguments developed by contemporary proponents of defamation of religion statutes.[84]

[82] ibid 658.

[83] ibid.

[84] Lord Scarman later changed his view about the desirability of maintaining and expanding the blasphemy offence. In a letter to *The Daily Telegraph* on 14 April 1990 he wrote: 'I suggest the way of reform is now plain to see: abolish blasphemy but strengthen the law … by including words of insult or abuse against another's religion as an offence under … the Public Order Act 1986 if the words are likely to provoke violence or public disorder.' After referring to his judgment in *Lemon* (n 80), he continued: 'On further reflection I agree with the Law Commission that [the extension of the blasphemy offence] is neither desirable nor possible. Such an extension would result in uncertainty (How many religions? What is religion?) and would lead to further restriction upon freedom of expression. In a plural society pledged to the protection of human rights the only acceptable restriction is if the insult is likely to provoke violence or public disorder. Let us consign blasphemy to the legal historian and concentrate on

To return to Robert Post's description of blasphemy as an assimilationist law, the general blasphemy offence advocated by Lord Scarman could be seen as an effort to re-establish it on a pluralist basis.[85] Pluralist law 'attempts to create ground rules by which diverse and potentially competitive groups can retain their distinct identities and yet continue to co-exist'.[86] Lord Scarman was proposing such a pluralistic ground rule which would provide that all religious groups enjoy the same level of protection from profanity and insult. Instead of structuring the blasphemy offence around the cultural values of the majority religion, a general blasphemy law embraces in an equal manner the distinct values of different religious groups and thus facilitates their peaceful and orderly coexistence.

A first criticism of this view is that the inclusive, pluralist model appears to presuppose a common metric of insult which can be applied to all cases of religiously offensive speech regardless of the faith involved. But, inevitably, that metric will reflect the dominant understanding of blasphemy—how far criticism, humour and satire can go, when the limits of 'decency' have been exhausted—an understanding shaped by the fact that the reasonable person relied on by the law when the blasphemy offence was transformed was the tolerant Christian who could put up with criticism of his faith if it was expressed in moderate language. This is the standard underlying the common metric and it is very doubtful whether all religious faiths which are currently present in Western societies share it; if courts were to apply it on all cases of religious offence, as Lord Scarman suggests, they would be imposing what is, in essence, an assimilationist rule.[87] Put differently, it is very difficult to disentangle the pluralistic model of the general blasphemy law which protects all religions from its assimilationist baggage.

public order', cited in Clive Unsworth, 'Blasphemy, Cultural Divergence and Legal Relativism' (1995) 58 Modern Law Review 658, 673–74. Thus Lord Scarman moves away from the protection of religious sensitivities as the reason justifying censorship and focuses exclusively on public order concerns. Under his revised standard, only communications likely to lead to violence can be prohibited. However, four years later, in correspondence with the legal academic Clive Unsworth, he reverted to his *Lemon* position: 'I continue to believe that the law should protect from insult the religious beliefs of the people. Why? The obvious point that such insults can provoke public disorder is not a sufficient answer-though it is important. The true reason is respect for other people's *bona fide* religious beliefs. Religious freedom is a human right. Interference with it is not to be tolerated', cited in Unsworth (n 84) 674. Here the concern is again about religious feelings and this time freedom of religion is used as a justification, with the right not to be insulted being seen as part of it. As we saw in ch 3 this is the justification that the European Court of Human Rights has relied upon to uphold the censorship of religiously offensive speech.

[85] Post, 'Cultural Heterogeneity and the Law' (n 5) 313.
[86] ibid 302.
[87] ibid.

Secondly, the justification for a general blasphemy law relied on by Lord Scarman and contemporary advocates of 'defamation of religion' statutes is based to a considerable extent on instrumental considerations. Silencing blasphemers is seen as a way to ensure if not harmony, at least some form of peaceful coexistence and mutual understanding in societies with a variety of religions. The problem with grounding a curtailment of individual freedom to a supposed good it will produce for society is that if the intended result is not achieved, there is no reason to continue supporting the regulation. Thus, if consistent and inclusive censorship of all religiously offensive speech fails, for whatever reason, to ensure 'internal tranquillity'[88] the justification for it collapses.[89]

A third, and probably more important objection, is that a general blasphemy law, although inclusive and protective of different religious beliefs, excludes from public discourse individuals who have non-religious or anti-religious outlooks and wish to challenge certain forms of religiosity, or the idea of religious commitment altogether. The argument that they can do so in a moderate manner, so as to avoid causing outrage and insult, is not convincing. As discussed in Chapter 4, the style of expression and the language used by the speaker are inextricably linked to the content of speech. It is certainly possible to communicate one's views politely and inoffensively, in ways which the average listener finds tolerable, but it should also be permissible to use humour, satire, irony, sarcasm, mockery, provocation or ridicule. Some of the powers ideas have lies in the means in which they are expressed. Therefore when the government is using its coercive power to proscribe words, the space available for ideas to be expressed and thinking to take place is diminished. The fact that the speaker chooses a certain mode of communication because she thinks it is the best way to express her views and get her message across is relevant for assessing the moral cost of censorship.

This is not meant to deny the importance of religious viewpoints for human affairs. It is precisely because religions address some of the most fundamental questions about what it means to be human that we should adopt, as Waldron suggests, a 'three-dimensional toleration'[90] which allows people to use all expressive means they have at their disposal for engaging with them. Religious

[88] *R v Lemon* (n 80) 658.

[89] As Jerome Neu, *Sticks and Stones: The Philosophy of Insults* (Oxford University Press 2008) 199–200 notes Macaulay's even-handed Indian legislation protecting all religions (which Lord Scarman in *Lemon* (n 80) considered as a model pluralistic ground rule) did not prevent the expression of hatred and violence between Hindus and Muslims.

[90] Waldron, 'Rushdie and Religion' (n 76) 140.

contributions are valuable because they 'go out into the world ... as public property, as part of the cultural and psychological furniture which we cannot respectfully tiptoe around';[91] they become available to everyone, including those who do not have a religious outlook or are decidedly anti-religious; and the different responses to religious claims, even when provocative or insulting, get to be part of how such claims function in public debate. In fact, those who view religious arguments favourably and wish to see them play a greater role in the formation of collective identity should be particularly worried about modern blasphemy laws. If prosecutors were to apply them seriously to all instances of provocative religious speech, religious contributions would face the danger of having their vigour and life drained out of them, of becoming museum pieces, suitable only for anodyne discussion or polite debate in academic journals but with limited relevance for exploring the difficult and messy experience that is human life.

Equal Censorship for All

The incompatibility of inclusive blasphemy laws with free speech principles was demonstrated by the US Supreme Court in *Burstyn v Wilson*.[92] The case concerned a First Amendment challenge to the refusal of New York state authorities to license a film for distribution in theatres because it was 'sacrilegious'. 'The Miracle', a 40-minute film by Roberto Rossellini, featured Anna Magnani in the role of a village girl who meets a stranger whom she takes to be St Joseph. While she thinks that he has come to take her to heaven where she will be happy, he gives her wine and the film 'briefly and discreetly' implies that he 'ravishes' her.[93] Sometime later she discovers that she is pregnant. Facing the hostility of the villagers she goes to live alone in a cave. Shortly before her labour she returns to the village and goes into the church where she gives birth to a child. The film ends with a close up to her face while she murmurs 'My son! My love! My flesh!'[94]

The New York statute provided that a film would not be licensed if it was 'obscene, indecent, immoral, inhuman, sacrilegious or ... would tend to corrupt morals or incite to crime'.[95] The state courts had interpreted the statute's

[91] ibid.
[92] 343 US 495 (1952).
[93] ibid 507.
[94] ibid 508.
[95] ibid 497.

proscription of 'sacrilegious' films to mean that 'no religion, as that word is understood by the ordinary, reasonable person, shall be treated with contempt, mockery, scorn and ridicule'.[96] Therefore, while the statute was not a traditional blasphemy prohibition imposed through the criminal law, it had all the characteristics of an inclusive blasphemy law: it was drafted in neutral terms which did not involve reference to a specific religious group or faith and targeted all communications which could cause religious offence because of the manner of expression.

The Supreme Court held that it was this very breadth of the statute which made it incompatible with the First Amendment: a rule of prior restraint was inherently suspect and could pass constitutional muster only in exceptional cases and provided that it was narrowly tailored.

> In seeking to apply the broad and all-inclusive definition of 'sacrilegious' given by the New York courts, the censor is set adrift upon a boundless sea amid a myriad [sic] of conflicting currents of religious views, with no charts but those provided by the most vocal and powerful orthodoxies, New York cannot vest such unlimited restraining control over motion pictures in a censor. Under such a standard the most careful and tolerant censor would find it virtually impossible to avoid favoring one religion over another, and he would be subject to an inevitable tendency to ban the expression of unpopular sentiments sacred to a religious minority.[97]

The concern expressed here is about the danger of unequal enforcement of a law which, although facially neutral and inclusive, is so broad that it cannot provide a discernible standard of conduct. As the Court explained, even a benign and fair censor called upon to apply an inclusive blasphemy law would inevitably tend to favour powerful religious groups.

But, the Court continued, this was not the only problematic aspect of the statute. Citing *Cantwell v Connecticut*, the case about the Jehovah's witness who had verbally attacked Catholicism (discussed in Chapter 4), it held that:

> [F]rom the standpoint of freedom of speech and the press, it is enough to point out that the state has no legitimate interest in protecting any or all religions from views distasteful to them which is sufficient to justify prior

[96] ibid 504. Another formulation adopted by the New York courts to describe the law was that 'all it purports to do is to bar a visual caricature of religious beliefs held sacred by one sect or another'. The term 'sacrilegious' was defined as 'the act of violating or profaning anything sacred': ibid 505.

[97] ibid 504–505.

> restraints upon the expression of those views. It is not the business of government in our nation to suppress real or imagined attacks upon a particular religious doctrine, whether they appear in publications, speeches, or motion pictures.[98]

Thus, the Court rejected the view that distress, annoyance, or anger arising from speech about religion can legitimize state coercion and that there is a corresponding right of believers to be protected from experiencing those mental states. That part of the judgment is of particular significance because the Court makes clear that inclusiveness and equality of application cannot save the law: even if 'all religions' are protected 'from views distasteful to them', censorship cannot survive constitutional scrutiny because in a liberal democracy governments should not be allowed to purify public discourse to make it palatable to those who take offence when what they consider sacred does not command general respect. As we saw in Chapter 4, this reflects an understanding of public discourse as a space where ideas and communities have an equal footing. *Burstyn* belongs to the same intellectual tradition as *Cantwell*, *Cohen*, and the flag desecration cases. Read together they provide a solid justification for the need to curtail state power to dictate the content or style of speech which is acceptable in public discourse. Censorship does not become acceptable merely because it is exercised equally upon every speaker who offends. In Harry Kalven's famous words, the First Amendment provides a 'first great principle of consensus' that 'in America, there is no heresy, no blasphemy'.[99]

Viewpoint Discrimination

One effect of general blasphemy laws which makes their partiality particularly apparent is that they punish references to and uses of religious symbols which are disrespectful or insulting but allow those which are respectful and exalting of those symbols. In American constitutional law, this is viewpoint discrimination which cannot pass First Amendment scrutiny. In *Schacht v United States*[100] the Supreme Court examined the prosecution of an amateur actor who, wearing an army uniform, participated in an anti-war street skit. The prosecution was based on a law which prohibited the wearing of a uniform

[98] ibid 505.
[99] Harry Kalven Jr, *A Worthy Tradition: Freedom of Speech in America* (Harper & Row 1988) 7 (emphasis in the original).
[100] 398 US 58 (1970).

without authority but exempted actors in plays and films provided that 'the portrayal [did] not tend to discredit' the armed forces. In an opinion by Justice Black, the Court reversed the appellant's conviction. It stressed that the effect of the law was to make it 'a crime for an actor wearing a military uniform to say things during his performance critical of the conduct or policies of the Armed Forces'.[101] If, however, he had praised the army while wearing the uniform, no issue would have arisen. Such a rule, Justice Black continued, which 'leaves Americans free to praise the war in Vietnam but can send persons like Schacht to prison for opposing it, cannot survive in a country which has the First Amendment'.[102] The right to free speech, then, includes a right to use, for the purpose of expressing criticism and disagreement, symbols which, for other participants in the public debate, should be treated with respect or veneration. The constitution creates a safe space where a military uniform is imbued with meanings constructed from the intentions of the user/speaker and the cultural environment in which it is being used, without those meanings being relevant for the question whether such communications should be protected by the law. Put differently, free speech norms preclude the use of state coercion for the establishment of a monopoly of interpretation: symbols can have several meanings and can be used by any individual or group to express opposing viewpoints.

A similar struggle between competing meanings of religious symbols is evident in blasphemy cases.[103] The claim that they can only be referred to with reverence implies that believers have a 'sectional monopoly'[104] over the function of and the message communicated by such symbols. Rival uses, which may take the form of humour, satire, criticism, or profanity, challenge the interpretations which religious groups give to them as an expression of their view of the sacred. Thus, blasphemy prohibitions become a weapon in the war of meanings, relied on by believers to fend off what they consider insulting.[105]

The Supreme Court applied the principle from *Schacht* to *Texas v Johnson*, which concerned the burning of the flag.

> We never before have held that the Government may ensure that a symbol be used to express only one view of that symbol or its referents ... We perceive no basis on which to hold that the principle underlying our decision

[101] ibid 62–63.
[102] ibid 64.
[103] Unsworth, 'Blasphemy, Cultural Divergence, and Legal Relativism' (n 84) 674–75.
[104] ibid 675.
[105] ibid 674–75.

> in *Schacht* does not apply to this case. To conclude that the government may permit designated symbols to be used to communicate only a limited set of messages would be to enter territory having no discernible or defensible boundaries. Could the government, on this theory, prohibit the burning of state flags? Of copies of the Presidential seal? Of the Constitution? In evaluating these choices under the First Amendment, how would we decide which symbols were sufficiently special to warrant this unique status? To do so, we would be forced to consult our own political preferences, and impose them on the citizenry, in the very way that the First Amendment forbids us to do.[106]

To *Schacht*'s condemnation of viewpoint discrimination, Justice Brennan adds here a concern about the lack of a constitutionally acceptable determinant of which symbols should enjoy special protection. This applies with even greater force to general blasphemy laws. Who is going to decide which religious figures, symbols, and beliefs are central enough to the respective faiths so as to punish offensive references to them? The task cannot be entrusted to the government or the courts because, first, we have no reason to think that administrative officials and judges are well-placed to analyse and evaluate theological doctrines[107] and, secondly, that practice would undermine the autonomy of religious groups and thus raise serious religious freedom issues.[108] The only workable option would be to leave the designation of the protected symbols to the religious groups themselves. But in that case we would be turning the law into a private mechanism for silencing anybody whose views are distasteful to believers.

It is true that nowadays many people who argue in favour of blasphemy and other similar laws are genuinely willing to extend protection to all religions, and support their enforcement in a truly non-discriminatory manner; this sensitive approach is certainly commendable. Ultimately, however, we should reject even general blasphemy laws because they adopt and embed a certain viewpoint about religion. They allow religious speech which vigorously promotes religiosity and exalts its importance, but such laws suppress competing messages which seek to challenge it with the same vigour. The Supreme Court's statement in *Texas v Johnson* that the state may not 'foster its own view of the

[106] *Texas v Johnson* 491 US 397, 417 (1989).

[107] See *Thomas v Review Board of the Indiana Employment Security Division* 450 US 707, 716 (1981): 'Courts are not arbiters of scriptural interpretation.'

[108] On the autonomy of churches and other religious groups see Rivers, *The Law of Organized Religions* (n 28) ch 2.

flag by prohibiting expressive conduct relating to it'[109] is the key to understanding why general prohibitions of religiously offensive speech are also unjustifiable: they foster coercively a particular view of religion.

Non-Religious Beliefs

A further complication arises if deeply held conscientious, non-religious beliefs are brought into the picture. Whether those beliefs should generally enjoy the same protection as religious beliefs is a broader issue which I will not discuss here. But a reasonable argument can be made that, in principle, the state cannot categorically deny secular beliefs the special protection it extends to religious beliefs because it would be violating its obligation to be neutral not only in the way it treats the various religious communities but also in its treatment of religion and non-religion.[110] Anti-discrimination law often includes within its scope conscientious, non-religious beliefs. For example, employment tribunals in England have held that beliefs in climate change[111] and ethical veganism[112] are protected philosophical beliefs, so treating employees less favourably because of them is unlawful. It can be argued that if the law restricts speech to prevent aggressive criticism of religious convictions it should do the same with secular ones.[113] This view is reflected in Article 166 of the German Criminal Code which protects not only religious beliefs but also ideologies and ideological associations.[114] This is a recognition that for some people ideological convictions occupy a position in their lives similar to that of religious beliefs in the lives of believers and that participation in an ideological organization can be

[109] *Texas v Johnson* (n 106) 415.

[110] In *Epperson v Arkansas* 393 US 97, 104 (1968) the US Supreme Court held that 'the First Amendment mandates governmental neutrality between religion and religion, and between religion and nonreligion'.

[111] *Grainger plc v Nicholson* [2010] ICR 360.

[112] *Casamitjana Costa v The League Against Cruel Sports* Case number 3331129/2018, Consent judgment (2 March 2020).

[113] Kent Greenawalt, *Religion and the Constitution: Volume 2: Establishment and Fairness* (Princeton University Press 2008) 322 draws a parallel between religious and secular beliefs in the context of religious exemptions from neutral laws: sometimes conscientious non-religious convictions are equally pressing as religious ones and, therefore, can also justify exemptions for non-religious objectors.

[114] Section 166 Criminal Code: 'Revilement of religious faiths and religious and ideological communities— (1) Whoever publicly or by disseminating material (section 11(3)) reviles the religion or ideology of others in a manner which is suitable for causing a disturbance of the public peace incurs a penalty of imprisonment for a term not exceeding three years or a fine. (2) Whoever publicly or by disseminating material (section 11(3)) reviles a church or other religious or ideological community in Germany or its institutions or customs in a manner which is suitable for causing a disturbance of the public peace incurs the same penalty'.

experienced as an element defining an individual in deep and pervasive ways which give rise to strong feelings of attachment to the group.

The protection of non-religious convictions also preoccupied the Law Commission, which reviewed the English law on blasphemy in 1985. The Commission recommended its abolition, noting, among other things, that it is questionable whether reverence for God is really different from 'other kinds of reverence, for example for the Monarch or for parents'; what they have in common is that one is 'unwilling to entertain grounds of criticism' in relation to the person who is the object of one's reverence. Thus:

> it ought to follow that the protection given to adherents of organised religion by a law of blasphemy should be extended to protect the susceptibilities of those who have a similar unqualified reverence for another person or institution, whether this be a person holding a unique position in the minds of a substantial number of people such as the Monarch, or an object which is the focus of similar feelings such as the national flag, or even a philosopher, artist or musician whose work has for some the spiritual significance which religion possesses for others ... it must be recognised that ... the equality of treatment which the law should provide, would mean that a substantial extension of the criminal law would be required to protect the feelings of individuals in all the cases to which we have referred.[115]

More recently, the United Nations Human Rights Committee has noted that blasphemy laws, in the limited circumstances where they may be acceptable under the International Covenant on Civil and Political Rights, should not privilege 'religious believers over non-believers'.[116] This tendency to treat religions and other deeply held beliefs and commitments in the same manner means that, if the response to offensive speech is the punishment of the speaker, the range of viewpoints whose disparagement can trigger a criminal conviction becomes extremely broad. Speech which is 'particularly offensive'[117] towards any system of belief or ideology, from communism to royalism, and from veganism to carnivorism, can be the subject of prosecution.

If this approach were to be accepted by courts, the power of the government to restrict speech would become practically unlimited. In modern pluralist

[115] Law Commission, 'Offences against Religion and Public Worship' Working Paper No 145 (1985) para 2.40 (citation omitted).

[116] General Comment No 34 CCPR/C/GC/34, para 48 (21 July 2011).

[117] Hillgruber, 'Legal Limits of a Permissible Criticism of Religion' (n 74) 272.

societies people pursue different ends, organize their lives around different values and give their allegiance to different ideas, persons and symbols. When those elements which make up one's conception of the good life, whether religious or secular, are criticized one may feel offended or outraged and what often follows is a claim to censor those responsible for causing the offence. A regime which gives in to such claims restricts freedom of expression to the point of extinction.[118]

Protecting a Sense of the Sacred

Perhaps the rationale for a general blasphemy law can be reformulated to focus on the protection of a sense of the sacred. The argument could develop like this: while religious believers have an immediate, personal interest in securing reverence of their religion's sacred figures and doctrines and extending the same respect to those of other religions, there exists also a more general societal interest in maintaining respect for a sense of the sacred; there is value for the community as a whole in protecting a spiritual dimension based on religion and this is something that even non-believers can recognize and benefit from; thus, there is reason for the government to censor sacrilegious communications through a general blasphemy law. This view has some similarities with justifications for blasphemy on grounds of public order, which is discussed later in this chapter—they are both about the effects of profanity on the community—but operates at a different level as it is concerned not with the practical arrangements for avoiding conflict but with ensuring the possibility of a transcendental element in human society.

Proponents of this rationale could attempt to link it to the general theory of value developed by Joseph Raz. Raz argues that we have reason to preserve anything that is of value regardless of whether we actually find it valuable.[119] He gives the example of Picasso's paintings: not everyone will be interested in them or like them but this does not mean that one can destroy them or treat them in ways which are inconsistent with the fact that they are aesthetically valuable.

[118] The same issue of what is to be protected also arises in the context of hate speech. As Eric Heinze, 'Viewpoint Absolutism and Hate Speech' (2006) 69 Modern Law Review 543 has shown, hate speech bans are themselves discriminatory because they prohibit hateful messages in relation to certain characteristics such as race or religion, but do not cover other characteristics, including obesity or mental illness, which make people who have them equally vulnerable. Adopting an inclusive, open-ended formulation which would ban any 'other form' of hate speech is not an answer because this would reach 'so far into everyday, colloquial speech and imagery as to require a fully-fledged Newspeak' (at 566).

[119] Joseph Raz, *Value, Respect, and Attachment* (Cambridge University Press 2001) 162–64.

Value is realized when we engage with valuable objects and practices but we do not need to engage with everything that is valuable. When we find something to be of value then we have reason to engage with it and also to preserve it and maintain the conditions which make such engagement possible. Those are reasons for engaging with a practice or object which apply to the person who finds the practice or the object to be of value. But there are also more general reasons for respect, which apply to everyone regardless of whether they themselves find the valuable object to be of value and wish to engage with it: 're-garding what is of value, be it instrumental or intrinsic, there is a universal reason for everyone to respect it'.[120]

If we have reason to preserve the spiritual element in human life which religion makes possible, then this is a universal reason which applies to everyone, irrespective of individual choices and preferences. Profanity and sacrilege undermine something of value which we have reason to preserve, even if we do not wish to engage with it. Therefore, censoring religiously offensive speech is a way of recognizing the value of the sacred. While I am sympathetic to this view, which attaches value to the public recognition of a transcendental element in human life, the argument cannot succeed in justifying a blasphemy law in contemporary societies where pluralism is the norm. People with entirely secular or actively anti-religious outlooks might not be expected to find value in any conception of the sacred, let alone consider the protection of the sacred as a reason justifying censorship.[121] This does not mean that it is always illegitimate for the state publicly to acknowledge religion and the fact that it is part of the ethical life for many of its citizens. I think that such recognition is appropriate and can be expressed through a variety of actions such as granting religious exemptions from general laws or designating religious festivals as public holidays. Those actions will have special importance for those who find religious practice valuable but will also convey the message that there is value in a spiritual dimension. Rather, my point is that the protection of a sense of the sacred cannot justify *this particular form of state action*—the exercise of coercion against blasphemers—if it is disconnected from the religious sensitivities of believers. What makes the protection of the sacred from sacrilegious speech relevant in a pluralist society is the fact that certain citizens who are committed to a religious life feel insulted when their beliefs are attacked or ridiculed.

An illustration of this point can be found in the Law Commission report which recommended the abolition of the common law offence of blasphemy.

[120] ibid 164.
[121] Eric Barendt, *Freedom of Speech* (Oxford University Press 2005) 187–88.

Two Law Commissioners agreed with the recommendation but suggested that English law should include a new, statutory criminal offence protecting all religions. But while they tried to justify it by invoking the interests of society in general and not exclusively those of religious citizens,[122] they were unable to define the new offence without reference to religious feelings: the new offence 'would penalise anyone who published grossly abusive or insulting material relating to a religion with the purpose of outraging religious feelings'.[123] Thus, even this supposedly reformulated justification which purports to be based on universal reasons turns out to be the familiar argument about the protection of believers from belief-mediated distress.

General Blasphemy Laws: Violence and Public Order

Even if the free speech arguments against modern blasphemy laws developed in the preceding sections are persuasive, an important aspect of the challenge posed by their proponents remains unanswered. When religious speech actually provokes violence, isn't it legitimate for the government to restrict the offensive communications? As discussed earlier, blasphemy prohibitions have always been seen as necessary for not only ensuring respect for God but also protecting the established civic order since the state identified with a specific religion. The contemporary version of the argument is that pluralist states, where many different religious viewpoints exist side by side, need to censor speech which, because it vilifies a particular viewpoint, can enrage people to such an extent so as to make them resort to violence. Thus, it is the need to avoid conflict provoked by religious speech and safeguard public peace which justifies speech bans.[124]

How Speech Causes Violence

A fundamental question is what 'provokes' (or similar expressions like 'results', 'leads to' and so on) means. The implication is that there is a causal relation

[122] Law Commission (n 115) para 3.2: 'We could therefore wish adherence to a religion, with the reverence for the sacred that goes with it, to be recognised by the State as deserving of such protection as the State can give without impairment of the rights of others ... the believer does not, we think, claim that protection for his own feelings as of right, or as essential, or even as important for his own spiritual well-being. The believers and those who have no religious faith can, however, join in wishing to afford that protection to all adherents of religion in the interest of society as a whole.'

[123] ibid para 5.2.

[124] This is the argument relied on to justify the German blasphemy law in Hillgruber, 'Legal Limits of a Permissible Criticism of Religion' (n 74).

between speech and violence in the sense that an actor sets in motion a process which results in changes to the physical world: a verbal or non-verbal communication about religion brings about a certain emotional state in the audience which acts out by resorting to violence. Causal concepts in general are important for a variety of issues on moral and legal responsibility but I think that, for the constitutional lawyer considering violence resulting from speech, the main concern is how strong the link between cause (speech) and effect (violence) need be before the government can legitimately censor the speaker. For example, if causation is to be established on the balance of probabilities, an approach common in private law, what would be the required standard of proof? In English negligence law the claimant needs to establish that it is more likely than not that the defendant's breach of the duty of care caused the damage. Is the 'more likely than not' standard appropriate for freedom of expression cases or a more exacting causal link should be required before speech is curtailed? A strict causation test is more restrictive of the government's power to intervene, while if the causal link is attenuated it will be easier to justify censorship.

Yet, it should be possible to think about speech and violence without having first settled the causal question.[125] Thus, I will focus on what the law's response should be *after* it has been established that it is speech that provokes the violence, assuming that whatever causation test is implied in the word 'provokes', is satisfied. Speech can provoke violence in, broadly, two ways. A speaker may address an audience which is friendly towards him and the content of his message and incite its members to attack a third party. In free speech literature, the classic example is that provided by John Stuart Mill in Chapter 3 of *On Liberty*: the law should not interfere with the publication of an article that corn-dealers are starvers of the poor, but it can rightly punish a speaker who says the same thing to an angry crowd gathered outside the house of a corn-dealer. The reason is that 'even opinions lose their immunity, when the circumstances in which they are expressed are such as to constitute their expression a positive instigation to some mischievous act'.[126] Accepting censorship in this context is consistent with Mill's earlier thesis that no opinion should ever be suppressed, because here the speaker has crossed the line dividing opinion and action. The absolute protection of speech covers all expressive acts but not all illocutionary acts as the latter may amount to instigation to engage in violence.[127]

[125] For a more detailed discussion of causation in relation to harms caused by speech see ch 6 on discrimination.

[126] John Stuart Mill, *On Liberty and the Subjection of Women* (Alan Ryan (ed)) (Penguin 2006 [1859]) 64.

[127] Daniel Jacobson, 'Mill on Liberty, Speech, and the Free Society' (2000) 29 Philosophy and Public Affairs 276, 286–87.

The context in which the opinion is expressed may turn it into something different than just the expression of an opinion.

It is probably uncontroversial that in situations analogous to the corn-dealer example the state can legitimately exercise its coercive power against the speaker. Some qualifications are necessary so as to ensure that speech bans are not motivated by governmental dislike of the substance of the opinion expressed[128] or that they are not overbroad,[129] going beyond what is necessary for averting violence. For example, we might ask whether there are other means, short of criminal punishment, which can achieve the same objective or how likely it is that speech will persuade the audience to turn to violence. A further qualification might relate to the speaker's intent. It is arguable that a speaker who unwittingly makes a statement which causes violence to break out should not be held liable for the harmful effect of his speech because, unlike an intentional inciter, he did not intend that consequence.[130] With those caveats in place, limitations on speech appear to be morally legitimate.

But violence may also erupt against the speaker himself, or against third parties, when his opinions reach a hostile audience. This is the *Charlie Hebdo* example. The argument is that when opinions about religion are expressed in a manner which can cause outrage and make the listeners become violent, the government should suppress the communication so as to protect public peace. It is with this claim that the rest of this chapter deals.

Hostile Audiences

The issue of hostile listeners who might react violently when they encounter communications they disagree with is not new, nor is it relevant for religious speech only. In 1949, the US Supreme Court gave judgment in *Terminiello v City of Chicago*[131] and reversed the conviction of an extreme right-wing speaker for breaching public peace. While addressing an audience of like-minded listeners in a Chicago auditorium, Terminiello made vicious attacks on various political and racial groups, denouncing them as dangerous for the

[128] For a discussion of the review of governmental motivation see Leslie Kendrick, 'Content Discrimination Revisited' (2012) 98 Virginia Law Review 231; Elena Kagan, 'Private Speech, Public Purpose: The Role of Governmental Motive in First Amendment Doctrine' (1996) 63 University of Chicago Law Review 413.

[129] On overbreadth see Richard Fallon Jr, 'Making Sense of Overbreadth' (1991) 100 Yale Law Journal 853.

[130] Leslie Kendrick, 'Free Speech and Guilty Minds' (2014) 114 Columbia Law Review 1255, 1270–71.

[131] 337 US 1 (1949).

nation's safety. The large crowd that had gathered outside the auditorium to protest became agitated, they attacked verbally those entering the venue and threw bricks through the windowpanes, while Terminiello called them 'slimy scum', 'snakes', and 'bedbugs'. Some protesters were arrested but Terminiello was also prosecuted and convicted under a city ordinance which prohibited misbehaviour causing a breach of public peace which courts had interpreted to cover conduct that 'stirs the public to anger, invites dispute, brings about a condition of unrest, or creates a disturbance'.[132]

In an opinion by Justice Douglas, the Supreme Court held that prevention of public disturbance or unrest was not a constitutionally permitted reason for punishing the speaker:

> [A] function of free speech under our system of government is to invite dispute. It may indeed best serve its high purpose when it induces a condition of unrest, creates dissatisfaction with conditions as they are, or even stirs people to anger. Speech is often provocative and challenging. It may strike at prejudices and preconceptions and have profound unsettling effects as it presses for acceptance of an idea. That is why freedom of speech, though not absolute ... is nevertheless protected against censorship or punishment, unless shown likely to produce a clear and present danger of a serious substantive evil that rises far above public inconvenience, annoyance, or unrest.[133]

Two years later, the Court reached a different conclusion in a similar case, *Feiner v New York*.[134] Feiner had spoken to a group of people gathered at a street corner in Syracuse, urging his audience to attend a lecture about racial discrimination at a local hotel, protesting the cancellation by the authorities of a permit to hold the lecture at a school, and making derogatory remarks about President Truman, the Syracuse mayor, and the American Legion. After a while, there was 'restlessness' in the crowd and some 'angry mutterings', 'pushing', 'shoving', and 'milling around'.[135] Two policemen approached the crowd and were told by a listener that if 'they did not take that "son of a bitch" off the box, he would'.[136] The policemen asked Feiner to stop speaking, he refused, and they arrested him on a disorderly conduct charge. The Supreme

132 ibid 3.
133 ibid.
134 340 US 315 (1951).
135 ibid 324.
136 ibid.

Court affirmed his subsequent conviction, holding that it served the 'interest of the community in maintaining peace and order on its streets'.[137]

The tension between the perspectives in *Terminiello* and *Feiner* was resolved in favour of the former in a series of later judgments on hostile audiences. *Edwards v South Carolina*,[138] *Cox v Louisiana*,[139] and *Gregory v Chicago*[140] all concerned peaceful protests against racial discrimination and segregation. When groups of unsympathetic onlookers became restless, the police ordered the protesters to disperse and, following their refusal to obey the order, arrested them. The Supreme Court reversed their convictions, holding that speech which is expressed in a peaceful manner cannot be prohibited regardless of whether the listeners may cause unrest because they find it unpleasant.

Those judgments establish a rejection of the 'heckler's veto':[141] the fact that hecklers might breach public peace when faced with the communications of a non-violent speaker which they consider insulting or outrageous is not a legitimate reason for restricting the speaker's right. An important point made by both Justice Douglas in *Terminiello* and Justice Black in his dissent in *Feiner* is that the provocation of at least some degree of dissatisfaction, unrest, and anger is inherent in the role speech plays in pluralist societies. When we publicly debate issues which go to the core of our individual and collective identity, as religion almost always does, strong feelings are inevitably stirred up, particularly when we encounter views which are so foreign to our own as to test our intellectual and emotional limits. Such encounters have 'profound unsettling effects' and, the more controversial the topic, the more likely it is for speech to affect us, provoking intense reactions. Thus, it is 'neither unusual nor unexpected that some people at public street meetings mutter, mill about, push, shove, or disagree, even violently, with the speaker'.[142] Feelings like antipathy, resentment, and anger are part of the mental life of every human being and it would be unrealistic to expect people to leave this experience behind when they enter public space as speakers and listeners. Speech is the medium through which such feelings can be acknowledged rather than denied. Instead of attempting coercively to enforce silence, it is preferable to put up with some unrest, accepting that it is part of living in culturally non-homogenous societies. The emotional costs involved in this approach are mitigated by the fact

137 ibid 320.

138 372 US 229 (1963).

139 379 US 536 (1965).

140 394 US 111 (1969).

141 The term was introduced by Harry Kalven in *The Negro and the First Amendment* (Ohio State University Press 1965).

142 *Feiner v New York* (n 134) 326.

that in our role as agents in public debate we can all cause outrage to others or experience it when faced with views or outlooks radically different from our own.

The rejection of the heckler's veto in English law is more qualified. *Redmond-Bate v Director of Public Prosecutions*[143] was about a fundamentalist Christian who was preaching from the steps of a cathedral in West Yorkshire when some people from a large crowd which had gathered there became angry and started shouting at her. A police officer, fearing a breach of the peace, asked her to stop preaching, she refused, and he arrested her. She was convicted of obstructing a police officer in the execution of his duty but the Divisional Court allowed her appeal. Lord Justice Sedley held that protecting public peace is a legitimate state interest but it is important to identify the source of the threat. Instead of arresting the preacher, the police officer should have directed his attention to the members of the audience whose conduct could have become violent. Passers-by did not have to stop and listen to the preacher and, if they did, they could express their view of her as she had the right to continue preaching. It was wrong to think, as the prosecution had suggested, that a non-violent speaker could not be blamed for a breach of the peace only if her message was inoffensive: 'Free speech includes not only the inoffensive but the irritating, the contentious, the eccentric, the heretical, the unwelcome and the provocative provided it does not tend to provoke violence. Freedom only to speak inoffensively is not worth having.'[144]

However, this rule was qualified by the following statement: 'It is only if otherwise lawful conduct gives rise to a reasonable apprehension that it will, by interfering with the rights or liberties of others, provoke violence which, though unlawful, would not be entirely unreasonable that a constable is empowered to take steps to prevent it.'[145] This seems to imply that sometimes violence against an unpopular, non-violent speaker is, although unlawful, a reasonable reaction, so the police may silence the speaker to prevent a breach of the peace. Thus, on the one hand, the judgment embraces the protection of offensive speech in a manner similar to the US Supreme Court's; on the other hand, it leaves the door open for the punishment of peaceful speakers who upset their audiences. But, overall, it points in the right direction, particularly as it affirms that the public expression of offensive ideas is not to be equated with a breach of the peace.

143 [2000] HRLR 249.
144 ibid para 20.
145 ibid para 16.

Where there is a real threat of actual violence erupting, the source of the threat is a morally relevant consideration for assessing the legitimacy of the exercise of state coercion. The speaker who incites a friendly crowd to violent acts is in a different position from the speaker whose message makes unsympathetic listeners violent.[146] In the former case, coercion should be exercised over the speaker but, in the latter, the object of governmental intervention should be the heckler who threatens the speaker (or third parties) with violence. As Justice Black said in *Feiner*, the government had an interest in safeguarding public peace but it should have been pursued by protecting the speaker and arresting the man who had threatened to 'take him off the box'.[147] While the premise that religious speech can lead to breaches of public peace is correct, it is wrong to conclude that the state ought to silence non-violent speakers whenever their views about religion or the manner in which they are expressed enrage some listeners who might react violently. Placating the aggressive audiences by silencing those they do not like is a way of having 'the police to do the work of the thugs in advance'.[148] Instead, what the police should do is arrest the thugs, the fanatics of all persuasions, who are ready to respond to what they dislike by beating up or murdering their fellow citizens.

The recent judgment of the ECtHR in *ES v Austria*[149] exemplifies this mistaken approach to the issue of a hostile audience. The applicant had given a public seminar in which she had made comments which, according to Austrian courts, could be construed to imply that Prophet Muhammad was a paedophile. She was convicted under Article 188 of the Austrian Criminal Code, which punishes disparagement of religious doctrines. The Strasbourg Court upheld the conviction, finding that it was a proportionate measure, necessary in a democratic society, with the aim of 'preventing disorder by safeguarding religious peace, as well as protecting religious feelings, which corresponds to protecting the rights of others within the meaning of Article 10(2) of the Convention'.[150]

There are many reasons to be critical of the judgment, including, as mentioned in Chapter 3, its unquestioning deference to the views of the Austrian authorities. What is important for the discussion here is the Court's treatment of the public peace argument and the link with the injured feelings of

[146] Jerome Neu, 'More Speech, Better Speech as the Best Defense' in Jerome Neu (ed.), *On Loving Our Enemies: Essays in Moral Psychology* (Oxford University Press 2012) 162.
[147] *Feiner v New York* (n 134) 327 (Black J, dissenting).
[148] Neu, 'More Speech, Better Speech as the Best Defense' (n 146) 162.
[149] *ES v Austria* (2019) 69 EHRR 4.
[150] ibid para 41.

the listeners. The national courts had held that speakers who are critical of a religion may be punished if their communication is 'capable of arousing justified indignation'.[151] The Court agreed both with the principle that the listeners' indignation is a reason justifying censorship and the conclusion that the applicant's message was capable of so doing, and, therefore, justifiably giving rise to criminal liability. The reasoning is perfunctory, mainly consisting of references to the judgments of the national courts, but the underlying idea could be reconstructed as follows: religious speech can make listeners indignant; they may seek to express their indignation by violent conduct which causes disorder and breaches public peace; and the government may legitimately silence the speaker so that the listeners do not become indignant and civic order is not disturbed.

This is an endorsement of the heckler's veto or, rather, its modern and much more dangerous version which Timothy Garton Ash has described as the 'assassin's veto'.[152] Like offence, indignation in this context is religiously determined. Every faith will have its own understanding of what can make its members indignant and how far they can go in expressing their indignation. *ES* allows religious groups to impose on society their views about what can be said publicly, lest the believers lose their temper and become violent. In fact, the more sensitive to religious insult one is and the easier it is for one's anger and indignation to be aroused, the more likely one is to succeed in silencing the critics of one's beliefs. The message *ES* sends to those who tend to become uncontrollably indignant and violent is that their threat of violence pays off: the violence-prone listeners need not become violent because the government itself will do the silencing of the opinions they dislike. However, a liberal democracy's morally appropriate response to the problem of hostile audiences is to arrest those who cannot control their indignation, not appease them by convicting those who upset them.

At the meta-level of the structure of a free speech theory, arresting the violent hecklers reverses the usual presumption that the state is the enemy of freedom of expression.[153] Constitutional and human rights jurisprudence on the legal right to freedom of speech has developed against the background of limitations on expression imposed by the government. The theory and practice of free speech have been dominated by issues such as what grounds can the state legitimately invoke to curtail speech, which techniques of restriction

151 ibid para 21.

152 Timothy Garton Ash, *Free Speech: Ten Principles for a Connected World* (Atlantic Books 2016) 130.

153 Owen M Fiss, 'Free Speech and Social Structure' (1986) 71 Iowa Law Review 1405, 1417.

are acceptable and how deferential courts need be to governmental decisions. Thus, the legal rules on freedom of expression were treated as a shield for those whose unpopular opinions attracted the enmity of the state. Protecting non-violent speakers from the hecklers' aggression introduces an alternative paradigm and promotes a more nuanced understanding of the role of the state. While the government remains the most powerful actor which can limit free expression, and vigilance against its measures is always required, it can also enhance the freedom to speak by using its power to maintain conditions which are necessary for the exercise of that freedom. One such condition is to be free from the fear that one's unpopular opinions will make one the victim of violence by hostile listeners.

Finally, the view of the link between speech and violence sketched here, has one further consequence about the usefulness itself of blasphemy provisions. If their justification is the protection of public peace, it seems that their existence adds nothing to the means available to police and prosecutors. The law already grants them the power to intervene whenever violence may break out. There seems to be no reason to have a special rule about breaches of public peace caused by reactions to speech which criticizes religious or ideological doctrines. Those who attack an unpopular speaker are no different from the drunken thug who attacks a passer-by outside a pub or the vandals who cause havoc at a football game. The appropriate response in all those cases is to arrest the aggressors and this is already possible without having separate provisions for each case. Nothing would be lost if blasphemy laws were abolished altogether.

6
Discrimination and Toleration

The discussion in previous chapters focused on arguments about the way free speech principles can help us think about claims that offensive communications which insult the religious feelings of the listeners should be prohibited. The idea at the centre of this debate is that those whose sensibilities are offended have a moral and legal right, grounded on religious freedom, to be protected from offence. Offence is understood as a belief-mediated unpleasant feeling caused by the content of the communication. If such a right exists, it is a reason which justifies the exercise of state coercion. I argued that, although religious freedom both constrains governmental action and sometimes requires the adoption of positive measures, it does not include a right to be protected from speech which upsets or insults one's religious sensibilities. This conclusion applies not only to laws which are partial and protect the religious faith of the majority, as the common law blasphemy offence did, but also to those which are drafted in an inclusive and general manner such as modern blasphemy and 'defamation of religion' provisions. The latter, although an improvement on their predecessors in terms of inclusiveness, are still to be rejected on free speech grounds.

Another argument discussed earlier in the book is that offensive speech stirs up anger and resentment in those affected by it and they are then likely to become violent towards the speaker or third parties. The government has a legitimate interest in protecting public order and peace so the prohibition of insults and profanity is justified as a means for securing for everyone a safe social environment in which to live. This idea still makes use of the emotional impact which offence has on the listeners but the focus has shifted from the protection of their mental peace to the protection of public order, which is now the aim pursued by governmental action. I suggested that this argument for banning offensive communications should also be rejected because, while it is true that speech can cause tensions and unrest, the morally appropriate action is to restrict those who resort to violence as a response to what they hear rather than coerce non-violent speakers into silence.

This chapter discusses two different arguments for censoring sacrilegious speech. The first is that allowing the satire and ridicule of religious beliefs can lead to acts of discrimination against those who hold them because it creates a

Offensive Speech, Religion, and the Limits of the Law. Nicholas Hatzis, Oxford University Press. © Nicholas Hatzis 2021.
DOI: 10.1093/oso/9780198758440.003.0007

negative environment where gradually it becomes acceptable to treat the believers themselves in a negative manner. This type of argument concerns the ways speech may affect societal attitudes and has been used in other contexts to support censorship. I will explore what exactly is meant by the claim that offensive speech leads to discrimination and what causal link between speech and action is required before the government can restrict speech.

The second argument is that sacrilegious speech is a form of intolerance towards those whose beliefs are insulted. Toleration is an important value which is usually thought to require, at a minimum, individuals and groups to engage in mutual forbearance so as to be able to live together in societies where a variety of beliefs, cultural identities, and ways of life is the norm. My focus will be on the moral obligations that the value of toleration grounds and whether such obligations can support the prohibition of offensive speech.

Both arguments are analytically distinct from those discussed until now. They do not depend on considerations about the mental and emotional discomfort suffered by the listeners of insults, nor are they linked to questions about the content of the right to religious freedom. The wrong which discrimination and intolerance might inflict on those whose beliefs are insulted is different from the belief-mediated distress they experience as a result of the insults. The issue that those arguments introduce is whether this different wrong provides a normative reason for censorship. Recall that in Chapter 2 we saw that the claim for banning offensive speech is a form of practical reasoning as it states what an agent (the government) ought to do under certain circumstances. Reasons derive their normative force from the values which underpin them. It is this relationship between reasons and values which makes it right to act in a particular way. The agent has reason to act because by acting she will realize a certain value. The reasons explored in previous chapters are underpinned by values such as respect for religious sensibilities and the preservation of public order and peace. The reasons discussed in this chapter depend on the values of equality and toleration. Does giving effect to those values require the suppression of speech which offends?

Preventing Discrimination

Like all claims about discrimination, the one relating to the potential discriminatory effect of religiously offensive speech is a claim about justice. It is based on the premise that profanity, harsh criticism, satire, and attacks on religious beliefs encourage and perpetuate societal prejudice against the members of the religious group having those beliefs. In turn, this gradually develops into discriminatory conduct against them in areas such as employment, housing, education, or the provision of services: landlords become reluctant to accept them as tenants, employers would not consider hiring them or bypass them for promotions, and so on. Thus, the members of the group are denied their fair share of opportunities and resources in their professional and social life, and this is a wrong that any legal system aspiring to justice needs to address. If that argument is correct, by censoring religiously offensive speech the government is giving practical effect to the requirements of distributive justice.[1]

A preliminary observation is necessary. The anti-discrimination justification for suppression of sacrilegious speech makes sense only where the speech refers to beliefs of religious minorities. It would be absurd to claim that Catholics in Tyrol, Anglicans in Britain, and Muslims in Turkey, in *Otto-Preminger-Institute v Austria*, *Wingrove v United Kingdom*, and *IA v Turkey* respectively, were in danger of becoming victims of discrimination if the communications which offended their sensibilities had gone unpunished. The argument from discrimination is based on concerns about the protection of vulnerable minorities, while those cases are examples of governmental interferences with free expression so as to protect majoritarian attitudes to religion.[2] Of all the censorship examples discussed earlier in the book, the only ones which could possibly benefit from an anti-discrimination justification are those of the Danish cartoons and the *Charlie Hebdo* publications or the seminar in *ES v Austria*.[3] The rationale would be that they were rightly suppressed because they reinforce negative stereotypes about Muslims who already face hostility and actual discrimination in many Western countries.

The obligation not to discriminate and the corresponding governmental interest in prohibiting discrimination mainly relates to discriminatory conduct.[4] The law imposes a primary obligation to not treat people less favourably than how others are treated on the basis of certain characteristics, including religion. Where those who are subject to the non-discrimination obligation fail to observe it, the law provides the victim with a set of remedies. Once it is

[1] On distributive justice obligations and anti-discrimination law see generally John Gardner, 'Discrimination as Injustice' (1996) 16 Oxford Journal of Legal Studies 353.

[2] Numerical minority status is not the only criterion of vulnerability. It is possible to think of cases where power relations are such that individuals within a dominant majority may be the target of negative treatment by other members of the same group. For example, in a traditionally Christian country, a nominally Christian secular elite may treat devout believers with contempt. The fact that the latter belong to the dominant religion does not mean that they are not vulnerable to hostility.

[3] (2019) 69 EHRR 4.

[4] Robert Post, 'Religion and Freedom of Speech: Portraits of Muhammad' (2007) 14 Constellations 72, 83.

established that the discriminator acted on a prohibited ground, he will be usually ordered by the court to pay compensatory, and possibly punitive, damages, and, in some jurisdictions, he may face administrative or criminal sanctions. The law focuses on the discriminatory conduct and the need to remedy the wrong it has inflicted on the victim of discrimination.

It is, however, arguable that the government has a legitimate interest in tackling not only discriminatory conduct per se but also the societal structures, prejudices and stereotypes which underlie it. The discriminator acts on a negative perception of people with a particular characteristic such as race, religion, or sexual orientation. This perception may be attributed, at least partly, to the fact that he has internalized negative societal perceptions of the people with that characteristic. By taking action to uproot the stereotypes and prejudices associated with certain minority groups, the government is addressing some of the factors which foster a culture that makes it is acceptable to discriminate against their members. In the Danish cartoons and *Charlie Hebdo* cases, and in *ES*, the argument would be that Muslim minorities face hostility in many Western countries; the publication of the cartoons perpetuates negative attitudes against them and actual discrimination flows from such attitudes; therefore prohibiting the publication is a way of protecting individuals from discriminatory conduct and giving effect to the value of equality.

Causation and Societal Attitudes

That argument cannot mean that all utterances which minority religious groups find offensive lead to discrimination and should be prohibited as this would turn the law into a private censorship mechanism. Rather, the argument should be understood to mean that the law needs to identify those offensive communications which are likely to cause discrimination. Tort law can provide a helpful analogy here. For a negligence claim to succeed, it is not enough for the claimant to show that he was owed a duty of care, which was breached, and that he suffered some harm. He also needs to establish that the harm was caused by the breach of the duty of care. English law distinguishes between factual and legal causation (or remoteness). The former is about the historical sequence of events in the real world which links the breach of duty to the damage.[5] The latter is a mechanism for limiting liability in cases where factual

[5] In English law, factual causation is determined by the 'but for' test: the defendant is liable if, but for his breach of duty, the harm would not have occurred. See eg *Barnett v Kensington and Chelsea Hospital Management Committee* (1969) 1 QB 428.

causation is satisfied but there are policy reasons to hold the defendant non-liable.[6] I am not claiming that the technicalities of application of causation in torts should be transposed wholesale to constitutional law but some form of a causal inquiry is needed before we allow the government to proscribe speech on the basis of its effects. An empirically verifiable nexus between speech and harm and a determination that the harm is close enough to speech are necessary components of that inquiry.

The US Supreme Court has recently reiterated the need for a causation test in free speech cases in *Alvarez*.[7] The defendant had falsely claimed in public that he had been awarded the Congressional Medal of Honor and was then convicted under the Stolen Valor Act 2005 which criminalized false statements that one was the recipient of a military award or decoration. One of the arguments relied on by the government was that the law was necessary to maintain the integrity of military awards since, if false statements were left unpunished, they could dilute the public's trust in the system for recognizing exceptional bravery and courage. In an opinion by Justice Kennedy, the Court agreed that this was an important governmental interest but concluded that it had not been shown that there was a link between the Act's restriction on false speech and the interest in protecting military awards. It was not enough to make a general assertion that the falsities would make people distrust the awards; 'there must be a direct causal link between the restriction imposed and the injury to be prevented'.[8] The government, Justice Kennedy continued, had failed to meet this standard and the Act was found to be incompatible with the First Amendment.

In cases such as the offensive cartoons, the burden on the government is to show that offence and discrimination are connected closely enough to justify censorship or, to put it differently, that the harm censorship is aiming to remedy (discrimination) stems from its alleged source (offensive expression) and is not too remote from it. Recall that the claim based on discrimination is not that an offensive film, book, or cartoon can turn the audience into bigots; it is rather that it affects the society's moral climate over time, with its pernicious effect taking shape slowly and demonstrating itself in the negative attitudes people develop and embrace towards religious minorities, which, then, lead to acts of discrimination. Thus, the outcome of the causal enquiry turns on whether the

[6] See eg *Overseas Tankship (UK) Ltd v Morts Dock and Engineering Co Ltd (The Wagon Mound) (No 1)* [1961] AC 388.

[7] *United States v Alvarez* 132 S Ct 2537 (2012).

[8] ibid 2549.

effect on society's perception of religious minorities is a strong enough link between offensive speech and discriminatory acts.

The Analogy with Political Speech

The view that the effect of speech on wider societal attitudes is a legitimate reason for curtailing expression and punishing the speaker is not new, nor was it developed in the context of religious or other offence. In American constitutional law, it was relied upon by the Supreme Court as a justification for the censorship of political speech in the infamous trio of *Schenck*,[9] *Frohwerk*,[10] and *Debs*[11] in 1919. The 1917 Espionage Act had criminalized acts capable of causing insubordination or disloyalty in the military or likely interfere with recruitment. *Schenck* concerned convictions for anti-war leaflets which denounced the draft in very strong terms describing it as 'despotism in its worst form and a monstrous wrong against humanity in the interests of Wall Street's chosen few',[12] and called on people to 'do [their] share to maintain, support and uphold the rights of the people of this country'.[13] The Court upheld the convictions against a First Amendment challenge. Justice Holmes wrote that not all speech is constitutionally protected and that what matters for First Amendment purposes is whether a publication poses a 'clear and present danger':

> [The] question in every case is whether the words used are used in such circumstances and are of such a nature as to create a clear and present danger that they will bring about the substantive evils that Congress has a right to prevent. It is a question of proximity and degree.[14]

Proximity was satisfied, he continued, even where no actual evidence existed that a publication had indeed obstructed the war effort; it was enough to show that it had the potential to do so: 'if the act (speaking, or circulating a paper), its tendency and the intent with which it is done are the same, we perceive no ground for saying that success alone warrants making the act a [criminal offence]'.[15] The causation test accepted here is very lax; even the possible

[9] *Schenck v United States* 249 US 47 (1919).
[10] *Frohwerk v United States* 249 US 204 (1919).
[11] *Debs v United States* 249 US 211 (1919).
[12] *Schenck v United States* (n 9) 51.
[13] ibid 52.
[14] ibid.
[15] ibid.

tendency of speech to affect people's attitude to war and their willingness to participate in it was found to meet it.

Frohwerk and *Debs*, which followed shortly after *Schenck*, raised similar issues. The first concerned a series of newspaper articles which criticized the decision to take part in the war, attributed it to a desire to protect capitalist interests, and argued that it was impossible to blame those who refused to enlist. There was no advocacy to breach the law, nor was there evidence that the articles had any appreciable effect on enlistment. However, Justice Holmes held that they were speech which government could proscribe because it might cause future harms: '[I]t is impossible to say that it might not have been found that the circulation of the paper was in quarters where a little breath would be enough to kindle a flame and that the fact was known and relied upon by those who sent the paper out'.[16] The 'kindle-a-flame' rhetoric was all the judgment offered in terms of the analysis of the nexus between the speech in question and the harm it might cause, thus depriving the 'clear and present danger' test of all bite and leading to wholesale deference to the government.

But the case that best exemplifies the dangers of using the possibility of future harm to justify censorship is *Debs*. The defendant was the leader and presidential candidate of the Socialist Party. During the party convention in Ohio he gave a speech praising socialism, criticizing capitalism and the war, and saying he was proud of his comrades who had been convicted of aiding and abetting others in failing to register for the draft. He was convicted of causing and attempting to cause insubordination and obstruction of the enlistment service. For the third time, Justice Holmes held that the government could punish speech relying on its probable effect. The fact that the defendant's statements were part of a political address on socialism was immaterial, if the 'manifest intent'[17] of part or the address as a whole was to obstruct enlistment. Even if there was no advocacy to breach the law, what the hearers 'might infer'[18] that the speaker meant was relevant. Where 'the words used had as their natural tendency and reasonably probable effect to obstruct the recruiting service',[19] Justice Holmes asserted, the First Amendment was no defence.

Debs not only continues the pattern of trivializing to the point of irrelevance the need for a causal nexus between speech and harm but applies it to what was a paradigm of political expression—a party leader and presidential candidate speaking at a party conference on a matter of the utmost public interest. It is

[16] *Frohwerk v United States* (n 10) 209.
[17] *Debs v United States* (n 11) 212.
[18] ibid 213.
[19] ibid 216.

this lack of a serious causal enquiry which turned the 'clear and present danger' test into nothing more than an exercise in predicting how speech may affect in the future the attitudes of citizens towards the war. Prediction, then, was based on such indeterminate and vague criteria as the 'tendency and intent' (*Schenk*) or 'probable effect' (*Debs*) of speech, what the audience 'might infer' (*Debs*) from was actually said and the danger of speech becoming a 'breath' that can 'kindle a flame' (*Frohwerk*).[20] It was against this indeterminacy that Learned Hand directed his criticism of the test taking the view that the permissibility of proscribing speech depends on whether 'the words were directly an incitement'.[21]

The clear and present danger test was also applied during the Red Scare era that followed the end of the Second World War. In 1940, Congress had passed the Smith Act which made it a crime to advocate the desirability or propriety of overthrowing the government of the United States by force or participate in groups which so advocated. When, after the war, anxiety about espionage and infiltration by Soviet agents in America increased, the Act was used to prosecute actual or suspected communists. In *Dennis v United States*[22] the Supreme Court upheld the convictions of several leading members of the Communist Party against a First Amendment challenge, holding that the fact that they were leaders of a well-disciplined, organized group advocating Marxist ideas, which included the need for the violent overthrow of government, was enough to justify the convictions, even though they had not actually taken any action or campaigned to destroy the government.[23]

Justice Douglas wrote a forceful dissent focusing on the issue of the causal link between the allegedly unlawful conduct and the evil the Smith Act was meant to prevent. His main point was the absence of evidence linking the

[20] A few months after the judgments in *Schenck*, *Frohwerk*, and *Debs*, Justice Holmes changed his mind about the application of the clear and present danger test in *Abrams v US* 250 US 616 (1919). Joined by Justice Brandeis, he wrote a dissenting opinion which emphasized the need for the danger to be immediate before the government is allowed to limit speech. This dissent contains the now famous reference to 'free trade in ideas', which was discussed in ch 5.

[21] Letter from Hand to Oliver Wendell Holmes cited in Gerald Gunther, *Learned Hand: The Man and the Judge* (2nd edn, Oxford University Press, 2010) 139.

[22] *Dennis v United States* 341 US 494 (1951).

[23] The Supreme Court adopted the interpretation of the clear and present danger test given in the judgment of the Court of Appeals which had affirmed the decision of the trial court to convict: 'in each case, [courts] must ask whether the gravity of the evil, discounted by its improbability, justifies such invasion of free speech as is necessary to avoid the danger', cited in *Dennis v United States* (n 22) 510. The author of the Court of Appeals judgment was Learned Hand. Given his earlier criticism of the clear and present danger test, his strict interpretation appears paradoxical. The explanation proposed by Gunther, *Learned Hand* (n 21) 516 is that Hand felt that his own incitement standard (from the judgment in *Masses*) had failed to attract support from the legal community and that he acted as 'a judge of a lower court who took seriously his obligation to follow Supreme Court precedents'.

defendant's speech to a real harm to the political system and institutions of the United States. He stated that the case had been argued as if the defendants 'were teaching the acts of sabotage, the assassination of the President, the filching of documents from public files, the planting of bombs, the art of street warfare and the like'[24] but 'no such evidence was introduced at the trial'.[25] Instead, the record showed that they had organized to teach the doctrine of communism using texts and books which were not themselves banned but this was construed as evidence of intent to overthrow the government:

> The Act, as construed, requires the element of intent—that those who teach the creed believe in it. The crime then depends not on what is taught, but on who the teacher is. That is to make freedom of speech turn not on *what is said*, but on the intent with which it is said. Once we start down that road, we enter territory dangerous to the liberties of every citizen.[26]

The effect of this construction, he continued, was to treat speech as such as if it were seditious conduct: '[W]e deal here with speech alone, not with speech plus acts of sabotage or unlawful conduct. Not a single seditious act is charged in the indictment. To make a lawful speech unlawful because two men conceive it is to raise the law of conspiracy to appalling proportions'.[27]

The *Dennis v United States* rationale was eventually eroded by a series of judgments in the late 1950s and early 1960s written by Justice Harlan, which, without declaring the Smith Act unconstitutional, construed it narrowly so as to require proof of advocacy of unlawful action as opposed to teaching of doctrine. In *Yates*[28] the Supreme Court reversed the convictions of the leaders of the Communist party in California on the basis that the trial judge had given the jury inadequate instructions as to the distinction between speech and conduct. It held that the Act required 'that those to whom the advocacy is addressed must be urged to *do* something, now or in the future, rather than merely to *believe* in something'.[29] The judgment of the Court of Appeals, which had recognized the need for some form of action, did not remedy the inadequacy because it had failed to require 'the *linking* of the

[24] *Dennis v United States* (n 22) 581.
[25] ibid.
[26] ibid 583 (emphasis in the original).
[27] ibid 584.
[28] *Yates v United States* 354 US 298 (1957).
[29] ibid 325 (emphasis in the original).

advocacy to action'.[30] The Court held that: '[mere doctrinal justification of forcible overthrow of government] even though uttered with the hope that it may ultimately lead to violent revolution, is *too remote* from concrete action to be regarded as the kind of indoctrination preparatory to action which was condemned in *Dennis*'.[31]

Four years later, in *Scales*,[32] the Supreme Court held that the membership clause of the Smith Act, which made membership in an organization which advocates the violent overthrow of government a criminal offence, did not apply to 'mere passive members';[33] it was, thus, necessary to distinguish between 'active' and 'nominal' membership.[34] And in *Noto*,[35] a companion case to *Scales*, the Court emphasized the need for convictions to be based on substantial evidence which 'is both sufficiently strong and sufficiently pervasive'.[36] A reference to the abstract teachings of the Communist party and their potential effect did not satisfy this requirement: 'it is upon the particular evidence in a particular record that a particular defendant must be judged, and not upon the evidence in some other record or upon what may be supposed to be the tenets of the Communist Party'.[37]

Finally, in *Brandenburg v Ohio*,[38] the Supreme Court did away with Justice Holmes' 'clear and present danger' test. The defendant was a Ku Klux Klan leader in Ohio who had been convicted under a 1919 state criminal syndicalism statute[39] for making threatening comments during a film that was broadcast by a local television station. In a short *per curiam* judgment, the Court held that the 'constitutional guarantees of free speech and free press do not permit a State to forbid or proscribe advocacy of the use of force or of law violation except where such advocacy is directed to inciting or producing imminent lawless action and is likely to incite or produce

[30] ibid 322 (emphasis added).
[31] ibid 321–22 (emphasis added).
[32] *Scales v United States* 367 US 203 (1961).
[33] ibid 222.
[34] ibid 223. On the facts, the Supreme Court concluded that the defendant was an active member and the conviction was upheld.
[35] *Noto v United States* 367 US 290 (1961).
[36] ibid 298.
[37] *Noto v United States* (n 35) 299. The conviction was reversed because of insufficient evidence.
[38] *Brandenburg v Ohio* 395 US 444 (1969).
[39] The statute criminalized advocating 'the duty, necessity or propriety of crime, sabotage, violence or unlawful methods of terrorism as a means of accomplishing industrial or political reform' and assembling 'with any society, group or assemblage of persons formed to teach or advocate the doctrines of criminal syndicalism'. A very similar California statute had been found to be compatible with the First Amendment in *Whitney v California* 274 US 357 (1927), which was overruled in *Brandenburg v Ohio* (n 38). In *Whitney*, Justice Brandeis, joined by Justice Holmes, wrote a concurring opinion which, although it affirmed the defendant's conviction for procedural reasons, provided one of the most influential defences of free speech.

such action'.[40] Given that the Ohio statute purported to punish 'mere advocacy'[41] as opposed to incitement to imminent lawless action it could not be reconciled with the First Amendment.[42]

The most unequivocal condemnation of the clear and present test is in the concurring judgment of Justice Douglas. After tracing the development of the test from *Schenk* to *Dennis* and its aftermath, he noted:

> When one reads the opinions closely and sees when and how the 'clear and present danger' test has been applied, great misgivings are aroused. First, the threats were often loud, but always puny, and made serious only by judges so wedded to the *status quo* that critical analysis made them nervous. Second, the test was so twisted and perverted in *Dennis* as to make the trial of those teachers of Marxism an all-out political trial which was part and parcel of the cold war that has eroded substantial parts of the First Amendment.[43]

The expression of beliefs and ideas, he concluded, are beyond the reach of governmental scrutiny: 'The line between what is permissible and not subject to control and what may be made impermissible and subject to regulation is the line between ideas and overt acts'.[44]

The cases on political expression show how threatening to the right to free speech is the substitution of a rigorous causation test with one based on the future effects of expression on society or a legitimate governmental interest. As the Supreme Court emphasized in *Noto v United States*, it cannot be enough to point to some form of unlawful action, as opposed to belief, to justify censorship. It is also necessary to demonstrate a link between the speech that is censored and the unlawful conduct, and that, even if the link exists, the conduct is

[40] *Brandenburg v Ohio* (n 38) 447.

[41] ibid 449.

[42] A rare case where a restriction on political speech was upheld is *Holder v Humanitarian Law Project* 561 US 1 (2010). The claimants wished to provide assistance and training for the humanitarian and political action of the Kurdistan Workers Party (PKK) in Turkey and the Liberation Tigers of Tamil Eelam in Sri Lanka. Both groups had been designated as terrorist organizations by the US government, and Congress had passed legislation which made it a criminal offence to offer material support to such groups. The Supreme Court held that the prohibition covered not only conduct but also speech—the claimants' communications to the PKK and the Tigers, i.e. a type of material support in the form of speech. The applicable standard of review was strict scrutiny but it was satisfied because the government's interest in combating terrorism was compelling and the statute was drawn narrowly enough. The Court noted that the government's determination of what measures were necessary had to be given considerable weight and that advocacy in favour of such groups was not unlawful. In dissent, Justice Breyer took the view that the government had failed to show that prohibiting this type of speech was necessary for achieving its anti-terrorism objectives.

[43] *Brandenburg v Ohio* (n 38) 454.

[44] ibid 456.

not too remote from the speech. Therefore, in a liberal democratic system, the permissibility of censorship so as to avert future harms ought to turn on the existence of empirical evidence linking speech and harm and an assessment of the closeness of that link. During the First World War and in the Cold War era, courts failed to perform that causal inquiry, being, instead, content to accept the government's invocation of a vague, future harm as a reason legitimizing censorship of provocative political ideas.[45]

Prohibiting religiously offensive speech because of its future effect on societal attitudes towards certain religious groups is problematic for the same reasons. Proponents of prohibition are right to point out that prevention of discrimination is a legitimate governmental aim but fail to appreciate the moral costs inherent in restrictions of liberty and the need to ensure that whatever harm is invoked as reason justifying such restrictions is real and actually caused by the speech in question. If we accept that the test for speech bans is whether a particular message has the tendency or probable effect to reinforce negative feelings about a religion which will then lead to acts of actual discrimination against its adherents, no communication that is robustly critical or satirical is safe. It will always be possible to claim that religious offence perpetuates negative perceptions of religious minorities making it likely for discrimination to occur. Where the required causal link between speech and harm is so attenuated, the power of the state to proscribe speech becomes vast and practically uncontrolled.

The concerns about discrimination triggered by offensive expression do not provide reason for censorship where the alleged harm is the effect expression might have on society's perception of religious minorities. The claim needs to be reformulated as follows: religiously offensive speech can be curtailed if it is a direct cause of discriminatory acts. The requirement for an empirically verifiable, direct causal link between the harm and the restriction on speech—reaffirmed by the Supreme Court in *Alvarez*—performs an important function as a limit on governmental power. It places on the proponents of prohibition the burden to show that offensive expression leads, as a matter of fact, to acts of discrimination and that the connection between the two is not too remote.

Thus, a standard similar to the one established in *Brandenburg v Ohio* is the appropriate test for deciding which offensive communications can be curtailed. While *Brandenburg* prevents the government from censoring messages

[45] Writing on *Dennis* (n 22), Gunther, *Learned Hand* (n 21) 517 also notes the lack of an evidence-based link between speech and harm as the judgments relied 'heavily on the world situation during the Cold War rather than evidence on the record, which consisted mainly of teachings of Communist literature'.

on the basis of their potential to cause future and uncertain harms, it maintains its power to intervene where such harms are real and imminent. That standard would protect criticism and satire of religion, even where couched in profane, intemperate, insulting, or aggressive language, but allow the state to restrict communications which call for discrimination against a specific group or individual and are likely to cause such discrimination.[46]

The Practice of Toleration

A similar argument in favour of censorship of religiously offensive speech can be made from toleration. In pluralist societies, people with very different cultural and religious sensibilities have to live and work together in a manner which ensures a reasonable degree of stability and social peace. To achieve that, individuals and groups need to engage in mutual forbearance and tolerate certain cultural and religious practices and opinions even where they disagree strongly with them. Part of this mutual obligation of tolerance is to avoid insulting the religious sensibilities of fellow citizens.

This is an approach endorsed by the European Court of Human Rights (ECtHR), which, in *Otto-Preminger-Institut v Austria*,[47] relied on toleration to justify the seizure of a film which, if shown in an art cinema in Innsbruck, could have offended Roman Catholics in the Tyrol area. The Court noted that believers 'must tolerate and accept the denial by others of their religious beliefs and even the propagation by others of doctrines hostile to their faith'. However, those criticizing religion must exercise self-restraint and avoid causing offence because '[provocative portrayals of objects of religious veneration] can be regarded as malicious violation of the spirit of tolerance, which must also be a feature of democratic society'.[48] This is a 'two-dimensional toleration'[49] which allows for criticism of religious beliefs and denial of their truth but imposes on critics an obligation to respect norms of civility so that the ensuing debate remains 'serious, earnest and respectful'.[50] The Court's point about toleration has similarities with the argument about the duty to respect the listeners'

[46] This determination, which involves questions of likelihood and imminence of harm, may differ depending on whether the speaker is trying to strengthen or activate existing prejudice or generate a new one. If the former, it could be argued that the effects of speech might be greater or more widespread among the population and, therefore, more likely to lead to actual discrimination.

[47] (1995) 19 EHRR 34.

[48] ibid para 47.

[49] A term suggested by Jeremy Waldron, 'Rushdie and Religion' in *Liberal Rights: Collected Papers 1981-1991* (Cambridge University Press 1993) 138.

[50] ibid.

sensitivities which was discussed in previous chapters but what is different here is the source of the duty: it is no longer grounded on the believers' right to religious freedom but on the value of toleration.

Invoking toleration in debates about religious speech seems particularly apposite because toleration, both as a political idea and practical attitude, starts with religious toleration. The religious wars that followed the Reformation left Europe deeply divided and struggling with the question of how to deal with religious differences. What emerged against this background were practical arrangements which 'enabled people of different faiths to live together in the same towns and villages'.[51] Thus, 'religious tolerance became the paradigmatic first tolerance in Western history, the matrix out of which emerged the modern concept of tolerance as applied to all forms of difference-ethnic, cultural and racial as well as religious'.[52] The best way to understand the claim that toleration is a reason for prohibiting profane speech is as an argument about the conditions for living together in contemporary societies where the encounter with the religious other 'strain[s] our resources of psyche and intellect'.[53]

Toleration can be both a public and a personal virtue. The latter concerns attitudes and ways of relating to others within close-knit communities such as friendships. By contrast, as a public virtue, it operates within the public sphere where members of the political community who do not necessarily have any personal ties to each other or share the same view of what constitutes an ethical life interact and often come together to decide on the arrangements for living in the community.[54] Toleration in the public sphere can be a characteristic of governments and individuals.[55] For example, a tolerant political regime will not suppress the expression of dissidents who challenge its authority and legitimacy. But individuals can also demonstrate toleration as a public virtue in the way they conduct themselves as citizens, both in the strict sense of performing political functions, such as voting or standing for election, and in the broader sense of entering public space, speaking publicly, and interacting with those who are not within one's circle of family and friends. The argument for censorship of offensive speech on toleration-related reasons concerns toleration as personal conduct in public space: those who participate in the public exchange of ideas, such as the makers of the film in the *Otto-Preminger Institut v Austria*

[51] Benjamin Kaplan, *Divided by Faith: Religious Conflict and the Practice of Toleration in Early Modern Europe* (Harvard University Press 2007) 162.

[52] ibid 4.

[53] Waldron, 'Rushdie and Religion' (n 49) 140.

[54] Michael J Meyer, 'Two Forms of Toleration: Tolerance in Public and Personal Life' (2002) 33 Journal of Social Philosophy 548.

[55] ibid 551.

case, ought to accommodate the sensitivities of other members of the community by not exceeding the boundaries of civility.

Toleration and the Dynamics of Power

The idea that we ought to demonstrate a tolerant attitude when we encounter others in public space makes good sense. But what kinds of obligations flow from that view and who is subject to them? A common theme in the very extensive literature on toleration is that toleration as a practice implies that someone who is powerful enough to interfere with an act or view that she disagrees with refrains from doing so; the person on the receiving end of toleration is usually the one who is, one way or another, less powerful than the tolerator. Bernard Williams emphasizes the asymmetrical nature of the relation between the tolerator and the tolerated: 'It is a feature of "toleration", as that term is standardly used, that it represents an asymmetrical relation: the notion is typically invoked when a more powerful group tolerates a less powerful group'.[56] Leslie Green argues that the main requirement toleration gives rise to is to 'put aside force, coercion and other forms of overbearing intervention that treat other people as if they were subjects of our own *imperium*'.[57] D D Raphael suggests that we can speak of toleration *only* where this asymmetry of power exists: 'One can meaningfully speak of tolerating, i.e. of allowing or permitting, only if one is in a position to disallow. You must have the power to forbid or prevent, if you are to be in a position to permit'.[58] Similarly, Susan Mendus says that the power to prevent is a condition for describing a decision not to interfere as an instance of toleration.[59] Therefore, if I find my neighbour's religious beliefs abhorrent or disgusting but I take no action because I know that he is far more popular in the community and if I try to persuade others to shun him I will come out badly bruised, you can hardly call me a tolerant person. However, if he is the unpopular one, and I choose not to exercise my influence over the other neighbours against him despite my very strong objections to his religion, I am probably demonstrating tolerant self-restraint.

[56] Bernard Williams, 'Toleration: A Political or Moral Question' in *In the Beginning Was the Deed: Realism and Moralism in Political Argument* (Princeton University Press 2005) 129.

[57] Leslie Green, 'On Being Tolerated' in Matthew Kramer, Claire Grant, Ben Colburn, and Anthony Hatzistavrou (eds), *The Legacy of HLA Hart* (Oxford University Press 2008) 278.

[58] D D Raphael, 'The Intolerable' in Susan Mendus (ed), *Justifying Toleration: Conceptual and Historical Perspectives* (Cambridge University Press 2009) 139.

[59] Susan Mendus, *Toleration and the Limits of Liberalism* (Macmillan 1989) 9.

This imbalance of power led Goethe to state that 'to tolerate is to insult'[60] and Thomas Paine to describe it as a form of 'despotism' similar to intolerance: 'The one assumes to itself the right of withholding liberty of conscience and the other of granting it'.[61] A contemporary, alternative understanding of toleration, one which does not focus on the power relation between the tolerator and the tolerated and the former's disposition to permit the latter's objectionable practices, makes respect the underlying feature of tolerant behaviour. Rainer Forst has described it as the 'respect conception' of toleration, as opposed to a 'permission conception'. 'The basic idea', he writes, 'is that toleration is a stance adopted by *the citizens toward each other*. They are simultaneously tolerating and tolerated'.[62] This is a form of public toleration among equals which can only be practiced in liberal democracies. However, as he notes, the emergence of modern democratic states did not make the permission conception of toleration obsolete, and the contemporary practice of toleration remains to a great extent a variant of it: 'the permission-granting side is now conceived as the *democratic* majority that 'puts up with' minorities'.[63] In such circumstances, power remains a fundamental element defining the relation between the tolerator and the tolerated.

One way of understanding the role of power in toleration is the distinction between toleration as a moral virtue and toleration as political practice. The former is about any individual's or group's stance towards another and is not limited to relations between the more and less powerful.[64] Thus, asymmetry of power is not a conceptual requirement for thinking about the virtue of toleration. However, asymmetry is introduced when we think of toleration as a 'political undertaking'.[65] Here, toleration is manifested as a refusal to use the law in order to interfere with, discourage or prohibit the expression of a belief or a practice, and the fact that this is a question of using the law implies that there is a group which has the power to do so.[66] Thus, toleration in politics is linked to the attitude of the majority: 'a democratic state can properly be said to tolerate x-ing only when those who dislike or disapprove of it are in the majority or could form a majority coalition. The politically powerless do not tolerate,

[60] Cited in Kaplan, *Divided by Faith* (n 51) 8.

[61] ibid 9.

[62] Rainer Forst, 'Toleration and Democracy' (2014) 45 Journal of Social Philosophy 66, 69 (emphasis in the original).

[63] ibid 70 (emphasis in the original).

[64] Bernard Williams, 'Toleration: An Impossible Virtue' in David Heyd (ed), *Toleration: An Elusive Virtue* (Princeton University Press 1988) 18, 19.

[65] Williams, 'Toleration: A Political or Moral Question?' (n 56) 129.

[66] Legal coercion is a paradigmatic, but not the only example, of intolerant behaviour through the exercise of power. Social power can also be used to express intolerance towards people or practices. See the discussion in Green, 'On Being Tolerated' (n 57) 278 and 283.

they merely accept'.[67] Imbalance of power is an aspect of the political practice of toleration and this explains the seemingly paradoxical fact that democracy has not transformed the practice of toleration into a relation between equals.

The imbalance of power can also explain why being tolerated can make one feel uncomfortable. Green has pointed out that toleration has common properties with other asymmetrical relations like offering mercy or pity.[68] While the person on the receiving end may be better-off, all things considered, where toleration, pity or mercy are extended to her (and where the alternative would be intolerance, cruelty, and ruthlessness) the very fact that she needs them is unpleasant; in an ideal world, she would not have needed them in the first place. It is in this sense that toleration, without being a form of power as such, 'is native to political environments in which power is, or may soon be, in play'.[69]

Let us go back to toleration in the *Otto-Preminger-Institut v Austria* judgment. Those who, like the ECtHR, make an argument for the prohibition of religiously offensive speech on toleration grounds are not thinking of toleration as a personal disposition and frame of mind but are answering the question of how one ought to behave publicly. Their response—that there is a toleration-related obligation not to insult the sensitivities of those with different beliefs and ways of life which the government can enforce—concerns the political practice of toleration and the reasons which legitimize the exercise of state coercion. Whether reliance on toleration is persuasive in specific circumstances will depend, among other things, on the relative position of the parties in the spectrum of power and their ability to intervene, by the force of law or other ways, with a practice they find objectionable.

In *Otto-Preminger-Institut v Austria*, the Court misconstrued the obligations that flow from toleration and misrepresented what was at stake in the case. It is impossible to claim with a straight face that the 87 per cent of Tyroleans who were Roman Catholics were subjected to intolerant behaviour by the film-maker and the director of the Institute where the film would have been shown. In fact, the power dynamics in that case were exactly the opposite: the latter were the outsiders who irritated the religious sensibilities of what the Court itself described as the 'overwhelming majority' of the population. Indeed, there was intolerance involved in what happened in Innsbruck: it was the intolerance exhibited by a powerful majority, in the name of which the Austrian authorities claimed to have prosecuted the director of the Institute and confiscated the

[67] Deborah Fitzmaurice, 'Autonomy as a Good: Liberalism, Autonomy, Toleration' (1993) 1 The Journal of Political Philosophy 1.
[68] Green, 'On Being Tolerated' (n 57) 284.
[69] ibid.

film following a complaint from the local diocese, towards people who did not show respect for what its members held sacred. While *Otto-Preminger-Institut v Austria* is a typical case of the more powerful failing to tolerate the less powerful, the Court turned the actual power relation between them topsy-turvy and portrayed the former as the victims of the latter, sanctioning the most draconian restriction on minority speech.[70]

There are situations, however, where those offended in their religious sensibilities are neither powerful nor influential; they may be members of a religious minority which other citizens regard with unfriendliness or open hostility. The Danish cartoons and *Charlie Hebdo* cases, and the seminar in *ES v Austria* are good examples. Muslim minorities in Western countries are often marginalized and may face suspicion or actual discrimination. Where a sacred figure of their religion is referred to with disrespect they may, understandably, feel wronged by a majority which appears to attack important aspects of their individual and collective identity. Is this, then, a situation where toleration requires the government to intervene and curtail offensive messages?

The Expression of Disapproval

Even where the group seeking to benefit from toleration is less powerful compared to the tolerating majority, it does not follow that censorship is justified. Toleration as a political practice places limits on the manner we act towards those whom we view in a negative manner. There is no consensus on what exactly this negative stance entails but toleration has been thought to involve 'disagreement',[71] 'adverse judgments about others',[72] 'disapproval or condemnation',[73] 'strong disapprov[al]',[74] 'disapproval and rejection',[75] 'dislike or disapprov[al]',[76] or the view that the other is 'blasphemously, disastrously, obscenely wrong'.[77] It is possible to think of these attitudes as expressions of essentially the same moral viewpoint, as parts of a spectrum with mild opposition

[70] For the same reasons, toleration cannot justify the censorship in *Wingrove v United Kingdom*, *Murphy v Ireland*, and *IA v Turkey*.

[71] Samuel Scheffler, 'The Good of Toleration' in *Equality and Tradition* (Oxford University Press 2012) 322.

[72] Green, 'On Being Tolerated' (n 57) 277.

[73] Post, 'Religion and Freedom of Speech' (n 4) 79.

[74] Thomas Scanlon, 'The Difficulty of Tolerance' in David Heyd (ed), *Toleration: An Elusive Virtue* (Princeton University Press 1996).

[75] George P Fletcher, 'The Instability of Tolerance' in David Heyd (ed), *Toleration: An Elusive Virtue* (Princeton University Press 1996) 159

[76] Fitzmaurice, 'Autonomy as a Good' (n 67) 1.

[77] Williams, 'Toleration: An Impossible Virtue' |(n 64) 18.

on the one end and vehement rejection on the other, differing only in intensity and degree. Or we might think of them as different moral categories which, although they have common properties, remain distinct. For the purposes of my discussion of offensive speech it is enough to note that that they all take some degree of negative feeling or assessment towards what is tolerated to be a necessary part of toleration.

The element of disapproval is what distinguishes toleration from scepticism and indifference.[78] If I think that no particular view about God or the good life can lay claim to truth, I will not wish to interfere with those whose religion or lifestyle are different from mine. Similarly, if I simply do not care how others in my community live their lives, there is nothing I need to tolerate. Both scepticism and indifference express a 'hands-off'[79] approach which leads to an outcome similar to that of toleration, namely non-interference, but on different grounds. Only in cases where I do care about someone else's choices and find them objectionable or repugnant but refrain from interfering with them can it properly be said that I am exercising toleration. George Fletcher has summarized the ethical content of tolerant practices as follows: 'To be tolerant . . . is to suffer what we cannot stand because we ought not, for a variety of reasons, intervene'.[80]

A possible criticism is that toleration conceived in this manner places excessive emphasis on non-interference with a practice we dislike and does not go far enough on what toleration requires of us. What we need instead is a richer conception of toleration which accords positive recognition to difference. This is a theory of toleration advocated by Anna Elisabetta Galeotti.[81] Galeotti offers a comprehensive, book-length argument whose details I will not discuss here; rather, I will focus on those points in her analysis which are particularly relevant for the issue of offensive speech.[82]

Her starting point is that the classic, liberal understanding of toleration emphasizes disagreement and conflict about values. Because individuals make different choices as to how to live, based on their view of the ethical life, we need political practices, such as toleration, which enable them to coexist in the community despite the tensions that the commitment to divergent values causes. By contrast, her theory makes identities and groups the

[78] Williams, 'Toleration: A Political or Moral Question' (n 56) 128–29.
[79] Fletcher, 'The Instability of Tolerance' (n 75) 158.
[80] ibid 159.
[81] Anna Elisabetta Galeotti, *Toleration as Recognition* (Cambridge University Press 2002).
[82] For this detailed discussion see Peter Jones, 'Toleration, Recognition and Identity' (2006) 14 The Journal of Political Philosophy 123.

aim of toleration. While acknowledging that conflicts of value are possible and do occur, she argues that 'the most genuine contemporary issues of toleration are ... differences between groups rather than between individuals'.[83] The characteristics which give rise to such group differences are ascriptive; they do not depend on individual choice but are part of the group's collective identity, so being a member of the group means partaking of those characteristics which make up its identity.[84] In turn, this means that the classic view's concern with securing for every individual the space to lead the life of her choice regardless of how others view that choice is inadequate. Cultural differences are 'sharpen[ed]' by the 'exclusion or the unequal and incomplete inclusion of various groups into democratic citizenship'.[85] Therefore, what is required is public, affirmative recognition of the identity differences of the groups which have been previously excluded or marginalized by a dominant majority.

Exclusion is the factor which determines which group differences raise issues of toleration. Galeotti writes:

> In general, toleration is needed when certain groups are 'different' in ways which are disliked by the majority in a society. First, the groups in question have to be genuinely disliked ... second, they have to be disliked by the majority, by people and groups whose characteristics, customs and ways of life are traditionally settled and dominant in that society.[86]

When those conditions obtain, the obligation of toleration arises; its substantive content is not merely to refrain from interfering with the practices of the minority group the majority dislikes but rather publicly to recognize the equal status in the polity of the minority with the disliked practices.[87]

The public recognition she is suggesting goes beyond the extension of equal rights to those who have been denied them in the past, because having the legal status of citizen and the formal rights that go with it 'does not automatically

[83] Galeotti, *Toleration as Recognition* (n 81) 5.

[84] ibid 89. By ascriptive, Galeotti means both characteristics which are objectively ascriptive, such as race and ethnicity and characteristics which, although elective, such as culture and morality, are construed as if they 'were ascriptive i.e. as a fixed characteristic of the group, which readily identifies and marks it off from other people'..

[85] ibid 6.

[86] ibid 88–89.

[87] Because of the requirement for positive acknowledgement of the difference which gave rise to past exclusion, Galeotti's theory is more demanding than the 'respect conception' of autonomy described by Forst which makes mutual forbearance and citizens' respect towards one another the core of the practice of toleration.

entail the ability to enjoy fully the status of citizen'.[88] Legal inclusion of such individuals is necessary and, in most cases, already granted, but it is incomplete if there is public disregard of the elements of their minority identity which caused their past exclusion. Public recognition can perform its symbolic function and count as a proper instance of toleration only if it is backed by appropriate reasoning:

> The right reason would be one that did not reduce the issue to a clash of values and cultures, but recognised that behind the clash there is an asymmetry between the dominant cultural standards and the different practices, attitudes, and lifestyles of minorities. It would also acknowledge that such asymmetry engenders a special injustice which results in less respect and dignity for minorities.[89]

The disliked practice is, therefore, acknowledged and included in the public sphere not because it is an individual's choice of the good life but because this is a way to remedy a past injustice, the dignitarian harm inflicted on minorities by a culturally and politically dominant majority. 'Public recognition', Galeotti says, 'ultimately aims to distribute the benefits of inclusion enjoyed by the majority to all citizens, whatever their ethnic, national, cultural or gender membership'.[90]

Galeotti is in agreement with the classic liberal view that imbalance of power and disapproval are necessary elements of the political practice of toleration, and that only the less powerful group can be said to need the toleration exhibited by the more powerful one, but sharply criticizes it for ignoring marginalization and exclusion of groups and reducing the conflicts that raise issues of toleration to the existence of competing conceptions of the good and the individuals' choices among them. There is, she claims, an 'institutional blindness' which is 'implicit in the neutralist liberal programme', making 'all differences equally invisible from a political standpoint'.[91]

While this criticism is probably exaggerated, I think she is right to insist on a full exploration of the dynamics of power in toleration and emphasize the different levels at which they play out. A very interesting aspect of her theory is the explanation of how dislike and disapproval are linked to the exclusionary practices of the majority. She persuasively argues that what the dominant

[88] Galeotti, *Toleration as Recognition* (n 81) 96.
[89] ibid 102–103.
[90] ibid 105.
[91] ibid 67.

majority finds intolerable is difference. Members of the minority group are 'seen to act in ways that depart from recognized social standards'[92] and this is experienced as 'unduly upsetting traditional and customary ways of life and thinking'.[93] The minority's insistence on its own practices and refusal entirely to assimilate into the prevalent social and cultural paradigm makes it a threat to established ways of thinking and living. The majority's intolerant response to that threat is to brand the less powerful group as the other, the outsider, the not-in-the-mainstream, and exclude it from the public arena. This is the evil that toleration as recognition aims to reverse.

Can Galeotti's theory of toleration support the suppression of offensive religious speech? As mentioned above, it is relevant only for cases where those insulted are a minority,[94] and the argument could develop as follows: Muslim communities in the West are faced with suspicion and hostility because they represent the 'other' whose presence in public space challenges the polity's generally accepted norms. This tension is not the product of the individuals' choice of a way of life but arises from the radically different collective identity of those communities, an important part of which is religion. If we think of ourselves and the political community we have established in a particular way, which includes, in conditions of Western secularism, the view that religion is a private matter, the encounter with the persistent, assertive, public religiosity of Muslim minorities, gives rise to a feeling of uneasiness, discomfort and threat. We respond by marginalizing those who do not fit in the framework of our collective thinking and we are, therefore, unable to grasp that satire or ridicule of their beliefs perpetuates their exclusion. The fact that Christian beliefs may also be treated in the same manner, the argument could go on, is irrelevant because, although individual believers may feel insulted, Christians as a group are not, and will never be, in danger of suffering the harm that Muslim minorities suffer, namely delegitimization and exclusion from public space. It is not enough to ensure that Muslims as individuals are full citizens in the legal sense; we also need to address the group dimension of the imbalance of power, and suppressing speech which insults what they hold to be sacred is a way of ensuring for them substantive, as opposed to formal, citizenship.

Whether this argument can work will depend on the obligations of political morality flowing from toleration as recognition. Inclusion in the sense required by this version of toleration cannot mean the public endorsement of the

[92] ibid 90–91.

[93] ibid 91.

[94] Galeotti herself considers the treatment of Muslim minorities as a paradigmatic example of a case raising toleration issues and devotes chapter 4 of her book to the headscarf controversy in France.

intrinsic value of whatever group difference is at stake.[95] First, identity differences are often irreconcilable and it will not be possible for the state to endorse all of them. Secondly, some practices and ways of life, even if they are constitutive elements of a group's identity, should not be tolerated in a liberal democratic state. For example, if beating one's wife and children in order to instil in them proper respect for the deity is part of one's religious outlook and identity, it would be a mistake for the majority to show toleration. Instead, what the enhanced view of toleration as recognition requires is 'the official acceptance of diversity within the normal range of viable options in society', so that 'all citizens [are] positively at ease with their full-blown identities in public as well as in private'.[96] This may entail, for example, a toleration-based obligation for the majority not to legislate a prohibition on wearing religious clothing in public, although it feels uncomfortable with or dislikes the sight of a woman in a veil or a burqa.

Yet, toleration as recognition does not require the elimination of all negative assessment of the practice being tolerated. We have seen that dislike is a necessary element for toleration issues to arise, and the fact that the majority does not act on it in order to 'hinder or interfere with [a] behaviour or practice'[97] is what makes its attitude of self-restraint an instance of toleration. Whether we adopt the more traditional view or Galeotti's toleration as recognition approach, there is 'always inherent in toleration' a 'conflict between disapproval and restraint'.[98] It follows that the practice of toleration should leave some room for the tolerator to express her negative assessment of the action or opinion which is being tolerated. I think it is not possible to give an abstract rule on how much room there should be or what form disapproval should take. It is, however, reasonable to think that disapproval expressed by speech, even intemperate or insulting speech, should be usually allowed. Perhaps there might be extreme cases where criticism is formulated in such a vehement or aggressive manner that it undermines the very standing of a religious minority and excludes it from public space. What is required then is an individualized assessment which takes into account what is being said, the medium used and the conditions that prevail in a particular society and political system. But it is difficult to see how humour, satire, and provocation, expressed in the framework of a liberal, democratic state, can be said to lead to the delegitimization of a minority group.

[95] Galeotti, *Toleration as Recognition* (n 81) 103.
[96] ibid 104–105.
[97] ibid 89.
[98] Williams, 'Toleration: A Political or Moral Question?'(n 56) 133.

If this is correct, the publication of the Danish or the *Charlie Hebdo* cartoons was not an act of intolerance of the majority against a religious minority. One may think that they were insensitive and insulting; certainly many Muslims thought so. But toleration does not require us to be kind, considerate, and sensitive with those we disagree with;[99] what it demands is to restrain ourselves from interfering with what we find objectionable. As such, toleration cannot justify proscribing speech and punishing the speaker because part of the audience finds the message offensive.

In fact, allowing offensive speech to be expressed publicly can have the effect of promoting toleration in public space in a broader sense. Lee Bollinger has argued that the thinking which underlies our wish to prohibit speech we dislike or find upsetting manifests itself in all aspects of human relations where we encounter the experience of difference. We find it difficult to accept that others think or live in ways different from our own, and our impulse is to restrict or excise difference altogether. 'Everyone who is perceived as being different, as having different values or beliefs or an interest in a different way of life, is a potential victim of an excess of this impulse'.[100] Speech is not special in this respect because even non-verbal conduct imbued with social meaning (and most of the things we do have such meaning) can trigger the wish to prohibit. The reason is that what we really find difficult to accept is the existence of minds different from our own. The speech we detest or the conduct we abhor are expressions of a mind with thoughts, values, desires, and priorities which are different from ours. Our immediate response is to suppress those expressions so as to eliminate the experience that there are other minds at work.

As intolerance is a mental element we all share, none of us is immune to acting on intolerant feelings. Bollinger suggests persuasively that we can carve out a specific field of human activity- speech—where it is possible to make a particular effort to moderate our intolerance and resist our wish to use coercion against those who enrage and insult us with their views. If we are successful in this effort, then we might be able to demonstrate the same increased capacity for tolerance in other areas of our life: 'to select a discrete area in which to develop a particular quality desired can have the advantages of concrete experience, offering the kind of practical knowledge that comes from actual experimentation'.[101] Thus, not suppressing speech we dislike is an ethical exercise and education in tolerance more generally. Another way

[99] That is not to say that we may never be morally required to demonstrate those virtues—clearly this is possible. The point is, rather, that those are not obligations flowing from toleration.

[100] Lee C Bollinger, *The Tolerant Society* (Oxford University Press 1986) 111.

[101] ibid 122.

of expressing the same idea is that by refusing to use the law to silence what we dislike we internalize an attitude and an experience which contributes to the development of a tolerant frame of mind. If tolerance becomes relatively well-established as a personal disposition, it is reasonable to hope that it will also translate into a tolerant attitude in public life. When we will come to decide, as citizens, which laws and institutional arrangements to support and what stance to adopt in matters of public interest we might be less inclined to consider those whose views or life choices upset, insult or infuriate us as worthy of punishment. We can still express our disapproval but we will be able better to control our impulse to coerce them into compliance with the norms we endorse.

This view of toleration elucidates some important features of religiously offensive speech, and offensive communications more generally, which we encountered in the first chapter of the book. The belief-mediated distress suffered by the offended listener is caused by the fact that the speaker challenges the sanctity of a figure, doctrine, or symbol. In this process there is an awareness that there exists a separate mind with thoughts which conflict with those of the listener. Very often, those who feel insulted have not actually seen the offending image or read the blasphemous text. Rather, they seethe with indignation at the thought that someone, somewhere, wrote a book which satirizes what they think is the true faith or made a film portraying a figure they revere as holy in a less flattering light. It is not enough to ignore the offending materials, because their existence functions as a painful reminder of a separate mind which thinks differently and is not under one's control. Silencing that which offends is a way to defend oneself against the experience of separateness and difference.

Of course, even if we are able on occasion to resist the impulse to suppress speech we find insulting, it does not follow that toleration will necessarily become the prevailing attitude in our private and public life. The intolerant part of our minds will not go away and, with it, the urge to control what others think and how they live will reassert itself whenever our encounter with difference makes us unbearably anxious. Religious toleration will present particular difficulties. When the source of dislike and tension are differences which are not religious in nature but, say, political, social, or ethnic, it appears easier to ask people not to demonize each other. But, for many religions, other people's deities are literally demons and those who believe in them are fatally misguided and destined for eternal punishment in hell. Within this frame of mind, the space for developing a tolerant attitude is severely limited. The hope is, however, that repeated experiences of self-restraint will somewhat modify our need to coerce others to conform to our view of what is a good life. This is not a straightforward, linear affair. Regression and throwbacks are inevitably part of it, and some ground which has been gained will subsequently be lost, making renewed effort necessary. Free speech, is, perhaps, the most important means we have at our disposal in this process.

Index

For the benefit of digital users, indexed terms that span two pages (e.g., 52–53) may, on occasion, appear on only one of those pages.